2200

POWER AND
POWERLESSNESS IN
INDUSTRY

POWER AND POWERLESSNESS IN INDUSTRY

An analysis of the social relations of production

ROSEMARY HARRIS

Tavistock Publications
London and New York

To the memory of my father, A. E. Harris

First published in 1987 by
Tavistock Publications Ltd
11 New Fetter Lane, London EC4P 4EE

Published in the USA by
Tavistock Publications
in association with Methuen, Inc.
29 West 35th Street, New York, NY 10001

© *1987 Rosemary Harris*

Set by Hope Services, Abingdon
Printed in Great Britain at the University Press, Cambridge

British Library Cataloguing in Publication Data
Harris, Rosemary, 1930–
    Power and powerlessness in industry :
    an analysis of the social relations of production.
    1. Industrial sociology   2. Interpersonal relations
    I. Title
    306'.36   HD6955

ISBN 0–422–60920–X

Library of Congress Cataloging-in-Publication Data
Harris, Rosemary.
    Power and powerlessness in industry.
    Bibliography: p.
    Includes indexes.
    1. Ammonia industry—Great Britain—Employees—Case studies.
    2. Industrial sociology—Great Britain—Case studies.
    I. Title.
    HD6956.A497H37   1987   338.4'766134'0941   86–14420

ISBN 0–422–60920–X

Contents

Acknowledgements

The research on which this book is based was made possible by financial support from the Nuffield Foundation which, under their Small Grant scheme, contributed towards the expenses and whose help I acknowledge with gratitude.

The study could not have taken place without the generous co-operation of ChemCo senior managers who permitted me to carry out my study as I pleased and, subject only to my getting the agreement of the shop-stewards, allowed me to come and go at Riverside as I wished and to talk to whomever I liked. To the shop-stewards, therefore, I obviously owe a great deal since they knew their powers and chose to be welcoming. My major debt, however, is to all those most closely associated with the two ammonia plants which form the focus of this study: the plant managers, supervisors, and operators, and the skilled tradesmen who from time to time worked on the plants. They were not only exceptionally kind but were also great educators, very ready to help me understand this wholly new environment in which I found myself.

I am also indebted to various people who have read the manuscript. Philip Burnham, of University College, London, read it as an anthropologist and offered helpful comments; and I am very indebted to the anonymous reader of Tavistock publications for his very perceptive advice. I am above all, however, indebted to Stephen Hill, Reader in Industrial Sociology at the London School of Economics for his generosity in taking the time and trouble to read an earlier draft and point me to certain writers whose work I had not considered, challenging me to look at my material in new ways. Needless to say the responsibility for faults is mine alone.

I dedicate this book to the memory of my father because my interest in industry dates back to the time when, at the age of seven or eight, I asked casually, 'Daddy what does "Ltd" mean?', and had the advantages and disadvantages of limited liability carefully explained! I had made the delightful discovery that I only had to ask questions on industry to be treated seriously as an intelligent adult, and it made the subject fascinating.

The 'Riverside' works complex

Ammonia Plant X

Ammonia Plant Y

1

Introduction: the innocent eye

This study gives an anthropological account of technology and 'culture' in two ammonia-making plants. The 'ethnography' of the chemical industry has for a long time been central to debates about the nature of industrial relationships, because it has been pre-eminently an industry that has been influenced by the techniques of advanced automation; and advanced automation, it has often been argued, transforms both the working environment and the social relationships between worker and boss. The work that originally popularized this view, Blauner's *Alienation and Freedom,* became a classic in its field. In recent years, however, the influence of technology as an independent factor affecting the relationships between manager and worker has been doubted.

It was this problem that first interested me and led me from the more usual fields of anthropological study to that of industry, and I shall begin this account, therefore, by giving an outline of my first impressions of the technology and culture of these ammonia plants. I have called this chapter 'The innocent eye' because it is the result primarily of attentive observation rather than theoretical reflection. Subsequently I shall consider in some detail the reasons that have been given for arguing that the significance of technology has been overrated, and why this initial descriptive account might seem somewhat simplistic. Briefly, there are two directions from which such a charge might be made. First there is the argument that it is naive to think that the culture of any work-place is determined by technological factors since it can be shown that if different countries are compared the same technology will seem to produce different cultural traits – in other words it is essential to consider any work-place in the context of national industrial culture. Second, there is the challenge from neo-Marxist theory. One form of this theory asserts that technology does not exert an independent influence on the relations of production because in a capitalist society the choice of technology is determined by management who design it not simply to fulfil certain productive tasks but to enable the bosses to control the workers. This view has been very influential in recent years, and I shall, therefore, attempt to deal with it with some care. However, it is not an argument that can be taken in isolation, for it is linked to a number of other concepts about the 'relations of production' in modern industry. Simplifying very much at this point, it might be said that this particular understanding of the role of technology is linked to a view of the work-place as a place of obvious oppression for the workers; an environment rigidly divided into management as 'the agents of capital', on the one hand, and the workers as the 'exploited', on the other; between them, it is assumed, relations are necessarily hostile. A second structural Marxist theory is more subtle. This acknowledges that much has been done in recent years to improve the lot of the workers, who may even enjoy what they do; but, it is argued, everything that has been done has simply had the result of strengthening management's position, and has been designed by management with this end. Thus, to ascribe co-operative shop floor relations to technological factors is absurd: they are manufactured by management.

The consequence, therefore, of setting out to explore the interaction of technology and culture is that we will, necessarily, have to examine in some detail, in later chapters, the nature of the relationships between 'management' and 'workers'. Thus, from a descriptive account of the two ammonia plants at the beginning, we shall have to move to a consideration of the significance, for their 'labour process', of 'consent' and 'goodwill'; and this will obviously involve reflecting on the merits of the different theories.

Since my original purpose in undertaking this research was to demonstrate the kind of insights that might be gained by studying an industrial situation to acquire data of an anthropological type and in their light examining theories about industrial relations, it seems essential here to discuss the techniques that I used. In describing the two ammonia plants which were the object of my particular attention, I have simply recorded impressions that came from close and careful observation; but the data that I shall go on to present will focus more directly on the behaviour of individuals and on specific situations; this perhaps needs justification.

What constitutes anthropological research? It is often assumed that 'micro-analysis' is the defining characteristic, but this alone does not make a study anthropological. The study of a single factory is not, *ipso facto*, industrial anthropology. Certainly social anthropology normally involves the detailed analysis of small-scale units, but this is merely a means to the end of understanding the 'culture' of the people being studied. Understanding any culture is far from simple since it involves *both* an analysis of the complex factors that structure the situation for the individuals caught up in it *and* an attempt to understand the 'meaning' of the situation for these individuals; the way, that is, that they understand it and how, in consequence, they try to manipulate the structure. Good sociology of course has similar aims (see e.g. Abrams 1981: ch. 1). The anthropological enterprise, however, has specialized in the way it has refined certain techniques of presenting material, especially about individuals, in order to overcome the difficulties inherent in this task; the problem, that is, of selection. If we accept the fundamental assumption that it is not legitimate simply to infer 'meaning' from structure but we must also grant significance to people's own understanding of their aims and actions, then we must in principle allow them to 'speak for themselves'. But since space is limited we obviously select the views of only certain people, and even the same person may not be consistent but say different things to different audiences, or at different times. It is only too easy for any research worker to select for presentation those views and those events that accord with the writer's own general theories.

The whole issue of the presentation of fieldwork data is one that has greatly exercised social anthropologists, who may differ radically among themselves in many respects but in general agree that their studies, made in considerable depth, of small groups of people, should conform to certain standards. Because of the often exotic nature of their work, they are expected to be meticulous in their study of the details of behaviour in order to avoid misunderstandings. Again, because so much of their work has been exotic, anthropologists are expected to present their fieldwork data in a great deal of detail, and in such a way that it can stand up to the rigorous scrutiny of deeply sceptical groups of colleagues who enjoy nothing so much as demonstrating publicly that the analysis under discussion is based on inadequate and/or misinterpreted data. I do not think that this behaviour means that anthropologists have been particularly cruel; it is simply that the only guarantee of the truth of the data that eventually finds acceptance is the perspicacious criticism of the author's peers. Anthropological fieldwork is judged to be really adequate only if it gives so much detail that it is possible to use it to subject any analysis that may be made of, say, a tribe, to critical review. There is good reason for this because one research worker may be the only qualified observer to visit some particular group. If the returned fieldworker states that the mother's brother among the Bongo Bongo did this or that, then other anthropologists, who have never been there, need to satisfy themselves as to the veracity and competence of the observer. Over the years the standard of reporting that was required rose considerably and, out of the critical comments passed on fieldwork, certain criteria came to be accepted by which fields reports have to be judged.

This is the background that does much to explain why good anthropological research is presented in the context of a wealth of detail. It is not regarded as sufficient to put forward a thesis and back it with 'apt illustrations', examples, however accurate, that simply confirm an author's argument. Anthropologists, as critics, tend to be very suspicious of data that totally confirm some particular abstract theory. Their own experiences of fieldwork lead them to be sceptical of any suggestion that individuals always conform either to the rules of their own societies or to theories propounded by research workers; therefore, exceptions and anomalies are expected. The student is firmly taught that mere apt illustration proves nothing except that the writer, having got hold of an idea, has then selected, from presumably a wide range of possible material, those particular instances that happen to support the point he wishes to make. The test is to present the critics with sufficient detail about individual behaviour to convince them that the particular analysis is tenable. 'Sufficient detail' broadly means that enough material is given for another anthropologist, holding a different theory, to test it on the same data. At all costs stereotyping, that is allocating to individuals within the society observed those characteristics the anthropologist assumes they ought to have, rather than those they actually possess, is to be avoided.

How do those who work within what may be called the 'traditional' framework of social anthropology seek to avoid the risk of 'stereotyping' and 'apt illustration'? To meet the best anthropological standards, the data presented should give well-described accounts both of the same individual interacting with a range of different people, and of the same kind of event being experienced by different groups. Generally it is considered that to illustrate key issues the best procedure is to present 'social dramas', a concept developed originally by Victor Turner (1957). In these, details are given of events in which individuals, some of whom have already been introduced in other contexts, are seen in action over periods of time dealing with sets of problems; the more complex these are the better.

Another anthropological defence against the danger of over-simplification that is at the heart of all stereotyping is to pay particular attention to the unintended consequences of actions and beliefs. Again this stems from the exotic history of the discipline. Anthropologists concerned with understanding so much that was strange paid great attention to all kinds of consequences that appeared to follow from particular actions, whether or not these consequences were comprehended by the actors. The legacy of this is a fascinated concern with consequences of actions that are to the actor, unintended, unwanted and, perhaps, unrecognized; and with relationships that regularly contain elements that are quite different from those that are formally acknowledged. The informal and the unintended are thus twin areas of particular anthropological concern.

There is one final and very important aspect of anthropological fieldwork. Because anthropologists have commonly tried to 'make sense' of exotic societies in which social relations take, to the research worker, strange and unexpected forms, any new society that is to be successfully understood has to be approached in a way that is relatively open-minded. Just as the apprentice anthropologist is taught not to impose a stereotyped view of the individual, so a stereotyped view of the society at a more abstract level is also to be avoided. It is essential to be alert to new forms of social organization not contained within the set of expectations that the research worker originally took to 'the field'.

This is not to suggest that the findings of anthropologists are essentially inductive; of course they owe an immense amount to the researcher's theoretical equipment. Perhaps the best way to put it is to say that there is a 'dialectical' relationship between theory and experience of the field. Initial perceptions are essentially guided by theoretical expectations, but these in turn will develop, and be altered by field experience. This should be true of all those who study society but perhaps anthropologists in particular are taught to expect the unexpected, and perhaps also it is they, especially, who develop an inner eye for unusual social patterning. These patterns are translated into abstract lines and circles linking those who are studied. Some of these links result from the unstructured whim of individuals. Others, that may at first sight seem just as idiosyncratic, turn out to be parts of regular patterns that are eventually seen to be quite crucial to comprehending the whole. I doubt if anyone can be really successful as a fieldworker who does not enjoy both the attempt to understand the intense individuality of the individual, and the study of the complex, abstract patterning of recurrently occurring relationships, above all when the patterns are unusual.

To put my aims in a nutshell, they were to discover how useful one standard technique of social anthropology, commonly called participant observation, might be in an industrial setting. In the strict sense of the term I was not a participant observer in that I made no attempt to observe *incognito* whilst appearing simply to be taking part in the activities being studied. Quite apart from any moral problems such an approach might have entailed, it would have been an impossibility. Indeed, when the question came up, as it did occasionally, as to whether I might be a management spy, I always countered by saying that if management had wanted a spy they would not have chosen someone who stuck out like a sore thumb, as I did. In a totally male, and largely working-class world I was a middle-class female, and in a predominantly young world I was middle-aged. Moreover, because the men I was working with wanted to avoid what they regarded as inappropriate language in front of me, their good manners meant that they tried constantly to be alert to my presence. However, I spent three months continuously at the works, and in this time the people on the two plants that I selected for intensive study did more or less get used to having me around.

I was a participant observer in the broader sense of the term since for my research I used neither questionnaire nor formal interview but instead spent long periods with people working shifts. I watched men in all the different grades and categories interacting with one another, and I listened both to what they said to me, noting especially what they said spontaneously, and what they said amongst themselves. It was an enormous help to me that I was particularly concerned with process workers, for by the nature of their occupation these men spent a large part of their time waiting for things to happen. They did particular tasks, but they were also waiting for things that might go wrong, and if nothing did go amiss then there was a certain amount of boredom and the presence of an outsider was more a diversion than an unwelcome intrusion. I provided a new ear for old stories, and a sympathetic ear for grouses. I think it was also hoped that I might provide a new channel of communication with senior managers. Whilst scrupulously avoiding repeating anything that I feared might cause trouble, I made no secret of the fact that I did sometimes talk to the top people, and my impression was that men on the plants tried from time to time to use me like a ventriloquist's dummy, to get their views expressed at a level they could not normally reach.

I studied in detail the two ammonia plants, that I call Plant X and Plant Y. Originally I had hoped to have attached myself to a particular shift on each plant and in turn to have done a complete shift cycle with it. This I found would have been an uneconomic use of my time since on night-shifts I became so stupidly tired that I remembered clearly relatively little of what I had heard and seen. Therefore, although on Plant X I did attach myself to a particular shift, and did most of the shift cycle with it, I completed only three full night-shifts. On other occasions, however, I did part of these shifts, remaining at the works late into the night, long after management had left. On Plant Y I stayed for no full night-shift, but again I linked myself particularly to one shift team, and stayed with them on the plant on several occasions until after midnight. Additionally, on each plant I did spells of work with other shifts; and naturally I worked over the week-ends as well as on week-days.

What I heard and saw I wrote up when I got back to my flat. At the plants I wrote down certain details about the technicalities of the work that I could not possibly have remembered. Often, however, it would have been wholly inappropriate to have attempted to take notes in the middle of events as they were unfolding. People knew I was there to observe, but nevertheless note-taking would have been disconcerting. Tape recordings would have been not only inappropriate but impossible, given the general level of noise, and I did not attempt to make such recordings.

This raises the question of the reliability of evidence that is not noted down immediately. I can say only that the ability to recall events accurately was a skill I had learnt from field experience on earlier occasions. I had learnt the hard way that it was absolutely essential to write up the details of events witnessed on one day immediately and that to accumulate mere outline sketches with the intention of writing up several days' activities was a recipe for confusion. Provided that on returning home I immediately jotted down brief notes, and then, after eating or sleeping, I at once wrote up all the details as fully as possible, I think I was able to recall conversations and events with considerable accuracy. Obviously I cannot vouch for every word of the conversations in my note-books, but I believe them to be substantially correct.

It was extremely hard work and meant that between one shift and the next there was no time for anything except eating, sleeping, and writing. Nevertheless this system of recording information has one great advantage over taping data. Because it demands a great deal of concentrated thought about what has just occurred it generates new questions and new ideas about the meaning of events. Such reflection was immensely useful and it is unlikely that it would have been as useful, even had it been possible, to put each day's tapes away, unconsidered, in the knowledge that they could be typed up at some future date.

In order to begin the task of presenting the data acquired through these techniques, ammonia production must first be described so that the non-chemist may be able to form some independent judgement on the extent of the significance of its technology for social relations. Put at its simplest, the argument for saying that it is important is that it is inevitably a potentially very dangerous process that can be operated with safety only by those who are well trained and responsible.

The basic purpose of the works, of which the ammonia plants

are one part, is to produce fertilizer, intended primarily for the agricultural market of the south of England. The plants I studied produced ammonia (NH_3) that could be used in two different ways. By far the greater proportion was used on the site, being converted first into nitric acid (HNO_3) in a separate plant, and then in that form used for the making of the actual fertilizers. A smaller proportion was 'exported' from the works (in liquid form, known as 'water-white') in specially constructed road and rail tankers. A by-product, liquid carbon dioxide (CO_2) was also 'exported'.

Ammonia is a combination of one molecule of nitrogen with three of hydrogen and the basic process involves the extraction of nitrogen and hydrogen in order to recombine them chemically with each other in the right proportions. Nitrogen can be taken from the air relatively simply, through a process of compression, and each plant has huge air compressors. Hydrogen was, when the works was built in the 1960s, produced at first from naphtha, a form of oil; but today natural gas, cheaper and safer, is used instead as a feed stock. (Water, which might appear to the layman to be a cheaper source of hydrogen, would in fact be prohibitively expensive because of the complex processes involved.

Put simply, ammonia production is concerned with the extraction of the required basic materials, and with the elimination (from the gases extracted) of various unwanted elements, of which sulphur, carbon and oxygen are the main ingredients. The oxygen presents little problem, being burned off in the heating of the gases required for other reasons. The elimination from the hydrogen feed stock of sulphur is much less of a problem than it was before the change to natural gas, for this contains little sulphur. It is the presence of carbon that causes most difficulty today. It is important to eliminate it completely since any that remained would be very detrimental to the final processes involved in combining the hydrogen and nitrogen to make ammonia. Within the production process as a whole, about fifteen different steps must take place before ammonia is produced. These steps involve variously: heating gases intensively, up to as much as 1000 °C, cooling them, passing them over or through catalysts which are easily spoiled ('poisoned') if the wrong impurities get to them. Ultimately ammonia gas is compressed to 300 times atmospheric pressure. As I am concerned only with the social implications of this technology, we shall look only at the general

Figure 1 Ammonia making: the key to fertilizer production

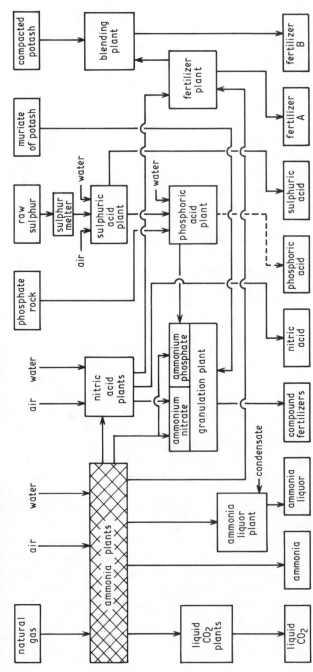

significance of all this heating and compression, and of the choice of the feed stock for hydrogen.

These heating and cooling and compression processes were not carried out on a small scale within the confines of a laboratory but in physically large complexes of machinery: the newer plant, X, the product of more advanced technology, covered two acres of land; the older plant, Y, covered five acres. Each had as its focus a control room with walls covered with clusters of instruments giving heat and pressure readings; so many dials and charts that by comparison those on the Concorde's flight deck appear simple. Round this centre were grouped one or two small offices, washrooms, kitchens and eating areas, since men on the plants could not leave them to eat in the canteen.

These centres were noisy, they smelt strongly of ammonia, but they were warm and dry. Outside, sometimes sheltered from the elements but often exposed to them, were the giant compressors, the huge furnaces composed of a multitude of gas jets, the cooling towers with their constant spray of water. To an outsider everywhere was noisy, but in some areas men were not allowed to work without ear protection because of the damage that would otherwise have been caused to their hearing. Everywhere outside the centre complex was considered dangerous enough to require men at all times to wear helmets. Because of the danger of fumes some areas might not be approached except by men carrying oxygen masks in case of accidents. Rules required that other areas might not be entered or particular tasks done except by those wearing full protective clothing; other regular monitoring jobs might be done only by those wearing goggles. Everywhere there were shower points so that in an emergency water might be immediately to hand to wash off noxious fluids. The men took care to warn me that if there were a leak of ammonia gas and it blew my way I must not follow my instinct and run downwind but must run towards the leak to get upwind of it or it would be fatal. But some said the greatest danger was probably that of a leak of steam being piped from one part of the plant to another: this was, of course, without any telltale smell, and so hot that if it escaped it was quite invisible and could cause severe scalding before a man knew that anything was amiss. I was quite impressed with my own devotion to research when I found myself climbing a fifty-foot outside iron stairway at 3 a.m., wearing a helmet and carrying an oxygen mask, all in the cause of finding out what it was like to check for a gas leak. Honesty, however, compels me to admit that that was on a pleasant summer night and there was no anticipation that the leak was particularly dangerous; it was a job that the men had to do no matter how foul the weather or serious the risk.

I found it significant that the men working on these plants took a pride in their complexity, stressing that they were much more complicated than any of the other plants in the works, and telling me, correctly, that after a shut-down the ammonia plants took the longest time to get back into full production: others might re-start in hours, but the ammonia plants' 'start-up' period had to be reckoned in days. I found that all those employed within the ammonia plants, whatever their rank in the company's hierarchy, and indeed whatever their attitude towards the ChemCo company, judged their worth *vis-à-vis* others of the same grade on the site in these terms. At its simplest their argument was that their machinery was more complex, therefore they were doing a more important job. Because they were involved in ammonia production they were superior to men on the same grade on other plants, even if this superiority could not be formally recognized.

Looking more minutely at the question of the social significance of the processes of production within the plants, it was obvious that the nature of the catalysts exerted a number of influences. The catalysts used in one ammonia plant are not necessarily identical to those in a different plant because there are various routes to the achievement of the same end. Basically a plant is designed from the beginning to work with a given set of catalysts which cannot subsequently be fundamentally altered. For example, Plant X used arsenic to remove CO_2, whilst Plant Y did not. Arsenic had been chosen when Plant X was designed because at that time it cost significantly less than other possible catalysts; its relative price advantage had gone and it had become relatively costly to use it, but despite its disadvantages there was no practicable way of changing it. Plant X is now, in some contexts, identified both by its own people and by outsiders as one that uses a particularly dangerous process. To outsiders in the works it gives the plant an unfavourable image: insiders, however, seem to take a certain pride in their situation, for by implication, 'We are the ones who can cope with danger.' Significantly, stories are told of real outsiders, contractors' men, who have displayed both unreasoning fear and have yet been prepared to take stupid risks. With some glee I was told the story of a bunch of contractors' men, with all the protective gear they had been demanding found at their tea break sitting down in the arsenic-contaminated section of the plant with their gloves off, eating jam doughnuts!

Contractors' men enter plant folklore because the life of all catalysts is limited and their efficiency deteriorates within a relatively short time. Therefore, every one or two years, an ammonia plant must be shut down, the catalyst vessels cleaned, and the catalysts themselves renewed. At the same time for safety reasons the machinery is completely overhauled. The 'shut-down' is apparently a period of social testing and tension. Everyone is extremely busy. Men judge the technical ability of their plant manager by his performance at this time: his chemical knowledge is gauged by his ability to suggest valuable modifications to catalysts or machinery; his general managerial skills are discussed in terms of his ability to get the best out of outside contractors. Men of one plant may at this time work with those they seldom see otherwise, for overtime work may be offered to men from the other ammonia plant, still working normally; this may lead to friendships but seems also to confirm the convictions of each group that the other fellows have some rather odd habits. It may also lead to resentment if the men of one plant believe that the others did not fully reciprocate the chances to work overtime that they had been given.

When the plant is running normally, the existence of the catalysts continues to have social significance because they can be easily damaged by 'operator neglect'. One of the main daily risks is that some act of carelessness may 'poison' a catalyst. Put simply, if some chemical element that should have been eliminated at an earlier stage is allowed through so that it passes a catalyst with which it should never have come into contact, then a great deal of harm may be done; such harm may be expensive even in the context of a very costly production operation. The consequence of this is both an obvious concern that operators should not be neglectful, and a less obvious influence on the reputation of individuals. Even if such damage cannot officially be traced to the fault of a particular individual, rumour quickly pins the blame on some operator and ultimately on the supervisor of his shift. Such stories become part of the gossip of the plant – as I realized when towards the end of my research I began to have the tales recounted to me – and build up or destroy the reputations of individuals, especially of supervisors.

The nature of the feed stock and the heating and compressing of gases involved in ammonia-making similarly exert a social significance because of the obvious danger of the processes involved, and because here too the alertness of operator and supervisor may make the difference between a minor hiccough in production and a major shut-down, or even a dangerous explosion. To take a simple and common example of something that may go wrong. Problems arise if even a small quantity of water reaches the gas compression stages, because water cannot be compressed. Therefore, if any water enters the compressor systems it causes great damage. An essential part of the compressor is a series of very finely ground steel valves, each costing about £500, and the water will wreck the first valve it encounters. After that the damage escalates, for if the production process is not stopped swiftly then bits of the broken valve will be carried on through the compressor, wreaking havoc on the other valves further along the system. The possibility that other acts of carelessness might cause far more significant damage is something that is always present in men's minds. So too is the realization that a simple lack of alertness to some malfunctioning of the machinery might also be both extremely costly and dangerous. At this point my data from the ammonia plants would conform wholly with recent data from a study of oil refineries that contrary to what was implied in some earlier studies of continuous process industries, automation does not eradicate the need for operator care – on the contrary, it can make the consequences of error spectacularly damaging. This is a point to which we shall return.

A quite different kind of social consequence was related to the fact that the the feed stock for ammonia production, natural gas, is both expensive and used in vast quantities, so that the process of ammonia-making, even apart from the high cost of the original plant, is extremely expensive. Operating costs alone involve millions of pounds a year, and this costliness influences both the attitudes of the workers and that of ChemCo.

In the first place the enormous costs involved influenced the attitudes of the men who believed that against this background the expense of their wages must be mere chicken-feed to their employer. The men themselves were genuinely impressed by the cost of the great amount of energy used. I was told that the plant consumed 35 million cubic metres of gas per day, and that this was one-tenth of the total consumption of gas in the region; I was also told that the daily consumption of gas at the works was more than the total national domestic consumption, and further that the works consumed 3 million megawatts of electricity per hour in its various processes. I am not concerned here with whether these are precisely accurate facts, but with what sensible people believed. Taking these running costs into consideration, and adding on the known capital costs of ammonia plants (currently in the region of £40 million), it was scarcely surprising that the men should conclude that the cost of their wages must be trivial by comparison. Indeed, the men had not been alone in this for it seemed that until relatively recently the management too shared this opinion; an attitude that is not surprising since this seems to have been a common assumption in the chemical industry.

The technology of ammonia production had further implications, or at least so I assumed initially; we shall see later the extent to which my assumptions may or may not have been justified. In the first place it was essential that the plants should, normally, operate continuously; there was no question of shutting them down every evening and therefore they were worked continuously by shifts of operators. Second, because of the potentially dangerous nature of the process, dangerous not merely to the men on the plants but to everyone in the locality of the works, there had always to be someone on the plant qualified by his training to take necessary decisions and issue orders in an emergency. Since clearly the plant manager could not always be present, the supervisor (foreman) of a shift had to fill this role in the manager's absence. Third, complex machinery such as that described, required not merely men to run it but also men to service it, men competent as fitters, electricians, instrument artificers, etc. and in consequence there are two rather different groups of workers on the plants. It became apparent to me very swiftly that despite the obvious connection between these groups, and the different types of work these men were doing, the barriers between them were almost as much due to the social construction placed on their activities as they were to these activities themselves. It also became obvious that these social distinctions were extremely important. Therefore, although my main concern in this chapter is with an account of the two ammonia plants and the differences between them, it is essential to begin by saying something about these two kinds of workers.

The process operators and the maintenance men (craftsmen) are distinguished both by their patterns of work and by their attitudes to their work. Much of the time, while the plant is running smoothly, the process worker is a mere minder of machines that should continue to work endlessly, round the clock, with little interference. Under such circumstances the operator's main job is to perform certain routine tasks responsibly. If things go wrong, however, he must be able to react swiftly, with efficiency, under conditions of stress and even danger; and any failure on his part may result in serious damage to machinery, enormous waste, and above all, risks to men. By contrast, and simplifying somewhat, the role of the craftsman is to service and repair instruments and machinery when they give trouble; and when they give real trouble they are taken out of service. Often these men work under considerable pressure and difficult conditions – idle machinery means lost production; badly repaired machinery can be dangerous. But their actual working conditions are different from those of the operator because quite obviously a machine that is out of action seldom threatens danger to those working in its neighbourhood.

Differences in the technology of their work seem clearly correlated with differences in attitudes and behaviour characterizing operators and maintenance men. The latter had a reputation for militancy, including a willingness to take direct industrial action; the operators did not. Less dramatically, but of literally everyday significance, were the different attitudes these two sets of workers showed to their tea and meal breaks – above all to the midday dinner break. To the maintenance men these breaks were sacred, in Durkheim's sense of the word, for they were times 'set apart and forbidden': they were set apart for the use of the men, and management was forbidden to encroach on these periods – indeed in a very real sense the dinner break belonged to the men since this period was not included in the hours of work for which the men were paid. By contrast the operators had no specified breaks at all. The process operators of course had many periods of slack time when they could and did take snacks. Indeed they were devoted to cups of tea at such times and the offering and accepting of tea was a social ceremony that sometimes had important consequences for patterns of relationships. Nevertheless, if it was necessary, work took precedence over eating and drinking, and an alarm bell would send men running from tables in the mess. The process workers were aware that this was one characteristic that distinguished them; when I asked what kind of recruit would not make a good operator, I was told of one who, because he was just about to start eating, thought he could ignore a summons over the loudspeaker. Their readiness to leave a meal to answer a summons was a pattern of behaviour that I saw repeatedly – most strikingly on one occasion when I was chatting to a new young operator who was just starting a snack. He suddenly got to his feet and rushed off with an apology. No call had come for him but he had heard a change in the noise of the compressor in his charge, and he had gone to investigate. In summary, therefore, in observing the 'culture' of these plants, I found myself observing two very different groups of men who were intensely aware of their differences.

The primary distinction between the process operators and the maintenance men was that only the latter could, properly, be called 'skilled'. This is directly related to a distinction, imposed by the unions rather than by management, between the workers, who had served a craft apprenticeship, and the process operators, who, whilst trained, had learnt 'on the job', after having been recruited by the company. The operators often spoke bitterly of being classed as 'unskilled', although officially they might more accurately be referred to as 'semi-skilled'. The reason for ascribing the distinction to the attitude of the trade unions, rather than to that of management, is that the works manager often found the division a costly nuisance, and a more flexible working system would undoubtedly have been preferred. Certainly the process men blamed the unions, saying that they thought that it was in the interests of the skilled unions to exclude them, and in the interests of the general union to which they belonged to insist on hanging on to them. The process worker receives on-the-job training that lasts several years and he may be extremely knowledgeable. Should he rise to be a supervisor, he will have almost sole charge for hours on end of machinery worth millions of pounds; as such he may find himself in a situation in which the safety of this machinery and of the men working on it, including the maintenance men, depend on his ability to make the right decisions under difficult circumstances. The fact remains that not having served an apprenticeship he has no paper qualifications and were he to find himself queueing at a labour exchange, he could not register as a 'skilled' worker. Men told me that at one stage ChemCo had suggested giving certificates of skill to those operators who had served satisfactorily as process workers for five years or more; but, they alleged, the hierarchies of the unions had joined in opposing the idea. The consequence was that the company had dropped the scheme.

It is at this point worthwhile stating what, to anyone with experience of working in British industry, is the obvious. To the skilled trades, the operator, as a man without an apprenticeship, is an inferior mortal who should be made constantly aware of his lower status and his lesser virtue. As is well known, the unskilled man is forbidden to use tools or to do any work requiring a trade skill. In practice this means, as the operators told me indignantly, that they were prevented even from using a screwdriver and they were not allowed to change light bulbs. Of course the main motivation behind such rules was undoubtedly financial – the skilled trades wanted the monetary advantages that came from forcing management to employ them on every occasion that could possibly be defined as needing 'skilled' labour. At times, however, it seemed almost reminiscent of a caste system, in which such regulations have a symbolic rather than a practical consequence; they made everyone continually aware of the sharp distinction between the superior and the inferior, just as apartheid regulations might, or prohibitions on the shadow of an untouchable falling on a person of clean caste. There was no doubt, judging from the conversation of many of the maintenance men, that they did regard themselves as, in a sense, morally superior to the operators because as lads they had given up the chance of easy money to become apprentices. They thought that on these grounds the rules that entrenched their superiority were fully justified. What was of real concern to me was to watch the interaction of these skilled craftsmen and the process operators, both in formal and in informal settings.

Not surprisingly there was hostility between these groups, but this was not the only factor of interest in their relationship. To the craftsmen, it seemed of intense personal importance that their superiority should be acknowledged; to the process worker, the skill of many so-called craftsmen was at best problematic, and they said so. The tensions and jealousies stemming from this very different perception of the 'real' situation manifested themselves in complex ways (and sometimes made the position of the process supervisor extremely difficult). Yet this was not the end of my concern with the maintenance workers. Anthropologists have a habit of making abstract mental images of social relationships, and in this context the abstraction seemed illuminating. Each plant provided the setting for intricately related circles joining process operators on the same and on different shifts. The operators seemed largely isolated from those on different plants but were interlinked by the skilled men who moved between the plants. They carried gossip, despite the antagonisms inherent in their relationship with the operators, and presented them with glimpses of a very different outlook on the company and on the world in general. All this was very important, as I realized when I began to try to understand the fact that the two ammonia plants I studied, if they were examined in detail, appeared to have very different 'cultures', despite having almost identical technologies. One factor that seemed to be significant was that minor differences in their design had led to different kinds of contact between the process operators and the maintenance men.

As a preliminary to describing these two plants, one further external influence must be noted: much that went on has to be ascribed to the fact that I studied them in a period of recession. This affected everyone, but its impact on these two groups of men differed. This was, first, because they had radically different positions in the labour market: skilled men had relatively strong positions in the external labour market; process workers had weak positions there.[1] Second, they were differently affected by the pattern of cuts in overtime working that had been introduced by management in an attempt to economize.

It was a very sore point with the skilled men that although the process worker had not been apprenticed, nevertheless his actual wages were equal to, or in certain circumstances greater than, those of the skilled trades. The reason for this was related to the special nature of process work, but was not wholly determined by it. All process workers were shift workers and were paid extra above their basic rate, which was usually lower than that of the skilled man, for their 'unsocial' hours. Moreover, as we shall see, process shift work also gives more chance of working overtime. It was because of all this that process operators could be the higher earners. This, as may be imagined, was bitterly resented by the craftsmen; it was not merely jealousy due to simple financial considerations, but seemed at least partly caused by the fact that the wage was commonly used to judge relative worth, so that to give process operators a higher wage threatened the skilled man's whole perception of himself and his place in the scheme of things. The situation had, however, been made a great deal worse because the maintenance men had recently been deprived of any chance to increase their earnings by doing shift work and there had been cuts in their overtime. Until shortly before I began my study, some fitters had been attached to shifts. These men had not only been paid extra for their unsocial hours, but they had also had reasonable opportunities for working overtime, and because they started from a higher basic rate, their pay had usually been above that of the process operators. An economy drive by management had, however, put an end to this system. The widespread resentment this caused amongst all the maintenance men, even those who had not been personally affected by the change, in itself suggested how great was the value to the skilled men that even a few of their number should have earned more than the 'unskilled'; whilst most of their resentment at the change was directed against management, it seemed also to spill over in their attitude to the process operators.

That management had acted to curtail the high earnings of the shift fitters was due to the fact that over the previous decade concern with marginal costs had grown, first rather gradually, but then much more urgently. ChemCo's trading position in the post-war world had worsened to the extent that it was recognized that its costs relative to its competitors had to be lowered if markets were to be retained. With this end in view, concerted attempts to economize had been made at all the company's works; every enterprise was involved. Ammonia production at the works I studied had, however, been particularly threatened by mounting costs. The fuel crisis of the 1970s had of course sharply raised the price of all fuels and had stimulated all ammonia producers to cut their expenses. The first target was, naturally, that of cutting the fuel bill, and to this end intense efforts went into designing more economical machinery, and more economical total systems. To save fuel, designers of new ammonia plants now included methods by which heat generated through chemical reactions in one part of the system, and formerly wasted, could be used to supply heat where it was needed, at other points in the production process. These new designs were in fact very much more economical in their use of fuel than were the systems that had been used in the plants I was studying, which belonged to an earlier generation. Here, too, a lot of redesign effort had been and was being put into improving the fuel efficiency, and had effected considerable improvements; nevertheless, they were severely handicapped in comparison with their newer competitors. These older plants were still producing well by the standards of their original design specifications but inevitably they operated at a severe disadvantage. Both plants, although not to the same degree, were being outstripped even by the performance of other plants owned by ChemCo. One figure quoted to me by a very knowledgeable worker was that the new plants produced ammonia at £48 per tonne, whilst one of the two plants on the site, Plant X, was said to produce it at £53 per tonne and the other, older one, Plant Y, produced it at £80 per tonne.

For this reason managers had developed a wholly new kind of concern over marginal labour costs. They believed that the future of the works might well be jeopardized by its high fuel costs; although it enjoyed a certain advantage in being close to the best agricultural markets for the fertilizer that was the ultimate product of their ammonia, this by itself was insufficient, and therefore labour costs, they argued, had to be reduced.

The management drive to cut labour costs was, however, causing friction with the employees, who undoubtedly recognized the problem of costs that existed but were inclined to think that most real savings must still come from greater efficiency in other aspects of production. By comparison with the astronomic costs of the fuel bills it seemed to them that wages costs could still scarcely have any more than a purely symbolic significance. Savings on wages might serve to demonstrate to ChemCo's senior management elsewhere that the works was doing everything possible to be 'good boys' but it was doubted whether in the long run this would prove to weigh with them. As the men still thought that their wages must be a very marginal factor, virtually irrelevant to ChemCo's calculations, they thought there was little they, as workers, could do to preserve their jobs. There was intense speculation as to whether the company would in the end build new ammonia plants on their site, or whether it would close down the whole place. They thought their future was endangered by two further factors. First, they knew that currently they were operating under an old and advantageous price agreement with the Gas Board that would shortly have to be renegotiated, on less good terms it was assumed. Second, it seemed that ChemCo's decision about the location of any new ammonia plants was likely to be influenced by government policy that gave substantial grants for developments in areas of high unemployment, which effectively discriminated against their district. Some men were optimistic, stressing the extra costs that would be involved if the company had to bring all its fertilizers down by rail to the agricultural south; such men eagerly read every bit of news about projected rises in freight charges. Optimists, however, were few, and not surprisingly they seemed to be concentrated in the more economical of the two ammonia plants.

Events in the history of the works that had entered its culture through its folklore made the men's anxieties worse. I was told that twice plants that had for a variety of reasons become redundant to ChemCo's plans, either through obsolescence or through a change in market conditions, had been shut down and the announcement of the closures had come without warning, when the men had thought their plants were in full and profitable production. In one case they said the decision had been made secretly at the highest level, and neither the plant manager nor the then works manager had known what was planned until the day of the announcement. In the past plant closures had not caused real hardship because the company had taken some trouble to try to find work for the redundant men elsewhere on the site, and because at the time jobs were readily available elsewhere. That was no longer the case, and so there was great fear of unemployment should the works close, and a considerable inclination to believe that this would indeed be its fate before long. The management repeatedly tried to reassure the men that, provided they ran the place as economically as possible, this would not happen. But although the present managers had not themselves been involved in the sudden closures of the past, the folklore generated by these events prevented any great credence being given to such reassurances. What had presumably been some former managerial strategy for keeping up morale in the short term had, not surprisingly, so entered the works' culture that it undermined morale in the long term. A sense of insecurity would have existed in any case, given that groups of highly perspicacious men, some of whom habitually read the trade journals, were assessing the economic future of plants that had so much to threaten their continuation; but the insecurity had been made worse by what was seen as former duplicity.

The process worker felt particularly vulnerable. He had gained his relatively high wage by learning highly specialized skills that were not marketable because they remain uncertificated. In any case automated chemical plants are so limited in number that the openings for employment are very few when compared with the openings that exist for the skilled maintenance men. Even had there been no recession, any threatened closure of the works caused them very grave anxieties, for with relative affluence they had taken on financial commitments, and they thought they had little chance of finding similarly well-paid jobs elsewhere. The occasional maintenance man might dream of doing rather well should the works close, for there would be redundancy money and the confident expectation of a skilled job with another firm, but the operator was in a fundamentally different position; a Sword of Damocles hung above his head. All this made it clear that on these ammonia plants two sets of workers existed. But did all process operators react similarly?

THE TWO PLANTS

I shall begin the descriptive account of the ammonia plants in this fertilizer works by comparing Plant X and Plant Y as fields of social relationships, for reflections on the nature of the differences between the two plants are very pertinent to the major theoretical debate about the relative significance of technology and culture for work-place behaviour. Cultural differences may be analysed at many levels. At the broadest level the focus of attention may be on differences that stem from national variations in the laws regulating industrial behaviour or, in relation to Japanese industrial patterns, for example, attention may be paid to an even wider cultural field. Here, however, I have chosen to examine very small-scale cultural variations, because by examining the questions of technology and culture in these two ammonia plants it is possible to limit the number of variables that have to be considered. These two plants are in the same works, Riverside (which earlier was the subject, as I shall describe, of a rather different kind of study [see Nichols and Beynon (1977)]), and are under the control of the same senior management; they recruit their employees from the same area by the same processes; they have an obviously very similar technology. It would scarcely seem possible for two plants to be more similar to each other. I shall argue, however, that if they are examined carefully, it can be seen that there are none the less small differences between them. These differences, although they may at first sight seem to be merely trivial and unimportant details of behaviour, when looked at more closely can be seen to be indications of significant differences of culture, and these can be related back to technological and 'environmental' differences. In effect I shall argue that the two plants provide rather different 'habitats' for those who work in them; and in detail they seem significantly different in the extent to which their operators are willing to co-operate with management. It is this fact that makes the 'ethnography' of the two plants of theoretical interest since an exploration of the relationships they display will help us to assess theories about worker–management relations. An analysis of the similarities and differences in behaviour and relationships amongst men on these two ammonia plants will bring into focus the two main themes with which we shall be generally concerned: on the one hand, the relative significance of culture and technology, and on the other, the meaning in the contexts of these ammonia plants of 'power', 'authority', and 'consent'; that is, the question of managerial authority and the extent to which it depended upon, or was independent of, the consent of the men.

Those whom we shall be studying in this account are primarily process operators. The job of ammonia operator is regarded as one of the best jobs open to men who have not served apprenticeships, and it is one to which men are promoted from other unskilled or semi-skilled manual grades; it is thus at the top of the internal labour market. In the normal course of events a vacancy in one of the ammonia plants was advertised first within Riverside and then, if it remained unfilled, more widely within ChemCo's other works. It was not inconceivable that a total outsider might be recruited, but it was very unlikely. Certainly no one currently employed had come directly from outside the company, although a few men had moved very quickly into the ammonia plants and had joined Riverside with the expectation of speedily becoming ammonia operators. Any applicant to either of the plants took certain personality tests, designed to measure his psychological and general suitability, and he also had an interview with a selection panel composed of the plant manager and two or three supervisors. The candidate was also taken round the plant and an effort was made to show him the nature of the work and the working conditions so that he might be able to make some kind of reasoned decision as to whether he would really be prepared to become an ammonia operator, with its attendant shift work, and its sense of danger. Management was concerned to recruit men who would not by any sudden panic turn a crisis into a catastrophe; who would be prepared to learn a rather complex set of operations and carry them out carefully (because any slackness, even if it were not dangerous, could be hideously expensive if, say, it resulted in the 'poisoning' of a catalyst); and who would complete their training successfully and not then simply get fed up and leave. It was reckoned to take three years before an operator could be fully trusted to work without close supervision, and the notional figure of £10,000 was quoted as the cost of the training a man received. It was obviously a situation in which the employer would seek the 'reliable' man, the worker with a stable background and young children who would think carefully before he threw up a well-paying job with fringe benefits.[2]

The process workers were internally differentiated by plant, by grades, and by shift. Each plant was administratively a separate unit under its own plant manager. The manager did not have his office on the plant but in the main administrative block. Each manager visited his plant each morning when he chaired a meeting composed of the supervisor of the morning shift and 'trade' supervisors (fitter, electrician, and instrument artificer) or their deputies to discuss any technical problems on the plant, and he usually called in during the afternoon to see the incoming shift supervisor; in addition, the manager was to be found on the plant at any hour if there was very serious technical trouble. In the normal course of events, however, the plant manager spent most of his time in his office off the plant where his major tasks were carried out. Here he kept checks on the statistics regarding the operation of the plant, did crucial technical work associated with the continual ongoing process of adapting the design of the plant, so far as possible, to meet changing energy conservation problems, and dealt with such items as new safety requirements introduced under the 'health and safety at work' regulations, or agreed with the unions. The plant manager might on any day have an informal conversation with the operators, but for the most part his communications were with the supervisors, who for the most part were left to get on with the more or less routine running of the plant.

On each plant, the operators were divided into four shifts. Each shift was under a supervisor who was on the lowest rung of the management ladder. Each shift had, in addition, a senior operator on the highest operator grade, that is grade 8 in ChemCo's company-wide scheme. Below this man were normally the 'team operators' (on some shifts four men; on some shifts three), who were regarded as fully trained to do any operator's work, including that of the control room operator. Until recently only the specially promoted operator had been allowed to do control room work. He was on grade 7 while the other trained operators were on grade 6, but now all team operators were on grade 7. In addition, on Plant X, which had introduced a pattern of somewhat more flexible working, the longest serving team operators on each shift had been trained to substitute for senior operators when necessary, and thus they had a kind of 'acting' grade 8 status for payment purposes. Below the team operators were, with one exception, only trainees on grade 5, but there were only two of these. One trained operator of long standing remained on grade 6 because he refused to do control room work.

Associated more loosely with each plant, but not exclusively linked to it, were the tradesmen. Because of the importance of the ammonia plants, each had as part of the building or close by, an office for the supervisors of the main trades, fitters and electricians. Each supervisor had jurisdiction over one ammonia plant and the plants associated with it. This was appropriate since that very different category of workers, the 'skilled' men, was essential to the work of the plants. They also were internally divided by trade and union into fitters, electricians, instrument artificers ('tiffys') and welders, etc. whose assistance was needed each day to cope with everything from routine maintenance to major repairs of machinery. The skilled men differed from the operators in ways additional to those already mentioned. They were not only recruited differently, often directly from outside the works as already qualified members of their unions, but they came under their own 'skilled' supervisors, and under their own engineer managers. Their work was not bounded by plants, although there was a pool of about eight fitters from whom a man was most likely to be called to work on one of the ammonia plants; similarly, out of the electricians on the site, there were about five who were most likely to be found working on Plant X or Y. However, as I have said, they were not fixedly attached to either plant but rather they moved between plants as their help was required on particular machines; and with very few exceptions they were on day work. Those who worked on the ammonia plants had to be on the highest grade, 8, that of 'self-supervised' worker.

By contrast, each process man, operator and supervisor, was attached to one particular plant, within which his whole career was usually spent. It is with the process men that we shall be particularly concerned in our analysis of the ammonia plants, although always, in the background, there are the 'tradesmen', playing an essential role in maintaining production.

I shall begin this part of my analysis by setting out what I perceived to be the differences in attitudes and behaviour of the men on the two plants. It was a search for an explanation of these differences that led me to develop many of the ideas that now seem to me to be of general importance. In setting these differences out, therefore, I am not seeking to lay for the reader a wantonly devious trail to conclusions that I really reached by other means. Rather I am setting out for inspection the paths down which I went in trying to find my own answers to teasing questions.

The cultural differences between the plants involved a great variety of attitudes and behaviour, but they could at one level be considered under just two headings: relationships between people; and relationships to place.

That differences of this nature did exist between the two plants was certainly something that the men themselves believed. I began my study on Plant X, and the supervisors there, when it was known that I was going to Plant Y, told me that I would find its organization much more hierarchical. They said specifically that the Plant Y supervisors were much more concerned to stress status distinctions between themselves and the men. In effect, the Plant X supervisors said, I would find these social distinctions symbolized in sharp spatial distinctions. It was stressed that Plant Y supervisors ate apart from their men, that they had a separate toilet, and that they kept the door of their office shut. On Plant X, they said, and as I could observe, the supervisors' office door always stood open; indeed, I was told it was shut only in the extremely rare event of the plant manager dressing down a supervisor. In contrast to this 'apartheid' on Plant Y, I was asked to note the good, easy, friendly relationships between supervisors and operators on Plant X. My first reaction to such assertions was scepticism; I expected to find that these perceived differences existed more in the minds of people on Plant X than in reality. In the event it seemed to me that although the Plant X supervisors were mistaken in believing that all the differences between the two plants really stemmed from the exaggerated status consciousness of the Plant Y supervisors, nevertheless there was at least something in the Plant X assertions. There did seem to be more concern on Plant Y with what may be called 'boundary markers'. I came to realize, however, that concern with such markers was not restricted to the supervisors on Plant Y.

I will begin by describing my first impressions of Plant Y. When I was a young post-graduate, setting out to do fieldwork in Africa, I was told to be sure always to record my first impressions of any place I visited. They might, it was said, offer crucial clues for a later analysis, and it was important to put them down at once, because after a fortnight I might come to regard as so normal the things that had at first surprised me that I might never notice them again. I, therefore, record here three things that, reading over the notes that I made when I first moved to Plant Y, I find struck me as odd. They seemed odd, I hasten to say, not because they were inherently peculiar, but because they differed from Plant X, which, after my few weeks' experience of it, I had come to regard as 'normal', literally the standard by which I measured any other ammonia plant. (Naturally, had I studied Plant Y first, then this would have formed the norm by which I would have judged Plant X.) Of course, this was subjective, but I am using these impressions of cultural distinctiveness as possible clues to more significant cultural differences.

One difference between the two plants relating to the use of space concerned the decoration of the rooms. Calendars, to which I had become accustomed on Plant X, were missing from Plant Y. These were not just any old calendars. British industrialists seem to regard calendars depicting nudes, varying from the pretty to the mildly obscene, as the best way of ensuring that pieces of cardboard advertising Blogg's steel tubes, or ball-bearings, or whatever, shall be pinned up rather than thrown into the waste-paper bin. The calendar itself is irrelevant but provides the excuse for keeping the nude, and therefore the advertisement, on the wall for a year. These calendars decorated several of the Plant X rooms, but there were none on Plant Y. We can exclude the possibility that Plant Y men had puritanical objections to nudes, and I made quite sure they had not been taken down for my benefit (a possibility that occurred to me because initially some Plant X men had seemed slightly embarrassed that I should see theirs). In fact the only decoration on Plant Y was a framed photograph of a guide dog for the blind, hung in the control room, presented in thanks for money that had been collected to provide such a dog. There was also a very large guide dog poster in the main mess. These apart, there was nothing to decorate any of the rooms, and I felt there had to be a reason.

One difference in the relationships between people on the two plants also struck me immediately. This was that a great deal less bantering occurred on Plant Y than went on in Plant X. I had become so used to it in all sorts of contexts on Plant X that its absence was something I repeatedly noticed in my diary recording my first few days on the other plant. Of course this is a subjective impression, and one that it is impossible to quantify. I can say only that on Plant X banter had seemed the small change of social interaction. There, what had been notable was that there were two men who stuck out because they could not be made the butt of jokes without losing their tempers. One was a supervisor and one was a senior operator, and this common characteristic had seemed to make them both, in very different ways, outsiders. By contrast, banter was so rare on Plant Y that I specially noted particular instances where it occurred. There was the incident, like a Bateman cartoon, in which a group I came to call 'the gourmet shift', while eating a particularly succulent supper in their mess, gazed in horrified amazement and joked at the expense of a man at the same table whose meal consisted simply of a can of hot baked beans tipped on to a cold plate. Then on a hot day, a keep-fit enthusiast who had come to work on his racing bike entered the control room wearing only a singlet and racing shorts; he was greeted with cries of derision, and there were calls to me to avert my eyes. These were entirely trivial incidents, yet I found myself paying them particular attention for no reason other than that here they were so very rare, whereas on Plant X it had seemed that no shift passed without such joking.

Why should there have been such a high incidence of joking and teasing on one plant, and relatively little on the other? The difference clearly meant something. No doubt once such a different pattern had been established it would perpetuate itself just through the way in which new recruits were socialized. Confirmation of this seemed to come from the fact that two men on Plant Y, each of whom had started originally on the same, non-ammonia plant at the works, commented spontaneously that when they had changed plants they had missed the horse-play to which they had been accustomed. They said they found the Plant Y men, by contrast, very serious, but (knowing nothing of the Plant X pattern of joking) they explained the difference in behaviour in terms of the superior quality of men on the ammonia plant: clearly they had been, in effect, taught to regard such physical joking as beneath them. Nevertheless, even if part of the explanation might be purely coincidental, it seemed unsatisfactory to jump to the conclusion that this general behavioural difference between the two plants could be explained away as due to some chance historical factor and therefore as non-significant. In the absence of banter, Plant Y seemed much the more formal of the plants. In the broadest sense of the term, it seemed that it must relate to the morale of the plant, and thus it seemed that some reason for the difference should at least be sought.

One other, to me curious, incident occurred on my first day on Plant Y that again provided an example of behaviour quite different from that on Plant X. There, during the period of change-over from one shift to the next, I had repeatedly been present in the supervisor's office when the man going off duty briefed the man taking over; naturally I had never interrupted such a discussion, but I had frequently been interested to listen to what was said about the state of the plant and any technical problems. Sometimes a third supervisor, not attached to any one shift, might be present and he might or might not interject a comment. There seemed to be nothing very remarkable about these sessions, and it had never occurred to anyone to notice my presence beyond exchanging a normal greeting. I was, therefore, mildly surprised during that first day on Plant Y, when, as I was in their supervisors' office talking to such an unattached supervisor, he suddenly turned to me and said that we must go out because it was 'the change-over'. Two men had come in and I realized that that next shift's supervisor wanted to discuss the plant with his predecessor. I assumed that the man who was talking to me thought we might interrupt the others, or that for some reason he did not want them to overhear his conversation. This latter seemed the most likely explanation because instead of taking me some- where on the plant, such as the supervisors' mess, he walked me round and round outside the perimeter of the plant until he judged that we could once more return to the supervisors' office and continue our conversation there alone. I was puzzled, however, since there seemed to be nothing either urgent or private in what he had to say. Subsequently I revised my opinion of why he had taken this action when I found that I was never allowed to be present in the office when one supervisor was handing Plant Y over to another. Moreover, my impression was not that I was, for some inexplicable reason, being singled out for exclusion, but that no one other than the two supervisors concerned could be in the office at this time. In my experience they were invariably alone, and whenever any supervisor wanted to talk to his incoming colleague he would simply say, 'I'm sorry, this is the change-over,' as if this statement were self-explanatory. This was another characteristic that seemed to give Plant Y a more formal atmosphere than Plant X.

The concern with privacy that I thus found among the supervisors was also clearly discernible amongst the men; indeed, it was expressed in a very obvious way in relation to their mess. The mess on these ammonia plants is a very important social space. The works has a good general canteen that is used by management and office staff and may be used by anyone who 'works days', that is anyone who normally works from 8 a.m. or 9 a.m. to about 4 p.m. and has a regular hour allowed as a meal break. This means that the maintenance workers may, if they choose, buy a meal at work. Process operators are in a different category because the nature of their work means that they must be continually on call. Often they may have much spare time during the course of their shift, if all is running smoothly, but it would not be safe for them to be away from the plant for any length of time; in any case the canteen is open only during a limited period of the twenty-four hours, and men on night-shifts also need refreshment. For this reason, as we have seen, each ammonia plant is provided with kitchen facilities and a place where the men may eat; all the operators use these and many maintenance men prefer to use such a mess than to eat the canteen food. Thus the mess is well used, and when, recently, the main mess on Plant Y had been redecorated and had had minor structural alterations there had been much concern with what had been done. One point that seemed to have caused general dissatisfaction was that the alterations had included the enlargement of the outside windows, and the fitting of new interior doors, which, instead of being solid, had glass panels at the top. The immediate response of the men had been to reverse all this. The larger part of the outside windows had been painted over by some of the maintenance men who shared this mess, and the glass in the main door leading to the rest of the plant had been covered over by the very large guide dog poster already mentioned. I found it was not regarded as decoration but had been supplied by the process operators as a screen. There was, in fact, talk of covering the glass of both the interior doors with hardboard. Further, I was told that while the mess had been closed for alteration, a large caravan had been supplied as a substitute mess, and that all its windows had been similarly painted over. By contrast, the window in the Plant X mess had been left untouched. The Plant Y men were quite explicit in saying that what had been done in their mess had been done to prevent anyone from checking up on what they were doing there. They were particularly anxious that nobody should be able to see if they dozed on the night-shift, and for this reason they said they planned to close one of the two interior doors permanently; the one they intended to leave open was guarded in a different way as it had a squeaky handle that could be guaranteed to wake any sleeper up if a supervisor did come round.

To understand what all this meant for the 'cultures' of the two plants, it is important to realize that Plant X and Plant Y each had both a small and a large mess, but that the uses to which they were put were significantly different.

On Plant X the small mess was used by all the process men, supervisors and operators equally. It contained a refrigerator, a small oven with pots and pans, and a sink unit. In addition, each individual had an identical locker for his tea, coffee, etc., and his china and cutlery. Sometimes the Plant X supervisors would eat in their office next door but they had to come into the mess to make their tea or coffee, to heat things up, and to wash up, and they were rather more likely to eat with the others, at the only table that could be fitted into this mess, than they were to carry their food away. If they stayed in the mess, I noticed that they usually, although not invariably, took charge of the conversation, but that the others always joined in. Senior operators always ate in the mess. Plant X had another, much larger mess that was better appointed. It was linked to the same building, but it was separated from the control room and offices of the process men, being built in a more or less independent unit that housed the showers that everyone used, and the offices of the maintenance supervisor and his assistants. Although all the process men had lockers in the shower unit and changed there at the beginning and end of each shift, and although the mess was, in theory, open to all, in practice it was used almost exclusively by maintenance men. The only exception to this was during the periods when the plant was shut down for its thorough biennial overhaul. At these times, apparently, when the plant was a hive of unusual activities, everyone ate in the large mess, but at all other times it was quite definitely 'maintenance' territory, and no process operator ever had a meal there.

The two messes in Plant Y were, by contrast, both in the same block but on different sides of it, and the pattern of their use was quite different from that on Plant X. In the middle of the main Y block was a large control room that was the hub of the plant and contained all its monitoring equipment. On one side of this room was the smaller mess (approximately the same size as the small mess on Plant X). It was adjacent to the supervisors' office and was used only by supervisors, senior operators, and, to a limited extent, operators who were on duty in the control room. On the other side of the control room was the large mess, divided into a slightly separated kitchen and an eating area. Behind the kitchen were the showers and lavatories. The eating area was set out with a number of separate tables and this mess was used by both the process operators and the maintenance men. Thus, on Y, instead of the division that existed on Plant X between the 'trades' and the 'process' sides, there was a division based on hierarchical status, as I had been led to expect by the Plant X supervisors. Moreover, this distinction was the more marked since this whole side of the building was used almost exclusively by those below the level of senior operator. Indeed, the main exception to this only served to underline the pattern because supervisors and senior operators came to the shower block behind the kitchen because their (locked) lavatory was located there. (On Plant X there was one small wash-room in the central block; sometimes men laughed and said it should be reserved for supervisors, but this was a joke; it was available to all and the only lock was put on specially for my benefit.)

The pattern of eating on Plant Y did not show quite that rigid separation of supervisors and senior operators from the others that I had been told to expect. Two senior operators chose to eat, some of the time, in the men's mess, although the others never did so. It was also customary for the control room operator to make the morning coffee or the afternoon tea in the supervisors' mess. This, however, was rather a relic of former status distinctions than a relaxation of the rules. Until relatively recently, control room operators had been a distinct grade of men, regarded as specialists in doing a particularly responsible job, but changes in the operators' job structure, that I have described, had meant that most operators were now ultimately trained to take their turn in the control room. Instead, therefore, of it being a special status-marking privilege, the right to enter the supervisors' mess was almost something of a chore, although it seemed not to be resented, perhaps because of its past significance. The man on duty in the control room would enter the supervisors' mess to make the drink and he would then carry his cup back to the control room where, sometimes, the supervisor might join him. As this perhaps indicates, the distinctions remained clear-cut and the rules, however informal, were apparently precise. There was a proper time for making this coffee and tea, and a proper person to do it. On Plant X matters were more flexible, and determined by shouts between the rooms of 'Have you/Shall I put the kettle on?', and ultimately a coded cry over the tannoy system would announce when the tea was ready so that all who were free might come into the mess to share it. On Plant Y the drink prepared by the control room operator was not on offer to all. Moreover, it was clear that the control room man making tea in the supervisors' mess was inhibited there. I made history, so it was said, by being the first woman ever to make tea there, and I did so simply because I stepped in to help a control room operator who wanted a slice of toast with his tea. Custom dictated that he must make the tea in his supervisors' mess, but it was apparently unthinkable for him to toast a piece of bread on the grill there – he felt he had to do that in the other mess at the opposite end of the building. Clearly his toast had been destined to be either cold or burnt unless someone helped him!

Plant X men were mistaken, however, in thinking that these distinctions were maintained solely by the supervisors. Whoever had initiated the rigidity of the system, it was clearly being maintained by the men as much as by anyone. One Plant Y operator, when I commented on the different eating pattern on Plant X, was horrified by the thought that his supervisor might use the same mess: 'I wouldn't *want* him in here.' Certainly I was given the impression that any move by the supervisors to use a single mess with the men would have been resisted as an invasion of privacy. Those men on one shift who took such pride in their cooking that I came to think of them as the 'gourmet' shift, were on sufficiently good terms with their supervisor to share their meals with him; but his food was carried over, course by course, by the senior operator (a cooking enthusiast who chose to eat with the other operators). The men chuckled at the thought of the supervisor eating alone in his mess with solitary satisfaction, but nobody thought of saying to him, 'If you want to share our meal come and sit with us at our table.'

It was quite clear, and obviously a very significant fact, that those most outspokenly concerned with, we might say, guarding the territorial integrity of the men's side of the building were the maintenance men. It was they who protested most clearly against any intrusion by process supervisors into 'their' space. It was they who had initiated the window-painting movement, beginning with the caravan. At one level this was a straightforward anti-management move. The maintenance men objected, in effect, not merely to the supervisor in person, but to the intrusion of managerial authority into space that they thought should be separated from the demands of work, for they resented even the control room operator calling another operator out of the mess to tend one of the machines. As we have seen, maintenance men had regular times set aside for their meal or tea breaks, which they were entitled to regard as their own; but the process operators had to be always responsive to any sudden demands made by their job, and accepted that they might be called at any time, if, say, warning lights alerted the control room man to trouble with a machine. Loudspeakers were installed in the mess so that operators might be summoned when necessary and this had become a symbolic *casus belli*. It was obvious that the maintenance men were deeply hostile to these loudspeakers, which to them represented the intrusion into their time and space of managerial authority.

It would, however, be over-simplifying the issue if we were to see it simply as one of men versus management. There was no suggestion here that the maintenance men were making any kind of common cause with operators because they felt sorry for them, pitying their indigestion or spoilt meals – far from it. Indeed, it seemed clear that one factor in their behaviour was resentment that, as tradesmen, they should have their meal-times interrupted by mere process operators, whom they persisted in regarding as lesser mortals; the maintenance men's anger could be directed very personally at an operator who disturbed them with calls to work. One man told me that he had sparked off a terrible row when, as control room operator, he had had a tannoy speaker installed in the caravan that served as the temporary mess during the redecoration period. He had been the first to call an operator out during the maintenance dinner hour. The result was that all the maintenance men had erupted into his control room and they had milled about there, shouting at him and taking no notice of his arguments that if there were a real emergency their own lives might be at risk if he were unable to get an operator quickly. They had dispersed only towards the afternoon knocking-off time – and was he glad to see them go! This man said it was no good for a control room operator to try to avoid annoying the maintenance men by going to call an operator quietly; the maintenance men objected strongly to the mere sight of the control room operator's head coming round the door of the mess!

The process men thought that the trouble over the shared mess had really resulted from the fact that 'tradesmen' were jealous that the process men, although they did not count as skilled men, could, because of their shift work and overtime, take home bigger pay-packets than the men who had served apprenticeships. This touches on a point that is absolutely central to the relationships with one another of different types of workers. We shall look more carefully at the factors that led to strain between them, but here it is enough to say that recent changes, initiated by management to cut labour costs, largely prevented maintenance men from working shifts or doing much overtime. Because such restrictions could not apply to process operators, symbolic differentials between the two types of worker had been upset; and in anger the maintenance men lashed out at operators as well as management.

Maintenance antagonism to the process workers was such that when management had asked for suggestions as to the alterations the men would like to see in their mess when it was redecorated, the maintenance men had, I was told, tried very hard to have the room cut in two, so that they might have their own mess, separate from the operators. When this idea had been turned down they had sought to have process operators barred from the room altogether during the maintenance dinner hour. In this attempt too they had been unsuccessful, but it seemed to me quite obvious that what they could not do officially they were trying to do unofficially. As the mess was normally used, one block of tables was, by custom, used by the process men and a different group of tables was used by the 'trades'. During the mid-day meal break, however, the maintenance men spread themselves out round all the tables and kept up a loud general conversation between the tables. Obviously this was the period during which the largest number of maintenance men were gathered in the mess. Nevertheless it was clear that they could easily have left one or two tables for the process operators. It was also obvious that if any unfortunate process operator did dare to eat at this time he was deliberately excluded from the conversation, isolated, and more or less forced into reading a book or newspaper. At other times there might be friendly chat between the two types of workers, but it was impossible not to feel the resentment between them during this meal break period.

So far in this discussion of the 'cultural' differences between Plants X and Y, I have concentrated on my subjective impressions of the distinctions between them. It was, however, the case that quite objectively the plants might be said to manifest very different degrees of willingness to co-operate with management. Such differences were shown in measurable differences in sickness and overtime rates (as we shall see, overtime might be generated by 'sickness' that was scarcely clinical in nature). Plant Y had an overtime rate of about 30 per cent which was linked to an operator sickness rate of about 20 per cent. On Plant X, I was told there was an overtime rate of 12 per cent and a sickness rate of 5 per cent. It was also significant that while the Plant X men and supervisors seemed rather proud of their low figures, Plant Y supervisors viewed their high rate as something inevitable, even if displeasing to senior management; and some of the men I spoke to boasted about them. Indeed, Richard, the dominant personality amongst the operators on the gourmet shift, commented on them with such pride, as being the highest of any plant on the site, that his colleague, Peter, who was personally opposed to many of the practices that went on, said ruefully, 'Oh yes, I fear we hold all the cups!'

The overtime rate on Plant Y was increased by the fact that it had stubbornly resisted management attempts to bring in more flexible working arrangements and agreements to reduce the number of men needed for certain tasks. The difference here between the two plants can best be shown by comparing their patterns of work.

On Plant X, the four shifts each had a supervisor and senior operator, as well as team operators (the name for fully trained operators), but the senior operator was not separated structurally from the team, and took operational responsibility for part of the plant. Moreover, each operator on the team had been trained to be able to take full operational responsibility for whatever section of the plant was put in his charge during his shift. The supervisor was there to take major decisions and give advice, but the operators carried out every task on the plant. It had been agreed, although with some misgivings, that senior operators might, under certain circumstances, deputize for supervisors. It had also been accepted that an experienced team operator might deputize for an absent senior operator.

On Plant Y the situation was very different because here supervisors and senior operators played a substantially greater role in the actual running of the plant's machinery. There was somewhat greater variation between the practice of different shifts on Y, but it is still possible to make certain generalizations about the basic pattern. The standard practice was for the team operator to be trained largely as a man who monitored and reported on the machines for which he was responsible, but any major manipulation of these machines, such as was occasioned by the starting up or closing down of any section of the plant, might be handled only by the senior operator or supervisor personally. Supervisors had not accepted, even on a trial basis, that senior operators might act as their deputies. Senior operators rejected any idea that operators might deputize for them – their response to the idea was that it was impossible as the operators did not have the necessary training. Indeed this was true, for only on one shift had a young supervisor, with new ideas, taken the trouble to try to train his operators for a more active role. Overtime on Plant Y was, therefore, generated from the top, for if a supervisor had to be absent from his normal work this meant overtime for another supervisor; similarly, an absent senior operator meant overtime for another senior operator, without whose presence a shift could not function. Perhaps it was because they themselves enjoyed the benefits of overtime that Plant Y supervisors appeared to be unwilling, or unable, to keep tight control of overtime generated among the operators by somewhat doubtful periods of ill health. Perhaps, as we shall see, they were less aware that certain bouts of sickness were dubious.

There was another measure of the difference between these two plants: the behaviour of the men at the change-over of the shifts when, ideally, each man told his relief how his section was running. On Plant X the norm was for the relief shift to arrive on the plant at least fifteen minutes before the next shift was due to take over; supervisors generally arriving even earlier. The scrupulous operator would be present, already changed for work; the less punctual would be on the plant but perhaps still changing. Anyone not ready by about ten minutes before the hour would be made the butt of criticism and jokes. By contrast, on Plant Y, while the majority were ready for work two or three minutes before the shift officially began, very few arrived much earlier and a few minutes' lateness was common enough not to be particularly remarkable. In conversation, Plant Y men rather deplored this. This was not true of everybody: one exceptional man, whose previous experience had been with a car body firm, rather deplored the whole system that, by making a man's right to leave work dependent on the arrival of his relief, meant that a man had to keep more or less to time if he were not to harm his mate. So far as this man was concerned, this aspect of shifting responsibility to the shop floor was simply a nasty trick on the part of management. Other men, however, thought that it would have been much better had operators got in earlier for their work; they spoke of having, initially, turned up much earlier themselves, but said they had become fed up when those who should have relieved them were not prompt. They said they had all gradually become later; it meant that the change-over was not as efficient as it should have been since the man whose shift was ending was unwilling to stay to discuss the state of the plant. He would just say 'everything's steady' and rush off, 'leaving you to find out what things are really like, but you manage'.

The two plants had behaved very differently when management had requested that a certain monthly 'holiday', called an 'ESO' (an Extra Shift Off) and usually worked at very high holiday overtime rates, should instead be taken as a day off. On Plant X it had been agreed to fall in with management plans (although this was put down, as we shall see, to rather clever manipulation of inter-shift jealousies by the plant manager), and the agreement was by a free vote of the operators who had accepted the new practice. On Plant Y, I was told, they had resolutely refused to co-operate, and had only in the end been tricked by management into doing so. It was said, and I had the story confirmed by the most pro-management operator, that after adamantly refusing to adopt the new practice, the operators had agreed to do so as a purely temporary measure, during a shut-down, on a promise that when the plant was restarted the former practice of working ESOs would also begin again. In the event, they were told, when the start up came, that management policy had now changed and they must continue to work the new system. Everyone regarded this as sheer duplicity. Those, including my pro-management informant, who had represented their shifts at the original discussions, were particularly angry because they felt that they had been tricked into telling lies to their shift mates, when they persuaded them to accept what they said was only a temporary change. The *fait accompli* had been accepted, but to the kind of dissatisfaction I found among the Plant X men was added, on Plant Y, a particularly angry sense of grievance.

It was, therefore, not very surprising to learn that Plant Y was the only one of the two ammonia plants ever to have taken anything approaching direct industrial action. It had happened at the beginning of the previous shut-down and concerned the proposal to change the four-shift into a five-shift system. The proposal, if accepted, was certain to bring a change to more flexible working and less overtime, and would be particularly drastic in its effect on Plant Y. The chief drawback of this scheme, so far as the men were concerned, was that it would mean less overtime. Management stressed that because there would be an extra shift, the proposed system would have the advantage, from the operators' viewpoint, that they would have to do fewer night-shifts, and that they would have more spare time that would be grouped into larger, and more useful, blocks. However, instead of having a free choice of holiday period, the new system would allot each man a break, sometime between June and September. Any man would be free to make a private arrangement with a mate to exchange his holiday period for another. But this was the rub, for, under this scheme, management would be able to spread holidays out: there would be no undermanned shifts, and so no large gaps to be filled by men working overtime. Union officials found themselves in the awkward position that they could not oppose such change because, in principle, the T&GWU was against overtime during a period of recession. Indeed on Plant X I heard the shop-steward tell some men off very sharply when one complained that the new shift system would cut his overtime pay. The men, however, resented the move bitterly.

The reactions of the men on the two plants to the prospect of the five-shift system was very different. It was disliked on Plant X, but there men seemed to assume that, since it was being generally backed by their union, the best thing they could do was to examine the different possible variations of the scheme to see which seemed likely to be the least obnoxious. By contrast, Plant Y men had reacted with an extremely brief, but very effective, 'strike' when attempts had been made to force them to consider the relative merits of these different schemes. The 'strike' had had nothing to do with the union. What, apparently, had happened was that on the very day on which they were to shut the plant down for its periodic overhaul, they had been told that they must at least consider the various five-shift schemes that had been proposed, and say what they thought about them. What the men feared was that if they were to do this they would afterwards be held to have given their approval, at least in principle, to the five-shift system. The men also immediately appreciated, as apparently management had not, that this was the one day in the biennial cycle when, simply by working normally, they could threaten disruption of a very serious kind. The works has large ammonia storage 'spheres' (something like immensely strong spherical tanks or gasholders), and these had been filled almost to capacity to tide the works over the period of Plant Y's shut-down. It followed that if production were to continue, the relief valve would blow, and they would start venting ammonia gas to the atmosphere. This would have been expensive to ChemCo, but, much more important, it would have constituted an intolerable threat to the environment.[3] Even if it had been possible for management to have circumvented this threat, any delay in shutting down the plant would have been extremely expensive to the company, because contractors had been hired to do the refit and to clean out the various catalyst 'vessels', and an army of expensive hired cranes was waiting for the work to begin. Therefore, the men, faced with this demand to discuss the five-shift system, responded by firmly saying that if that demand were forced then they would continue production as usual. In the end management had, allegedly, climbed down completely, and had issued a hastily typed statement saying that the men did not, 'at that time', have to discuss the proposed shift changes. Most men assumed this was a victory. However, Peter, the pro-management operator, who was against industrial action and was keeping his thoughts to himself in order not to cause more trouble, privately told me that he feared that the very wording of the note might trap them. He thought that perhaps because they had accepted it when it said 'at this time' they did not have to consider any change, they might be held to have agreed in principle to the idea that they would, at some other time, have to accept it. However, most men thought they had won their point and were satisfied, and so far there had been no further talk of forcing them into accepting the new five-shift scheme.

One further contrast seemed to exist between the two plants. The attitude of the operators to senior management was generally critical, but criticism appeared to be particularly strong on Plant Y. Again the impression has to be subjective, but the difference was, for me, neatly summed up in two stories that were, I think, variants of the same 'folk-tale' about the works manager. The story told on Plant X related to the abolition of the old system by which day workers (by definition 'not us') had had to clock in and out. It was common gossip that these men had taken advantage of the new leniency, and that those who should have stayed at work until 4.15 p.m. knocked off at any time after 3.30. Plant X operators had a story that there had been an occasion when the works manager had intervened personally to try to reduce this indiscipline, and had stood one afternoon by the main gates, to note those who were leaving early. There were chuckles at the dramatic account of drivers panicking, and trying to make U-turns when they saw who was watching. On Plant Y it was a rather different tale, concerning socks. The company issued various items of clothing, of which the most trivial were socks, for those doing contaminating tasks, especially on catalysts. Such clothes were supposed to be returned after use and be laundered on the site, but allegedly they often did not come back, and since the socks had a distinctive pattern, I know it was the case that they were commonly worn at work by many men. The Plant Y story was that the works manager had stood at the main gate, not just to look at those leaving, but to examine the socks of all the men going home, and had actually sent a man back because he was wearing 'company' socks. The point of the story was its illustration of the ridiculous, pettifogging behaviour of the man – how absurd of him to (literally) stoop so low! Not only was the story inherently unlikely, but had it been true it would scarcely have been passed over in silence on Plant X, where, because such socks were commonly given out to those who had to deal with the arsenic, they were generally worn. I assume, therefore, that the two stories are really one and the same, the elaboration on Plant Y being the result of cheerful embellishment by their myth-makers. The Plant X story laughed at the works manager, but also with him. The Plant Y story was simply concerned to hold him up to derision, and was happy to twist the evidence to do so.

The men on these two plants, as I have already indicated in the case of Plant X, recognized the existence of 'cultural' differences between them, and had their own 'explanatory models' to account for them. As may be supposed, there were however considerable differences in what were perceived to be the differences, and in the explanations put forward to account for them. There was considerable rivalry between the two plants, apparently just because they were basically so similar. Each was convinced that it was the pattern to which the other should aspire, and said so, more or less openly.

The men on Plant X claimed superiority to all non-ammonia plants at the works, on the grounds that the system of ammonia production was more complex; and they claimed superiority to Plant Y because they asserted that their own plant was the more efficient producer of ammonia. In social matters they also thought their own plant superior. In summary it may be said that they asserted that Plant Y was riven with petty distinctions between the different grades that had long ceased to apply on Plant X, which was altogether a better place on which to work.

Plant X men explained the benighted condition of Plant Y men in terms of history. Plant Y, the first plant to be built, had been staffed originally by foremen and assistant foremen who came from the north, and were dictatorial and hierarchical in their attitudes, and they had established a tradition that had never altered. By the time that Plant X was established, the local area had, as it were, started to exercise its civilizing influence. When they started up, the Plant X supervisors decided, quite deliberately, that they wanted to do things differently, in a much more friendly and democratic manner. Hence the whole ethos of Plant X was different.

Men on Plant Y acknowledged that Plant X might be a more efficient producer of ammonia, but they asserted the superiority of Plant Y because producing ammonia was only part of its functions; they supplied vital services (which will be described below) to the rest of the works. Therefore Plant Y was the more important, and those men on Plant X were suffering, more or less, from delusions of grandeur if they thought their plant superior. Socially Plant Y was a better place because they got on much better with the rest of the works than did Plant X. Plant Y men boasted that their relations with the others were so good that when they had had their 'strike', they had immediately had offers of support from other sections of the works, although not, of course, from Plant X. It was asserted that if the men on that plant had tried to take any such action then nobody would have supported them because they themselves were so unco-operative and unwilling to help others. The explanation was simple – Plant X men were selfish, concerned about no one but themselves.

Neither of these 'home-made models' can simply be dismissed out of hand. I thought there were grains of truth in both, although each also needed to be taken with grains of salt.

There is an element of truth in the assertion that differences between grades were less marked on X than on Y, and it is perfectly possible that this has arisen because of the historical determination by some individuals that Plant X should be more egalitarian than Y. Certainly Martin, a Plant X supervisor who originally moved from Y to X when the latter was started up, was quite emphatic that there had been discussions between the original core of foremen and assistant foremen in which they decided both to move with the times and to run a plant in a way that was appropriate for their egalitarian area. He said the foremen decided that they would not have a separate mess but would eat with the men. Yet this cannot have been the whole story, for it seemed to me that Plant X was, in fact, less egalitarian than its supervisors liked to imagine. I listened to one of them discussing his new plant manager and gloomily forecasting how difficult he was likely to be. Sitting in the supervisors' office, its doors as usual wide open, he nevertheless said, 'I don't care what he does so long as he doesn't upset them out there.' 'Them out there' were the plant operators, and that phrase was significant. The office door stood open, true, but from my observation the only people, apart from supervisors, who came in for any length of time were the senior operators. Ordinary operators, of course, came in but were quite clearly conscious when they did so that it was a place where they came only on business, and not to relax. Their demeanour was thus not so very different from Plant Y operators who had to open a door to get into their supervisors' office.

It might seem that we could dismiss out of hand Plant Y's explanation that Plant X was different because its men were 'selfish'. However, as one way of describing the situation that existed the remark was not as far out as might appear. It was certainly true that Plant X was clearly much the more isolated from the rest of the works, and although there was a spatial element here that made Plant X literally slightly further away from the hub of things, the difference was minimal. It was a curious fact that while on the 2 p.m. to 10 p.m. shift, Plant Y men quite often sent one of their number over to the canteen to bring back a cooked meal, I never saw this done, nor heard of it being done, on Plant X, where it was said that the canteen was too distant to permit this. It was, in fact, an extra two minutes walk each way. Plant X and Plant Y were separated only by a small footbridge across major pipe-works; in terms of distance they were a mere stone's throw apart. Yet a very perceptive Plant X supervisor, whom I encountered on the path between them, jerking his thumb said, 'It's a long way over that bridge!' He was right; the geographical space was minimal, but the social space was considerable. Perceptions of selfishness and unselfishness were undoubtedly related to this fact.

Plant X was not merely spatially somewhat more isolated than was Plant Y, but Plant Y was, structurally, rather more involved with the rest of the works, simply because of certain characteristics of its physical and technical design. Plant Y was the first of the ammonia plants to be built and the product almost of a different technical generation. It was set out with a lavish use of space, and in consequence a lavish use of pipe-work that had come to seem very extravagant. Moreover it occupied a prime site, with its administration building and main machinery adjacent to the main gate. It was centrally involved with the rest of the works for two main technical reasons: first, it produced the compressed air vital for the operation of many machines used in the other plants on the site; second, Plant Y's ammonia was piped directly to the nitrics plant and was vital to its functioning – and the nitrics plant was the major source of surplus steam for the whole site. In an era in which the cost of all fuel had risen sharply, surplus steam had become vital, as a source of cheap power, on other plants. For these reasons, as I witnessed, anything threatening production on Plant Y brought anxious senior men from elsewhere to hover in its control room watching the dials. By contrast, Plant X was a much more compact unit, and instead of lying adjacent to roads that were common works' territory, its office block was effectively an island, surrounded on all sides by different sections of its own plant. Few outsiders had business there, or went there if they did not have business.

If we rephrase in sociological terms the differences between the two plants that were picked out by the assertions made by each group of men, we could say that Plant X is notable for the sense of vertical cleavage that separates those who belong to it from the rest of the works; Plant Y, by contrast, is notable for the intensity of the horizontal cleavages separating operators from supervisors. I was struck, for example, by the fact that the two Plant Y men whose comments on the lack of horse-play I mentioned earlier, also contrasted Plant Y with their first plant, Plant Z, by remarking that there was a much greater them/us distinction on Plant Y than they had experienced on Z. I found this particularly striking since, on Plant X, Z had been held up to me as an example of a plant having particularly bad operator–supervisor relationships. If there is, indeed, such a broad difference between the two plants, other questions are prompted. Why do operators and supervisors on Plant X have, apparently, such a strong sense of common identity? Conversely, on Plant Y, why do the operators seem to feel a sense of identity, not with the plant, but with other employees, providing they share the characteristic of being 'not-supervisors'?

One factor making for the special character of Plant X may have been its technical history, which has been rather different from Plant Y. The latter, everyone agreed, having been designed by the company's own team, always performed reasonably well. Its machines operated with so much spare capacity that they produced ammonia at levels comfortably above those they were supposed to meet according to their original specifications. By contrast, I was told on every side that Plant X, for all the millions it cost, was from an engineer's viewpoint, a cheap and nasty plant, bought for the company off the peg, as it were, when it was in an earlier economizing mood. Therefore it was a plant that gave a great deal of trouble in its start-up period. By the time I did my study, most of the snags had been ironed out by the company engineers and, with the change to natural gas, production had become a relatively smooth process. Keeping it 'on line' in the earlier days, however, had been an extremely difficult task. It is a cliché that unity is most easily achieved when there is an external enemy and, from all accounts, the plant itself was initially a fairly redoubtable enemy. Running the plant well required the real co-operation of men and supervisors.

Technical factors may have been significant also in that they almost certainly led Plant X supervisors to introduce their special system used in running the plant, by which, as we saw, the operators themselves were here trained to cope with the machines and did not rely on the supervisors and senior operators to perform all the tasks of shutting down and starting up. In a plant where things seemed to go wrong so often, it was only sensible to have operators who were particularly well trained. The fact that they had this training in turn gave the Plant X operators a personal involvement in the efforts made to keep it 'on line'. It may not have been the same kind of involvement as that of the supervisors whose personal pride, as we shall see, seemed to be linked to success. The men were primarily concerned, or so they asserted, with saving themselves trouble, for it took much more effort to start up or shut down the plant than it did to keep it running normally. I suspect that they did, in fact, take a pride in keeping their plant going, even if it were 'not done' to talk about it. But even if their motives differed, however, they were of one mind with the supervisors in wanting to keep things running smoothly. By contrast, on Plant Y, because the supervisors and senior operators had elected to keep these major tasks in their own hands, there was inevitably less sense of common purpose in the effort made to keep the plant on line. Indeed, a Plant Y supervisor, Bert, hinted to me that there had been a time when his men had deliberately got at him by tripping part of the plant. When I mentioned this to James, a Plant X supervisor whom I knew particularly well, he snorted and suggested that the men had merely been scaring Bert, whom James thought rather self-important and easily frightened; James had never heard of anything like that on Plant X; but then, he added, he could not really rule out the possibility of such behaviour on Plant Y, for whereas on X the men would merely have been making more work for themselves, on Y they might relish the prospect of sitting back and watching the supervisors sweat!

The differences in the architectural designs of the two plants seem also to have exerted a certain social influence, for Plant Y was much the more closely linked to the rest of the works, physically as well as functionally. The core of the Y building is the very spacious control room. As already described, on one side lie the supervisors' office and mess, and on the other the men's mess. The inner wall is covered with dials, but opposite, in the outer wall, are large windows that look on to the plant itself and also give a view to the rest of the works. Doors at each end of this wall give access to the external world.

Men coming to see the supervisor could walk along a pathway outside the building to the door nearer to the office, but tended to enter by the door near the men's mess and then walk through the control room. The managers, other operators, and maintenance men of various sorts, tramped through, or chatted to one another, or stood at the windows, reading the papers, without reference to the control room operator, who was often socially isolated, working at his desk or dials. One operator, who had come to the plant from a totally different ammonia unit in another works, commented that he had, initially, very much resented the way in which men came through without apologizing for their intrusion. He had been used to thinking of the control room as 'his', but he had had to change his outlook. I remarked to one operator that it was like Waterloo station; to which he replied that I should 'see it in the shut-down – it's like a clearing centre for refugees'. It was essentially a public room with the control operator very conscious of his exposure, both to outsiders and to his foreman because the door into the supervisors' room had a glass panel; the operator could be constantly observed, if any supervisor so wished. This fact was said, by one supervisor, to make the control room job very unpopular.

The contrast here with Plant X was particularly striking, for the control room on X was very much smaller, and was separated from the supervisors' office and the other rooms by a little twisting corridor. The control room could fairly be described as pokey, and apparently inconvenient; yet the only times that I ever heard anything about X praised on Plant Y were when two operators on separate occasions remarked how very much better the Plant X control room was than their own. Certainly on Plant X the control room operator was always, as it were, the host in that place, and if he were not actively engaged with his work he was always involved

Figure 2 Ammonia control block X

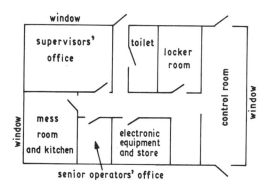

Figure 3 Ammonia control block Y

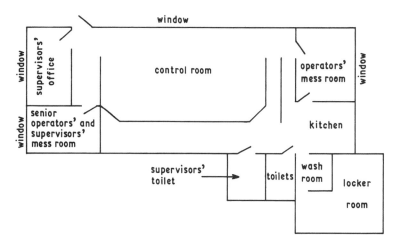

in whatever activity or conversation was being carried on.

There is thus a paradox here. Plant X boasted of its 'open doors' policy, and disparaged Plant Y because its doors were shut. Nevertheless, in practice, there was much more privacy built into the design of the Plant X rooms; on Plant Y, however, any privacy had to be fought for. This was most notably so in the case of the men's mess. As it was designed, the Plant Y mess had big windows in its outside wall that looked on to a busy path, commonly used by men who did not belong to the plant; and in its inner wall half-glazed doors looked on to the very public control room. By contrast, on Plant X, the process mess, although it was adjacent to the supervisors' office, was open to view only if the visitor actually stood in the doorway and looked round; its external windows were high and gave out only on to the middle of the plant. It was not really remarkable, in one sense, that it should have been the Plant Y men who sought to blank out their windows. Yet this had become an issue that increased the sense of antagonism between operators and management because it could be seen as a permanent symbolic challenge to one expression of management authority.

Even within the Y mess there was a problem about the control of space. Here the process operators had to share the facilities with the maintenance men, which led to considerable friction. This had a significance of its own to which I shall return, yet here too there was a paradox, because it seemed evident that, in so far as their defence of this space led Y operators to try to keep management authority out, they were in fact simply borrowing the attitudes of maintenance men. Design factors that on Plant X had physically separated the socially divided maintenance and process groups, had, on Plant Y, thrown them together, because to the architectural plan had been added a social factor, the Y supervisors' determination to keep the small mess as exclusively their own. Certainly, despite all the friction between them, process operators here seemed to have borrowed maintenance workers' attitudes. Thus the latter started the exclusion of outsiders by painting over the windows, but the process operators took the initiative in separating the mess from the control room by blacking out the door with the guide dog poster. For all the men, the mess had become 'our' territory, from which 'they' ought to be rigidly excluded, 'they' being both the supervisors and, in a certain sense, managerial authority in general. It might be argued that Y operators were simply showing what might be thought of as typical industrial attitudes.

In this case, what requires explanation is why the process men on Plant X had a more co-operative attitude in relation to management. Granted that part of the explanation may lie in the technical links that bind Y so strongly to the other plants on the site, and in the pattern of messing facilities that brought the Plant Y process operators into so much greater contact with the maintenance men, can we be content with an explanation that rests ultimately on the purely negative argument that X operators had less to do with 'skilled men', especially since we must not forget the real degree of hostility that did exist between these two types of worker? This is, at best, an inadequate explanation.

A more satisfactory explanation seems to emerge if the relationships between supervisor and operator are looked at carefully. Clearly, these too differed between the two plants. This was most obviously so in relation to their eating patterns. On Plant X the mess was an area in which operator and supervisor could be relatively relaxed in each other's company. I am not suggesting that status differences were forgotten, or that tension was necessarily absent, or that conversations were necessarily unguarded. Meetings between them in the mess did, however, quite obviously take place on neutral ground, and led to chat about everything from work and family life to what was in the newspapers. It was the setting for a two-way interchange of ideas – it was not simply a situation in which supervisors could influence operators, for it provided the perfect setting for an operator to express his own opinions to the supervisors. On Plant Y, by the very way in which space was defined, the mess was not, indeed it could not, be used in this way, since it was virtually out of bounds to supervisors, a kind of 'no go' area for them, just as their mess was out of bounds to the operators. How important was this? True the control room on Y partly replaced the X mess, for in the Y control room supervisors and operators could meet fairly freely. On the other hand, because for much of the day it was a very public room, status consciousness seemed to be particularly marked here. Even after the day men had left and the atmosphere became somewhat more relaxed, the control room could not be an adequate substitute for the Plant X mess just because Plant Y operators without much to do tended to drift back from the control room into the mess. One subjective indication of the difference between the two plants is that when I was studying Plant X, I felt I had to make a special effort to talk to operators by themselves because wherever I went for a chat, it was seldom long before a supervisor would appear and join in the conversation. The reverse was the case on Plant Y. I found there that I spent long periods chatting in the men's mess where I simply did not encounter supervisors; I had to make a special effort to meet them.

I began this comparison of the two plants by noting what at first seemed to be three quite unconnected peculiarities about Y: the absence of nudes, the absence of banter, and the curious behaviour at the change-over of the shifts. I came to think, odd as it may seem, that in fact they were all manifestations of a plant characterized by a combination of formality and tension over the use of space.

Formality, I think, accounted for the privacy that supervisors demanded at the change-over of the shift. It might, of course, have been indicative of a certain defensiveness, but I am inclined rather to see it as a symbolic statement of the importance of what they were doing, and of the importance of their own positions. Their discussion could concern no one else, and should be interrupted by nothing. Like two baton carriers in a relay race, only the two leaders, one of the outgoing and the other of the incoming shift, could effect a proper hand-over – anyone else would get in the way. Hence the demand for privacy. The urge to keep the door shut was probably a simple reaction to the fact that the office opened on to such a very public room; but if they were going to exclude a lot of other people, perhaps it may have seemed natural to exclude all but those directly involved.

The curious case of the missing nudes relates, I suspect, both to the degree of formality on the plant and to the tensions over space. First, I would guess that a room will have pin-ups on its walls only if the individual or group using it can claim 'ownership' in a fairly clear-cut sense; to decorate a room successfully there has to be a measure of consensus about the use of the space concerned. If that is lacking then the act of decorating may constitute a claim to the room that some who share it might regard as unacceptable, even though the decoration might be acceptable to all. Hence, perhaps, the undecorated nature of the Y mess. Further, since nudes are by definition, we might say, unbuttoned, they are perhaps suitable only for situations in which men are relaxed. If rooms are public, or in any important sense are settings for the assertion of status, then the calendar nude may seem out of place; and the absence of these calendars from the Y control room and the Y supervisors' rooms may be explained.

The different degrees of banter on the two plants seemed to me to be very significant indeed. It appeared to be the most obvious manifestation of the fact that on Y informal interaction between operator and supervisor was very limited, while it was common on Plant X. Although banter was not exclusive to relationships of this kind, yet in fact where it occurred it very frequently involved supervisor and operator in some interchange. Much banter, in fact, involved elements of the typical 'joking relationship' found world-wide, and essentially related to ambivalence, to a combination of friendly familiarity and tension between two individuals. In the joking relationship licence is given to speak, in 'jest', the true word, and to hide strain in physical horse-play. In fact, when I analysed the content of the Plant X banter, I found that a considerable amount involved supervisors and operators in situations where the joking was a mild form of sanction. Thus the man who did not turn up for his shift in good time was 'teased', both by his mates and by his supervisor; and the teasing might reoccur at various times in the shift if the man were thought to be becoming really slack. Even more marked was the one occasion when I saw a supervisor come late: then the whole period of the shift was punctuated by jokes his men made at his expense, and he had to take their laughter in good part.

It would be wrong, on the strength of such a difference between the two plants, to suggest that they were socially entirely different places. It is clear that there did exist between supervisors and men on Plant X a 'joking relationship', whereas on Plant Y this relationship was one of some formality, but it is accepted that these two patterns, far from being entirely unconnected, are, universally, two sides of the same coin. Each represents a way of handling relationships that embody both divergent and common interests. To give these a stable, ordered form the parties may maintain 'an extreme mutual respect and a limitation of direct personal contact' or they may accept that their behaviour may properly display 'mutual disrespect and licence', serious hostility being prevented by 'the playful antagonism of teasing' (Radcliffe-Brown 1952:92). In so-called 'primitive societies' relationships with in-laws are commonly handled in one or other of these ways – and anthropologists recognize the similarity of the attitudes behind these very different ways of behaving. It is not, perhaps, entirely fanciful to see supervisors as structurally like tribal mothers-in-law in the case of each plant.

Nevertheless, I do think there was a connection between the joking relationship with supervisors that men had on Plant X and these operators' markedly greater willingness to co-operate with management. I shall argue that a very important factor in Plant X was that it had come to provide a social environment within which supervisors could exercise informal social skills, and that they had generally an interest in doing so in such a way that they raised the efficiency of the plant. On Plant Y some of the supervisors were technically excellent men and were keen to run their shifts efficiently, but it was very difficult for them to exercise the same kind of influence over their men because of the formality of the relationships that had developed there. Excluded, initially by their own wish, from informal contacts with the operators, the Y supervisors, from the operators' viewpoint, so symbolized management authority that their very presence reminded men of it; thus informal social relationships must have become increasingly difficult. In so far as informal ties were lacking, the supervisor's influence was minimal, for, as we shall see, power had been removed from him. The result was that Y supervisors seemed incapable of effecting those changes that had been accepted on X, not because as individuals they were less keen to do so than were the X supervisors, or more anatagonistic to management policy, but because their social situation was very different.

I want to make immediately a point to which I shall return later. I found no evidence that the men of Plant Y in any general sense 'rejected management authority', or that they were particularly influenced by some politically militant shop-steward or operator. Plant Y, indeed, had had, for the most part, shop-stewards who did not stay long in the job and were not particularly opposed to management. Plant X, on the other hand, had a shop-steward of long standing who had a not altogether undeserved reputation for outspoken hostility to management. He was a man who rejoiced, it seemed to me, in opposing supervisors if he thought he had an excuse to do so. So far as operators were concerned, I could discern no significant difference in political outlook between men on the two plants. Specifically, on Y I found only one such 'militant' operator and he seemed to be without influence. The great majority of Y operators accepted equally with those of X

INTRODUCTION: THE INNOCENT EYE   *55*

that it was the proper job of management to manage. Mostly they obeyed that authority without question when it manifested itself in the demand that they should do particular tasks at particular times. They differed only in what may be called their general morale and in the degree to which they showed a firm disinclination to co-operate in trying out new working practices. But in no sense could the different patterns of co-operation on the plants be related to differences in the political views of the individuals concerned, or to some quality of 'militancy'.

It is now time to turn our attention much more to theoretical writings on industrial relations in order to assess what has here been described. The account in this chapter will already have been classified as 'sheer empiricism' by some. They will be outraged that the words 'capitalism' and 'capitalist' have not so far occurred, and scandalized that supervisors have been linked with mothers-in-law rather than identified as the 'agents of capital'. This is sad. Nevertheless it seems to me to be important to give a general picture of the situation before considering its theoretical implications. Of course, what I saw was influenced by my general ideas about the relations between technology and culture; nevertheless I attempted to avoid restricting what I saw to what I had expected to see, and it is my first impressions that I have set down here. The next chapter will, however, be concerned with a discussion on Marxist and non-Marxist approaches to the study of industrial relations that will provide a basis for the analysis of the ethnography here presented. I shall also discuss a specifically anthropological approach to data collection that exerted a very considerable influence on my research, in order that the reader may follow the kind of dialectical relationship between theory and ethnography that is here being presented. Subsequently we shall come back to the ammonia plants, and particularly to the supervisors on Plant X, for I shall argue that the data from the plant on the details of the relationships between the supervisors and the operators on the one hand, and between the supervisors and senior managers on the other, do much to clarify the differences between the plants that have here been described. I shall go on to argue that the material on the supervisors does more than this, however, for I think it can be shown that it has a real contribution to make to theories about the exercise of managerial authority, and indeed the nature of management power.

NOTES

1. The process operator is weak in the external labour market because his *de facto* skills are job specific. For the concept of the differences between the internal and external labour markets see Doeringer and Piore (1971) and Blackburn and Mann (1979).
2. On the costs to employers of recruiting to skill-specific jobs see Doeringer and Piore (1971:30).
3. In the last resort management would have had to 'throw the switch' on the plant to bring it to a halt, but this would have done considerable damage to it.

2

The social impact of technology: theoretical viewpoints

The 'ethnography' of the chemical industry has for a long time been central to debates about the nature of industrial relationships, because it has been pre-eminently an industry that has been influenced by the techniques of advanced automation; and advanced automation, it has often been argued, transforms both the working environment and the social relationships between worker and boss.[1] Against this view, however, increasing criticism has been heard so that it is now time to try to begin to assess, as objectively as possible, the merits of the different arguments. To do this it seems essential to move 'dialectically' between an ethnographic base and the various theories. After the brief account of the two plants, therefore, we must look at these theories before turning, more informed, to look at further ethnographic detail; finally coming back, once again, to reconsider the theories.

In 1978 Gallie, in his book *In Search of the New Working Class* sought to deal on an empirical basis with the question as to whether automation did influence in a particular way the workers' attitudes to management. He looks very carefully at the nature of automated work as operators experience it. He also tries to answer the question as to whether this common experience leads to common responses from the work-force, irrespective of other aspects of their culture. As the result of a very careful comparative study of French and British oil refineries, he concluded that so far as three major areas of industrial relationships were concerned (the 'social integration of the work force within the capitalist enterprise', the 'structure of managerial power', and the 'nature of trade unionism') technology seemed to have very little influence. In these three crucial respects, the French and British oil refineries differed significantly, despite their virtually identical technologies. In consequence, Gallie argues that the factors determining industrial relationships appear to be the 'wider cultural and social structural patterns of specific societies' (Gallie 1978:295) and thus concludes that automated technology must be somewhat irrelevant. He also concludes that the benefits to the workers of automation had been considerably exaggerated in earlier discussions, because little had been said about certain inherent disadvantages involved in running continuous process plants, however automated.

Summarizing what had earlier been the commonly received opinion about the social influence of technology in the chemical industry, Gallie (1978: 9–13) says that it was believed that automation influences the integration of workers because it makes the work a man is called on to do both more complex and more intellectually demanding than most other industrial work, and yet it is work that is physically less exhausting. Moreover, because the men must be skilled, and because their wages represent only a very small part of the total costs of production, managements grant their employees great job security, and high wages. The worker has, in effect, a career akin to that of a manager, and therefore the relationships of manager and worker are altered because conflicts between them are much reduced. This is particularly the case, it is argued, because the manager becomes less of a disciplinarian than a technical adviser. Control systems are built into the machines themselves so that the 'managerial hierarchy is spared its police function', thus altering the structure of managerial power. Indeed, it was even held that so many causes of conflict had been removed that it was likely either that trade unions would disappear, because men would simply not be interested in joining them, or, at least, that unions that did exist would be notably accommodating to management, and certainly not militant.

Against this Gallie quotes French writers who believed that

the new technology would lead the workers in a very different direction. For example, they argue that it re-unites workers previously divided by differences in skill, so that operators, maintenance workers, and technicians have a common sense of identity and are as one in their bitter revolt against the existing structure of managerial power. These writers see the workers in the technologically advanced industries as particularly likely to become active in trade union affairs, and believe their unions will spearhead the revolution (Gallie [1978: 16–24] discussing Mallet [1969] and Naville [1961, 1963]). The differences between these French authors and the others, Gallie argues, reflect not only differences in their theoretical and political positions, but the fact that they are generalizing from their experience of different countries with different national industrial cultures.

This does not wholly account for the differences between what we might call French pessimism and the optimism of Blauner and his followers. The latter initiated the discussion and Gallie argues that part of their optimism arose from a certain misunderstanding of the nature of process work and led to naive expectations about the extent of automation's benefits.

Summarizing Gallie's (1978) views, we may say first that he believes harmony in the relationship between management and process operator could not be expected simply to result from the technology of a continuous process system. In the first place, although this eliminates some traditional sources of grievance, it introduces others. Sheer ignorance of the actual working conditions was demonstrated by those earlier writers who believed that process workers inhabited a brave new world of such high pay and security and comfortable working conditions that they saw their managers, we might say, as their friendly neighbourhood advisers. Gallie agrees operators have relatively high pay and security for manual workers. On the other hand, he argues, those who wrote about the pleasant conditions of the chemical industry studiously avoided discussing the serious disadvantages of the shift work that is the essential concomitant of continuous process work (Gallie 1978: 94–105).

Gallie also argues that such work leads to real causes of dispute with management. He cites, for example, the problem of determining manning levels of shifts. For various reasons it is almost impossible to determine objectively what is the 'right' level. On a shift where nothing goes wrong few men may be needed, but if there is a breakdown a lot of labour may be required, and undermanning may increase the risks the men have to run; clearly the interests of management and men are at variance here (Gallie 1978:100). Moreover, it is wrong to assume that work performance is so determined by technology that it no longer gives rise to disputes. Process workers are sufficiently skilled, and sufficiently in charge of their own responses to information provided by the technology, to influence production; of course, this can lead to trouble with managers.

If serious disputes emerge then their course is not predetermined; technology does not eliminate strikes. At this point national industrial culture must be considered, for British workers did not strike, saying it would be dangerous, but the French workers did. Against this background, Gallie (1978) argues, differences between the French and British refinery workers in their attitudes and behaviour become very interesting. French refinery workers were objectively better paid than their British counterparts and there was, in France, a greater differential between ordinary manual workers and process workers than existed in Britain. Nevertheless the French workers were much the more dissatisfied and were less ready to acknowledge management's authority. The conclusion reached is that the French worker was directly influenced by the more militant ideas of his union leaders, and the complementary hostility of French management towards unions. This had led French managers to strive to retain various prerogatives, particularly that of determining the pay of individual workers. French workers, both craftsmen and process operators, were graded on bases agreed with the unions, but managers retained a right to alter pay packets to take account of a man's age and individual skill as assessed by his manager. Therefore, men formally on the same grade might, at management's discretion, get very different wages for similar work. (Gallie 1978: 55–72). The situation was very different in Britain. Here management had quite given up any right to determine an individual's pay. Craft workers, classified as 'skilled', were grouped in a single grade and paid an identical salary. The process operators were still classified into a small number of different grades; nevertheless, what was important was that all workers on the same grade had to be paid on the same basis (Gallie 1978: 65). Gallie argues that the French pattern, that left the decision on an individual's wage to his manager, led both to great rivalry between individual workers and to a lot of hostility directed at management. The British system, he thought, largely eliminated the rivalry between individual workers, and protected the relationship between manager and worker from resentment. This was so despite the fact that Gallie also shows that many of the early assumptions about automated work were false: shift work tired French and British workers equally; operators' career structures were not like managers'; management had become concerned about wage levels (Gallie 1978: 97–9).

Gallie argues, however, that a real difference between the French and British refineries existed in that in Britain the unions had achieved such power that they could deal with management from a position of strength. If British management wanted to effect changes they had to win agreement, based on financial inducements and extensive discussions, with shop floor representatives. Consequently, British workers, confident in their negotiators, and undivided by the kind of jealousies that disturbed their French counterparts, could be self-confident enough to admit, with equanimity, management's right to manage. Thus Gallie argues that it was management's acceptance of the power of the unions that played the crucial role in gaining the British workers' acceptance of managerial authority (Gallie 1978: 170, 180, 182–84).

Gallie's study is relevant to our general discussion in two ways. In the first place, his data and arguments provide a foil against which it will be very useful, later, to set neo-Marxist arguments about capitalist control and the role of unions. Second, Gallie makes it abundantly necessary for anyone who would assert the influence of technological factors in industrial relationships to take cognizance of national industrial culture. Obviously, for example, distinctions such as those that have been described between maintenance and process workers cannot simply be related to differences in the nature of the jobs that have to be done. If attention is once turned, as Gallie turns it, to the structure of union organization and power, then all that has been said about these men on Plants X and Y must be seen in this light. Attention must be turned to regulations, agreed nationally with the various unions, that only men who had served apprenticeships could join skilled unions, because only such men were allowed to 'use tools'. In many cases it was such agreements, and not the real quality of skill demanded, that made this work the possession of the members of these unions. That this rule was essentially the result of national industrial culture is proved beyond all doubt by a recent study by Halle (1984) of an American chemical works where the interchange is common between the two kinds of work. A distinction exists between process operators and maintenance workers, but if a process operator is under forty-five years old and will forgo the high pay of shift work, he may take a general intelligence test in arithmetic, and, if successful, may then put his name down for the next trade vacancy, for which he can be trained on the job and at night school and finally receive an official certificate. Obviously, under such a system the social differences between 'process' and 'trades' are far less apparent than in Britain (Halle 1984: 130–32). Thus the distinction that seemed such clear evidence of the influence of technology turns out to illustrate Gallie's arguments regarding the significance of national industrial culture.

From a quite different standpoint Braverman (1974) argues that it is the essential nature of capitalism that is a far more important determinant of industrial relationships than any kind of technological factor could be. He argues that capitalism ensures that the working environment is ruled by the imperatives of the 'class structure', for his central thesis is that technology, far from being an independent variable causing change, is itself designed with the primary objective of supporting capitalist power within the workplace. Taking a global view, Braverman (1974) sees technology as the handmaid of 'monopoly capitalism'; monopolistic corporations, having freed themselves from many of the constraints of the free markets in raw materials and from the competition of rivals, use new technology to free themselves from any constraints that they might meet with from workers in the labour market. Braverman's central thesis is one that has a much larger application than just to the chemical industry, but it is particularly striking if set in the context of the arguments about technology that have just been reviewed. Braverman asserts that work-place technology is determined by the desire of capitalists to control proletarians. The possession of skill that is essential to production gives the workers power and, therefore, new technological developments are continuously being designed to eliminate workers' skill. The 'deskilling' of work may accompany technological change but this change is essentially inspired by the management's concern to free itself from any dependence on its employees' skill. For Braverman the deskilling of work is a major element within the overall capitalist strategy that aims to achieve a totally controlled proletariat outside as well as inside the work-place; he sees the tactics of large corporations as inspired initially by Taylor writing in the early years of this century. (Braverman [1974: ch. 4] discusses Taylor's works in the 1947 collected edition.)

Braverman's Marxism is functionalist in that for him the correct analysis of any aspect of industry in capitalist society demonstrates *how* (not if) it serves the ends of capitalists. In this light he discusses 'deskilling', arguing that there are no real distinctions between the skilled and the unskilled; such distinctions, even when made by the workers themselves, mask the truth; indeed they are designed to mask it. Today, he argues, there exists, for those with eyes to see, only an undifferentiated mass of workers who are more or less interchangeable with one another, for this suits the needs of capitalists. He assumes that the workers are powerless to resist 'deskilling', and that unions do so little to defend workers' rights that they scarcely deserve a mention in the discussion. All such 'functionalist' arguments, however, assume what should be proven, and Braverman's (1974) position has been criticized, by Marxists as well as others, for doing too little to support his assertions with hard data. Clearly, however, his contribution to the analysis of industrial relations is valuable in that no one now can discuss technology and assume its design to be free of the influence of managerial strategy. Braverman goes to an extreme in that he argues that management, or at least capitalist management, in order to control the workers, has abolished skills and has been able to do this without incurring any significant opposition from the workers who are assumed to be powerless. Nevertheless his arguments have to be considered carefully in any discussion on the significance of technology.

Despite the value of Braverman's contribution, however, any careful examination of the details of industrial relationships seems to come to the conclusion that his arguments are seriously over-simplified. This comes out very obviously in relation to the assumption that workers have been defenceless in the face of deskilling. It has been pointed out, for example, by Lazonick, that Braverman 'whole-heartedly roots his own analysis of the twentieth-century capitalist labour process in Marx's analysis' (Lazonick 1983: 114); and that this, in turn, relied on a somewhat inadequate account of the British cotton industry of the 1830s. Marx's argument regarding the way in which capital was able to dominate labour through the use of technology was illustrated by references to the introduction of the automatic mule in place of the hand mule; but Lazonick points out that this argument quite overlooked the fact that still in the 1860s 'the highly competitive character of the British cotton industry enabled mule spinners to retain rigid *craft control* in their work processes – control over the pace, organization, and remuneration of work – despite the fact that the actual *craft* basis of this control had been substantially undermined' (emphasis in original). Nevertheless, having determined, to his own satisfaction, that machinery solved the problem of getting work out of the workers ('appropriating labour') Marx assumed that '[l]abour disappeared as an active force in shaping the social and technical organization of work' (Lazonick 1983: 113). Similarly, argues Lazonick (p. 114), Braverman assumes that 'the problem of getting work out of the worker is resolved by mechanisation and automation'; in this he quite overlooks the fact that if modern managements are to achieve their ends of 'capital accumulation' they need 'dependable, reliable, attentive and loyal workers' (Lazonick 1983: 115); the 'capitalist cannot manipulate wage-rates and work-loads with impunity precisely because he still has to deal with a labour force whether unionised or not. He has to get his workers to work for the company' (Lazonick 1983: 117).

The arguments of Lazonick, and of those like Littler (Gospel and Littler 1983: 171–96) who take much the same position, are significant because they immediately suggest that any research into the 'relations of production' involves the researcher in the analysis of relationships that are far more complex and subtle than Braverman (1974) would have us believe. To do such research is to enter not the simplified field in which it is open to management to impose its will without negotiation, and by installing machinery to dictate how workers will behave. Rather it is to enter a situation where negotiations are being carried on, often at an informal level, and where the prize is that element which Taylor thought he had banished, the worker's 'goodwill'. I shall argue that it is just this topic that is of central interest to my own work. It is this topic that has been tackled by another Marxist writer, Burawoy, in his book *Manufacturing Consent* (1979). Burawoy's work is something that I find particularly valuable precisely because I read it only after I had written the first draft of my own study; because of the total independence of the two accounts and their very different viewpoints, the extent to which they are clearly talking about similar phenomena is quite striking.

Lazonick is concerned with the transformation of production relations that took place in America when craft production disappeared and mass production took its place, at the end of the nineteenth century. He argues that by the 1870s 'conditions of supply and demand had emerged that promised enormous profits to those capitalists who could introduce systems of high speed through-put into vertically integrated series of manufacturing processes'. Managers had to redesign the flow of work as well as the division of labour, and they had to motivate their workers. This latter task gave them considerable problems. They tried the technique of close supervision through tough foremen, but this was not very successful. Ultimately, with the shortage of labour experienced during the First World War, employers apparently suddenly became concerned to win the goodwill of their employees. They wanted to take full advantage of the new mass production techniques, and so needed a worker who could be won over to being a competent, dependable, alert operator, loyal to his firm and in many cases able and willing to exercise his judgement on its behalf. Even if he did not have a real craft skill and was classed under the vague heading of 'semi-skilled', a man of this calibre could be very valuable to his firm. In other words Lazonick is arguing that the mere introduction of machinery embodying human skills did not either solve managements' difficulties or render all workers interchangeable. On the contrary, since such men were relatively expensive to train and not easily found, one of the major consequences of mass production, and indeed of 'monopoly capitalism', was the development by management of various strategies aimed at so restructuring the working environment that what was gained was a co-operative work-force (Lazonick 1983: 116, 124, 126).

Lazonick does not, of course, suggest that managements were motivated by altruism (he shows very clearly that their goal was increased productivity), but he stresses that no management could increase productivity whilst remaining unconcerned about the reactions of its workers. One strategy was simply to give workers more pay (i.e. a share in the 'surplus value' they produced), but other more complex strategies were also introduced. To encourage workers to remain with a firm, various benefits, included under the heading of 'welfarism', were brought in. Another development was that of creating for loyal employees a career structure based on security of employment and the possibility of promotion within the firm. A worker with several years invested in one firm, and his feet one or two rungs up a career ladder, was much less likely to throw up his job to move elsewhere because very often his experience was not easily marketable with another company. Thus the so-called internal labour market was introduced as a response to problems faced by a management employing the new technology. A further response was the curtailing of the dictatorial hiring and firing rights of foremen, because in order to keep a co-operative work-force it was advisable to convince them that promotions and sackings were reasonably fair (Lazonick 1983: 123, 125, 126–27).

Lazonick discusses all this in the context of the American experience. He shows that unions there were particularly weak in the period he examines, the late nineteenth and early twentieth centuries, for many of the new centres being developed were not unionized, and the rate of immigration meant that the supply of workers clamouring for employment put established union labour in a weak bargaining position. Nevertheless, despite the inherent weakness of many of the so-called 'company unions', which lacked strike funds he points out, management could not disregard them. Indeed even when a work-force was totally non-unionized, it was impossible just to ignore the way in which the men responded. The men's co-operation was essential to successful utilization of new techniques (Lazonick 1983: 117).

It was evidence of just such co-operation that led Burawoy (1979) to develop his ideas to account, in terms of Marxist theory, for the evidence he accumulated as a participant observer working in an American engineering machine shop. Here men were paid on the basis of piece-work, the classic condition for the development of great antagonism between workers and management. Nevertheless, he thought that the evidence was that their situation had objectively improved in recent years and that their relationships with management were comparatively good, despite the obvious fact that workers and management had good reasons for disagreement over piece rates.

Burawoy is particularly interested in the extent to which management in this factory may be said to have gained the 'consent' of its work-force, for he says that they demonstrated a willingness to co-operate with management objectives. In the context of my own concern with the existence of evidence of consent and goodwill on the ammonia plants, which are continuous process chemical plants, Burawoy's data are particularly welcome. Because they relate to such a very different technological system, it necessarily follows that many of the elements of the 'relations of (or 'in') production' were different. However, despite the fact that his informants were paid on piece rates and not time rates, as were the ammonia plant workers, what is of particular interest is that Burawoy argues (against the views, as he says, of Marx himself and even more of 'twentieth-century Marxism' and obviously of Braverman), that wage labourers co-operate with management not because they are the mere objects of its manipulation, incapable of resistance because of their absence of skill, and the victims of the 'inexorable forces of capital accumulation'; rather they co-operate because they are *willing* to fall in with management's wishes (Burawoy 1979: 77–94).

The crux of Burawoy's position is that he seeks to destroy what he sees as an erroneous Marxist view of workers without falling into what he believes to be the error that has engulfed non-Marxist writers on industrial relations. He is willing to accept that genuinely good relations exist between workers and management, but argues that these are nevertheless always contrived by management in its own interest. Boldly, he confronts the issue of the shop floor fiddle as a test case for his arguments. Non-Marxist writers have noted, he says, much that goes on 'on the shop floor' that suggests that there are 'supposedly autonomous responses of workers to the demands of Capitalist work' particularly certain 'games' (English 'fiddles') associated with piece-work. These apparently give the workers great enjoyment both because the men get more in their pay packets than they would do otherwise, and because they 'beat the system'. He quotes another writer's view that 'in a wide variety of industrial settings "uncertainties in the labour process are exploited by subordinates, leading to power struggles and non-co-operative games aimed against management"' (Burawoy 1979: 79). Burawoy's concern is not to duck the evidence that men do play such games, and enjoy doing so, but, whilst accepting it, to deny that in any ultimate sense this is against management's real interests. Thus he seeks, as it were, to maintain his integrity both as an observer and as a structural-Marxist theorist committed to the idea that what is done in capitalist industry is ultimately done for the benefit of capital. He achieves both these ends by arguing that although workers may genuinely believe that what they are doing is against the boss's interests, and even get a kick out of this belief, they are playing capital's game even when they think they are playing their own. It will become clear that I have reservations about these arguments, but they are nevertheless of great interest.

Burawoy disputes the apparently obvious fact that if workers seem to be succeeding in ganging up to break management's rules and to fiddle higher wages this must be against management's interests. He knows better, on *a priori* grounds. He also believes that he has evidence to support his position for in various descriptive accounts where these 'games' are described, it is sometimes clear that foremen and assistant foremen 'either connived [at] or actively assisted in playing' the game. Since these men are 'management', he argues that it follows that these practices could not really have been 'against management'. Further, Burawoy can refer to other writers who have asserted that 'management' may be deliberately slack in maintaining the rules that should inhibit such games; slack, that is, not out of indolence but because the very atmosphere of uncertainty thus created allegedly enhances management's power. Burawoy believes he is right partly because he can show that fiddles that threaten to cripple a firm are stamped on, and he thinks this is evidence enough that where fiddles are allowed it is because it is recognized that they really assist management. On this basis he reaches a preliminary conclusion that these games/fiddles 'are usually neither independent of nor in opposition to management' (Burawoy 1979: 79–80).

However, he goes on to use his own data to develop this proposition further. In the first place, he puts forward quite precise details to show how the game being played in the workshop he studied worked ultimately to management's benefit. The men, as we saw, were on piece-work rates and their foremen, and even the shop manager, actually helped the men to work a fiddle that enabled them to do very well out of 'slack' rates for particular jobs. The background was that in this large factory, men had considerable freedom to ask for, and to get, transfers to different shops should it be believed that they offered relatively easier work. Burawoy's foremen and shop manager were therefore encouraged to assist the fiddle because they wanted to keep up a steady production rate in their shop, and this would have been threatened had there been an unnecessarily high turnover of personnel as men requested moves to easier shops; even had they simply been disgruntled output would probably have been threatened. Nobody wanted the bother of having to recruit and train new workers. In fact, as Burawoy says, shop management at all levels 'loved the [time-study] engineer no more than the operators did' (1979: 80).

Burawoy, however, explicitly aims to trace the significance of 'games' beyond the realm of piece-work production, and his argument is both subtle and, in part at least, convincing. It is that 'consent' (and he has quoted with approval the definition of consent as 'voluntary servitude') to authority (Burawoy 1979: 81) is generated by the very fact that workers do participate in the game/fiddle, despite the fact that they believe it to be contrary to management's interests. His argument is that in so far as the 'game' becomes an end in itself, attention is focused on it and is deflected away from any concentration on management's or capitalists' misdoings. Thus the workers' interest in the game serves to make them acquiesce in their role in the process of production; the social relations of production necessarily define the rules of the game and therefore game-playing generates consent to these rules (Burawoy 1979: 85–6). Similarly, he develops a complex argument about the role of trade unions in industry. He argues neither that they are ineffective, nor that their members have been 'bought' by management, but rather that senior management permit unions to have just enough real power to enable them to keep the confidence of their members. Thus, as negotiators, the unions can carry their members with them, and workers thus become voluntarily co-operative with their employers (Burawoy 1979: 110–14). This is an argument we will look at again in the last chapter.

At this point, however, it seems necessary to take stock of the arguments that have so far been reviewed. This debate started in relation to a discussion on the role of technology in industry, and it seems clear that this cannot be discussed on its own. Any attempt to think about its significance leads into a debate about the nature of the influence of unions and, more generally, into a debate about the nature of the relationships between workers and management.

If we look first of all at what has been said about trade unions we can see that opinions differ considerably both about their actual effectiveness and the extent to which they may be said to act on the workers' behalf. Braverman clearly regards trade unions as so toothless that no one was capable of putting up any effective resistance to management's plans to increase its control of the work-force. Lazonick, whilst acknowledging that under certain historical circumstances unions have been weak, visualizes managements as forced to negotiate since they had to win the co-operation of workers who may not have been skilled but nevertheless had considerable power to do harm. Burawoy acknowledges management's concern to achieve willing compliance, but assumes that if management appears to give way to union power this is indeed only an appearance designed to give the workers a false confidence that will keep them happy. Burawoy does not refer to Gallie, but it might be supposed that he would see in Gallie's work on the British refineries evidence for the argument that if men have confidence in their unions then they will be cheerfully co-operative workers. The difference between Burawoy and Gallie on this issue is, however, significant: Gallie (1978: 291–92) argues that British managements have been forced into negotiation by union power; Burawoy would assume that they choose to make it seem that this is the situation. Burawoy might even point, as evidence for the rightness of his position, to Gallie's assertion that British management are willing to negotiate with the unions because British unions are not committed to revolution. Such an argument, however, becomes complicated, because the obvious retort would be that if indeed it is to management's advantage to present this face to its workers, and Gallie certainly makes this case, then why did the French management not achieve the same happy position? And there the answer must surely be either that they could not, because of the intransigence of the French trade unions (in which case unions would seem to be capable of acting autonomously), or French management did not know where its own best interest lay.

This latter point is one of particular interest and leads us to consider the main point of difference between Gallie and Lazonick, as non-Marxist writers, and Burawoy and Braverman as structural Marxists. Between Burawoy and Braverman there are very fundamental differences, yet they are united against the other two in this, that both assume that at least senior management, almost we might say as manifestations of capital in the flesh, always know what is in capital's interests and unfailingly order things so that they work together for its greater good. Thus, in discussing the attitude of these authors to unions, we are brought to the point where we have to consider their attitudes to the general relationships between workers and management. Gallie is explicitly concerned with whether men think managements have a right to manage, and, as we have seen, believes the major factors to relate to managements' responses to the unions both nationally and at the level of the refinery. He makes no implicit assumption that management, at any level, or in any context, is all wise. Neither does Lazonick, who quite explicitly sees management as grappling with very difficult problems. While he does not doubt that leading industrialists were very concerned with trying to react to the new mass production technology so as to derive the greatest profits from it, and that part of this reaction involved them in thinking up new ways of dealing with their workers, Lazonick makes it obvious that in his opinion their strategies were not always crowned with success. Braverman, on the other hand, quite clearly assumes that in the interests of capital accumulation, management wants to dominate, and succeeds in dominating, its work-force. Burawoy's position, although more subtle, seems equally to depend on a kind of papal inerrancy in management when dealing with its workers.

This can be shown by looking once again at the main steps in Burawoy's arguments about how it was that the men working in the machine shop that he studied came to co-operate voluntarily with management. He argues that such co-operation can be assured only where it is possible for workers to feel they exert a measure of control over 'the labour process' that enables them to take advantage of some 'uncertainty' in the situation. He argues that the 'game' that the men played to fiddle their bonus payments gave them just this sense of control. It also introduced a kind of gamble into life at work and gave a spice to it which gave them a real enthusiasm for their work in general; thus one effect of game playing was to eliminate much of the drudgery and boredom otherwise associated with industrial work. The true role of the 'game' was brought home to him by his own experience of learning to operate a machine; this taught him how much his personal reputation with other workers depended on his ability to become so competent at his job that his output rate came up to a standard that enabled him to play the game. This had little to do with the small amount of extra money he thereby earned, but it had everything to do with 'prestige, sense of accomplishment, and pride' (Burawoy 1979: 89). *Ergo* even though it might seem that the aim of the men is to get more money for themselves than they should, officially, have this is not the real reason for the fiddle's existence; it is explained by its result – higher productivity on the part of the workers and hence profitability for capital. The 'game' exists because it benefits management. Thus, in effect, while actions of Burawoy's workers may be dogged by consequences that are, to them, unintended and unwanted, 'management' is perceived to have manipulated in its own interests all those things that can be construed as having a positive influence on profitability. Later in his book, as we shall see, Burawoy accepts that the interests of foremen and even shop managers may diverge from those senior to them in the hierarchy. Nevertheless, because he can show that foremen participated in, or connived at, the 'games' on the shop floor, he believes that this shows that they are somehow due to senior management engaged in 'manufacturing consent'.

This argument is teleological and is not self-evidently true; it requires further substantiation in relation to his own data, and it certainly cannot be accepted as a valid generalization. Nevertheless, it raises both a general issue that is of great interest – the extent to which senior management are involved in 'manufacturing consent' – and a particular issue that is very relevant to this study – the role of foremen. In the examination of the two ammonia plants, I ended by stressing the apparently contingent differences in the relationships between supervisors and operators on Plant X and Plant Y. Burawoy would certainly assume that the great degree of worker co-operation on Plant X had somehow been created by senior management, and that it had something to do with the activities of the Plant X supervisors, whether or not they knew this. This is something to which we must eventually return.

When I began my research I was, as I have said, originally interested in studying the significance of technological factors and my attention was directed primarily to Gallie's work, because it seemed that it would be interesting to test his ideas about the significance of national industrial culture by studying the extent to which 'cultural' variations were possible within two plants that were not merely in the same country but within the same industrial complex. However, my attention was also directed to Braverman because the ammonia plants I studied were within a works that had previously been the subject of research which was, in part, apparently intended to provide evidence for Braverman's thesis about the subordination of technological factors to the exigencies of capitalist control.

The book in which this aspect of the research was published is *Living with Capitalism* by Nichols and Beynon (1977). The authors, while not explicitly saying that they are testing Braverman's ideas, write a descriptive account that has been welcomed for providing the necessary test of his work (Elger 1982: 48–9). Nichols and Beynon take issue with the idea that the nature of automated work somehow in itself integrates the worker within the capitalist enterprise. They present their data from the works, which they call 'Riverside', to stress the discomforts and disadvantages of jobs in this chemical complex, especially the drawbacks connected with shift work, that they, like Gallie, believe seriously limit the benefits of a relatively high pay-packet (Nichols and Beynon 1977: 25–7). Moreover they show that process work is not as secure as has been depicted. In particular, however, they give strong support to Braverman's arguments about deskilling. Against the previously accepted ideas that chemical process workers are really skilled in the new technologies (and indeed against Lazonick's arguments about the real capabilities of the so-called semi-skilled workers, and my own subsequently developed views on process operators) Nichols and Beynon suggest that process workers may, in a real sense, be lumped together with 'the generalized labourer', whom management, they thought, deprives of any chance of becoming skilled. They 'have nothing like the same skills as a nineteenth-century craftsman' (Nichols and Beynon 1977: 24, 68).

These authors deny any idea that new automated technology has altered the structure of managerial power. Rather, they believe technology is to be seen as a tool of that power, for they support Braverman's idea that the interests of managerial control determine the choice of technology. In support of these views they bring specific evidence to suggest that in one or two cases the type of machinery actually used was determined simply by managerial judgements about its cost-effectiveness in relation to company profits and that the management did not necessarily feel constrained to employ the most modern technology (Nichols and Beynon 1977: 13, 45).

Their main argument, however, is that the overriding concern of management with the profitability of a capitalist enterprise means that relationships between management and worker can never really be transformed, but are essentially those of mutual hostility. Even at the lowest level of management, that of the foremen, they argue that hostility clearly structures relationships (Nichols and Beynon 1977: 6, 57, 141–46). Thus it is obvious that Nichols and Beynon are to be seen as followers of Braverman rather than of Burawoy's more subtle approach.

On the subject of the nature of trades unions, Nichols and Beynon similarly take Braverman's position. Unions are seen as serving the cause of capitalism: not only do they effect a reconciliation of the worker with the capitalist system by innocently, as it were, negotiating with management because they believe this to be in the workers' interests; rather unions are management's tool: corrupted by management, they exercise no independent power. In *Living with Capitalism* data from Riverside are used to argue that the union officials had been more or less rendered powerless by management (Nichols and Beynon 1977: 147–60).

However, in the view of Nichols and Beynon there was effective opposition to the bosses at Riverside but it came not from the formal union machinery but from the informal operation of real class warfare on the shop floor. This is where their insistence on the mutual hostility of management and worker is so important for this, they say, is the basis on which effective resistance to management power is generated (Nichols and Beynon 1977: 107, ch. 8). Although the authors do not themselves, in *Living with Capitalism*, debate this theoretical issue explicitly, this argument is of considerable theoretical interest. Indeed, it is particularly for this pattern of argument that the book has been praised. For example, Elger, believing Braverman's analysis is flawed mainly because it overlooked evidence for workers' counter-action (1982: 24), very much welcomes this study of Riverside because in his view it redresses the theoretical balance. It shows, he thinks, that it is possible to take a broadly Bravermanian position and yet escape from a position that is intolerable for a mainstream Marxist, that of giving up all hope that the proletariat can be expected to bring in revolutionary changes. If class warfare can be found burgeoning on the shop floor then, despite the ineffectiveness of the unions, there is still hope for the future.

Since Riverside had been studied previously I obviously have to answer the question as to the extent to which this account may be said to be a 're-study'. That I chose to study the same place was in no sense fortuitous; yet I did not set out to make a 're-study', for I did not intend originally to debate the findings of *Living with Capitalism*. Instead, I planned to do something that would be more relevant to Gallie's data, looking at the 'technology versus culture' issue in a way that would not entail making more than a passing reference to Nichols and Beynon's book. Mine is still a study which sets out to do a very different kind of research and largely pursues its own different line of argument; yet it will become apparent that in certain specific instances I do inevitably say things that are relevant to some of the themes introduced by Nichols and Beynon, and that I come to somewhat different conclusions. It is obvious, therefore, that I must say why I chose to study the same works and what the similarities and differences are between the approach I adopt here, and that of the first study.

It was an interest in *Living with Capitalism* that led me to visit Riverside in the first place. Once there, however, I realized that it was just the sort of works that could provide a suitable setting for the kind of research into industrial relations that I had long wished to carry out. I wanted to use an approach of the social anthropologist rather than that usually adopted by the industrial sociologist. This means, at its simplest, that I had wanted not so much to ask questions as to observe how the people involved behaved in their relationships with one another. However, to derive real understanding from such observation requires the prolonged study of a group that is small enough to enable the observer to come to know the members as individuals. The value of this kind of approach is that it generates a real respect for the people involved that is one of the best protections against the danger of reconstructing informants as stereotypes who conform to particular theoretical presuppositions. Before I went to Riverside I had feared that this kind of research would have been practicable only in a small firm, which would have precluded the analysis of much that is most interesting in industrial relations. However, the Riverside works, I discovered, was composed of several different 'plants', each small in the number of the men it employed, and structurally somewhat isolated from its neighbours. In other words, to my eyes the works was, in effect, an archipelago of those semi-isolated islands beloved of anthropological researchers. Nichols and Beynon while at one level studying the works as a whole, had concentrated their detailed attention on a plant concerned with bagging the final product, fertilizer. What I wanted to do was to try my anthropological techniques on one or two of the other plants in which more complex technological processes were carried out. That is why I say that I did not plan my research as a re-study of *Living with Capitalism*, but as a very different project.

I must make it clear that I was not recruited by the company, that Nichols and Beynon call 'ChemCo', to do any research on their behalf. I say this to dispel any suspicion that might arise because my study is much less concerned with criticisms of management than is theirs. Indeed, far from being recruited by the company, I had a great deal of difficulty in getting their permission to do any research at all. Riverside's management felt somewhat let down by *Living with Capitalism* because they thought it in part unfair and because they believed that the guarantees of anonymity that the authors had given when they began their research had not been honoured. (Names had been changed, but in a setting in which Christian names are constantly used, little anonymity is given by a published account that alters only the individual's surname). Let me say categorically, therefore, that the company has in no way supported this research or its writing up.

It is, of course, likely that the Riverside management may have hoped for something from my researches. I think that as they thought they had been unfairly treated they hoped that in some unspecified way I might set the matter straight. Their expectations were, I think, as vague as that and if perhaps they have not been wholly disappointed this is not because I make no criticisms of management, but simply because I do not cast them as the villains of a drama. That I was unlikely to do so was almost certainly clear to them from the preliminary conversations that we had. Nevertheless, I think they were quite unsure what form my analysis would take until I showed them the first draft of my report.

Before I began my study I had some longish interviews with senior managers in which I outlined the kind of work that I wanted to do, but as I explained that my ambition was to try to use anthropological techniques to study a chemical works in a way that had not been done before, it is scarcely surprising if they remained in some doubt as to what it was that I would actually be doing. Therefore it was particularly necessary that they should be prepared to trust my impartiality; and in all the circumstances I have outlined I had to rebuild their belief that social scientists could be 'fair', in the traditional academic sense of that term, that is that I would try to look objectively at both sides where I discovered any conflict of interest between management and work-force. I thought it only reasonable, therefore, to say something about my own background, and it seems reasonable that I should be equally explicit here.

The most important point is probably that I made it clear that my basic outlook on industrial relations is different from those, academics and politicians, who appear to see them essentially in terms of a 'zero-sum' game. According to game theory, in a zero-sum game one side can gain only at the expense of the other, and it must, therefore, be impossible for workers and management to derive mutual benefit from any given decision. In the course of my discussions I saw no reason to hide the fact that I would agree with C. S. Lewis when he said that to believe that 'My good is my good and your good is yours. What one gains another loses' is the basic philosophy of Hell. I do not think the manager is always the enemy of the worker. Rather than seeing the employer as being inevitably the exploiter, in the layman's sense of the term, of the employee, I would argue that it is sometimes perfectly proper to see him in the role assigned to him in German, as *Arbeitgeber*, 'Giver of Work'. I say this both on general principles and from experience as the daughter of a man who, in the aftermath of the first world war, founded a small engineering company because, in a very Weberian sense, he saw it as his 'calling' to direct his technical abilities to provide work by designing socially useful and marketable products. Probably Riverside managers decided I was not a member of the Workers' Revolutionary Party. Nevertheless, they scarcely had grounds for expecting that I would be motivated by some comic desire to rush to the support of a large multinational company (of the type that habitually consumes small family businesses) and to this end do research with the intention of whitewashing its management. They could reasonably hope, however, that I would not regard management as the enemy.

I must reiterate that having been given general permission to do work at Riverside, no pressure whatever was put on me by the management to pursue my researches in any particular direction. The design and scope of the research was left entirely to my own discretion. Once it was agreed in principle that the management were prepared to let me work there only two conditions were made: that I should get the permission of the shop-stewards, and that I should agree to show the local manager anything I intended to publish. I did not feel this to be inhibiting, and in the event not the slightest attempt has been made to persuade me to change my analysis in any way. The only alterations suggested have related to any factual slips I may have made relating to the organization of the plants or their chemical processes.

In what ways do the particular approaches and research techniques that I described in the opening pages of this account lead to the acquisition of different kinds of data, differently presented from the more usual study of an industrial situation? This is something that will, I think, become clear as the complexities of the social 'relations of production' at Riverside are gradually unfolded through this essay. However, it has to be said at once that it is immediately obvious that my findings will inevitably differ substantially from any presented by those who, like Braverman, believe that the only value of industrial research is as a vehicle for the demonstration of the truth of Marxist class theory. This approach is adopted by Nichols and Beynon in their study of Riverside. It means that to them data are relevant only if they support the thesis that, properly understood, Riverside's technology is not designed to make chemicals, but to make chemicals for profit; that its hierarchy of decision-makers is not necessitated by any problems of chemical production but by capital's interests in preventing the balance of power from being altered in favour of the workers; and that were it not for the divisive class system of a capitalist society the management function could be rotated (Nichols and Beynon 1977: 69–70). Because the authors are trying to say something about the forces that fashion social classes in modern capitalist society, where, by definition, in the interests of capital, management, on capital's behalf, 'exploits' workers, they are trying to convey the message that the 'structure' of the situation and its 'meaning' for the participants cannot be analysed separately. It follows that to talk of people's understanding of their position is to talk of 'class-consciousness'; 'exploitation' and 'understanding' cannot be separated, they say (Nichols and Beynon 1977: 76–7). Therefore, when Nichols and Beynon introduce individuals into their account, and they do so liberally, their central concern is to show how these people manifest in their opinions and their actions the influence of capitalist class relations. Their data are rich but they are essentially only 'apt illustrations' of this central thesis. Their book revolves, therefore, round a technique of analysis that anthropologists regard as highly suspect.

From its opening pages *Living with Capitalism* adopts a

Bravermanian position, focusing attention on the system of human control at Riverside rather than on the technology of chemical production. There are brief descriptions of smoke and pipelines and the unpleasant smells associated with sulphuric acid and ammonia. What are described at greater length, however, are the manifestations of social hierarchy. We are told how it is embodied in the working environment, manifested in the differences between the pleasant offices of the managers in the administrative block, the grimy foremen's offices on the plants, and the noisy, and noisome, working places of the men. The threefold division implicit in this description is, moreover, rapidly diminished to a dual structure, for the foremen, although they inhabit the plants with the men, are nevertheless symbolically differentiated from them by the fact that they wear white coats, and these coats link them indissolubly with management. Thus the outlines of the two sides of a zero-sum class game are early foreshadowed (Nichols and Beynon 1977: 3–6).

Nichols and Beynon strive to link both managers and foremen with capital. They accept that the local managers occupy relatively lowly positions within capital's hierarchy, with correspondingly low rewards. Nevertheless they are to be classed clearly as agents of capital since they are seen as essentially concerned with maintaining the pattern of social relations necessary to capitalist production (Nichols and Beynon 1977: 72). The manager may be a technical expert but he is to be seen primarily as a controller of labour who acts in the financial interest of ChemCo. Managers are, therefore, not so much 'chemists' as 'accountants', whose essential task is to make labour profitable to the company. Because managers seek to buy their men's labour power as cheaply as possible when (it is implied) it is obviously in the men's interests to sell it dearly, managers are really capitalists in conflict with their workers. The fact that managers do not own the means of production gives no basis, in Nichols and Beynon's view, for asserting that they are not capitalists. The supervisors are similarly depicted as opposed to the workers, despite the fact that they have proletarian origins and may work with their hands. They are described as using their working-class culture against their class of origin, as capital's paid agents (Nichols and Beynon 1977: 72). It is asserted that the essential role of the foreman is not that of technical supervision, but of helping managers to exercise social domination in production. To this end the supervisor collects and processes information that the manager needs in order to be able to monitor his system of control. Supervisors who are outstandingly good at their jobs use their contacts with their men to set workers against one another to management's advantage, to find out men likely to make compliant shop-stewards, and somehow, in ways unspecified, to see that they are elected. The overwhelming significance for the supervisor of this social control factor is illustrated by the comments of a man newly promoted to this position. He is quoted as saying that he only realized how to do his new job efficiently when it dawned on him that he must become more conscious of the power he now wielded over his former mates, and must be prepared to use that power (Nichols and Beynon 1977: 57 and ch. 4 *passim*).

Opposed to these manifestations of capital stand the workers. In line with Braverman's assertions, Nichols and Beynon lay emphasis not on the process operators but on the unskilled manual workers. They stress that many of the employees at the works do jobs such as those involved in bagging fertilizer and loading it for transport. In discussing process operators, the disadvantages of their position are underlined. Nichols and Beynon refer to the difficulties the operator experiences if he wishes to move his job, because his training tends to be so specific that it is not easily marketable; they stress the noisy, isolated, and sometimes dangerous nature of the work, giving an account of an explosion that had occurred earlier on Plant X. More dubiously, it is noted that operators are classed as 'unskilled' and the impression is given that under a capitalist system only the work of the 'controllers' is valued and that all workers are assumed by management to do donkey work. What is remarkable is that in all this discussion on the role of the workers and the extent to which they may or may not be regarded as skilled, there is scarcely any reference to the maintenance men, the one group that is called skilled. It is not argued that they are not really skilled – they are simply ignored (Nichols and Beynon 1977: 12, 24).[2]

The justification for the rigid dichotomy depicted between 'management' and 'worker' is the existence in the authors' view of unbridgeable divergences of interest, for they see management's aims as necessarily entirely contrary to the interests of workers; even the possibility of any convergence of interest is unthinkable. This view is particularly obvious in relation to a description of the introduction of a new productivity deal in the 1970s, an account of which forms the core of the book. Under this deal the company initiated a scheme to simplify the previous complex payment structure, by which bonuses were earned on many different bases. The scheme's stated aim was to make work both more efficient and more rewarding. This is called a trick to increase the 'exploitation' of the men (without any explanation being given that in Marxist jargon the term means merely that productivity is increased, without necessarily implying that men are worse off). It is admitted that they gained very substantial increases in pay in return for accepting a new, simplified pay structure, like that which Gallie (1978) describes for the oil refineries. It is argued, however, on the basis of a remark by one manager, that some rise in wages would have occurred in any case because it was a time of labour scarcity (Nichols and Beynon 1977: 7–10). The authors' viewpoint comes out, perhaps, most obviously in their comment that the men were disadvantaged by the very fact that the new scheme reduced friction between workers and management, therefore serving to hide from the men's perception the reality of the conflict dividing them from the bosses.

It seems to epitomize the opinion Nichols and Beynon have of the attitude of ChemCo's management towards its work-force that it is said that a highly sophisticated management chose the Riverside site in order to be able to man it with an industrially unsophisticated labour force, the more easily, presumably, to be able to take them for a ride. The authors write, summing up much of their book:

'. . . it is well to begin by remembering two important facts. "Chem-Co" is not a small-time, one-off firm: it is a giant multi-national producer and one of the largest companies producing in Britain. Its strategies are the strategies of large-scale, progressive, corporate capital. The other fact has to do with the location of the Riverside site. It is situated miles away from the nearest urban centre and has recruited a green labour force widely dispersed across an area in which there is no militant trade union tradition. It is hard to think that these factors weren't important ones in determining Chem-Co to purchase its 1000-acre site; harder still when you consider that Riverside is but one of several new chemical complexes that have been located in such situations.'

(Nichols and Beynon 1977: 161)

One answer to any question that asks what difference anthropological research standards might make to industrial research is that they make a statement such as that just quoted, no matter how theoretically relevant, preposterous because it deliberately omits that which does not fit the theory. Ammonia production is potentially hazardous, as we have seen, and Riverside is sited in an area designated for industrial deveopment and as close to the city outskirts as the city authorities would permit. It is located close to port facilities through which, originally, it brought in most of its raw material, and close also to a point at which it can discharge noxious effluent and be sure that it will be carried out to sea; it is close to the junction of two motorways and adjacent to a main railway line. Regarding the 'greenness' of the labour force opinions might be divided, but it is surely relevant to mention that the men see themselves as a self-confident, egalitarian bunch, not given to being over-deferential to management simply because they have never known conditions of high unemployment.

Rather than following through Nichols and Beynon's ethnography, however, to give any point by point account of where I agree or disagree on factual grounds, I want to take up general issues that are of much greater significance. I have to argue that the omission of theoretically 'irrelevant' data results in a distorted picture being given in *Living with Capitalism* of the reasons for the selection of the Riverside site. Similarly, I have to argue, and morally this is rather more serious, that the omission of theoretically 'irrelevant' data about people results in their being distorted into stereotypes; and that this is particularly the case with regard to the depiction of supervisors, who seem to be treated with particular severity, perhaps because their position is anomalous. (It is widely accepted amongst anthropologists that many people regard whatever is anomalous as dangerously polluting and therefore abhorrent.) I am not very concerned to present material that will enable me to say, 'Supervisors are not necessarily betrayers of the working class or the lackeys of management.' I shall, however, be concerned to present, as the result of detailed research, material that will show that the position of the supervisor is very complex, and that an analysis of situations in which supervisors interact with one another and with men and management raises a number of issues that have considerable theoretical implications. This will lead not merely to a rejection of the stereotype of the foreman given by

Nichols and Beynon but to debates on the wider issues of managerial control.

The position of the foreman or supervisor seems to be one that repeatedly comes up as being of especial interest. On empirical grounds I have argued that it seems likely that somehow or other supervisors play a major role in making Plant X and Plant Y surprisingly different places in which to work. Burawoy (1979), understanding the day-to-day reality of friendship and co-operation between worker and foreman sees the latter as the perhaps unwitting tool of a senior (and apparently all-wise) management engaged in manufacturing consent. Nichols and Beynon (1977) show by their treatment of the subject, their intense awareness of the theoretical problem presented by foremen for those who believe that industrial relationships must be depicted in terms of a thoroughgoing dichotomy between worker and an almost all-powerful management. They go further, however, for they centre their hope for a revolutionary future on signs they thought they saw of workers acting, independently of their union, to take up the struggle of class warfare on the shop floor; and their evidence for this focuses on acts of indiscipline and hostility that were, for the most part, directed against foremen (Nichols and Beynon 1977: 135–37).

I will take up this issue of 'hostile' attitudes and behaviour in relation to supervisors because I too have empirical evidence on these matters and yet I think they are to be interpreted in a way that puts a radically different construction on them from that given by Nichols and Beynon. In order to show the kind of argument I shall seek to make, let me refer back (p. 61) to Gallie's assertion that there is a link between the workers' acceptance of management's right to manage and the strength of trade unions. Gallie believes this acceptance of management authority exists because workers have confidence in the ability of their union to negotiate on their behalf with management. I shall show that this cannot explain the attitudes of Riverside process operators since they manifested little trust in their union, but nevertheless appeared to agree that management ought to manage. With perhaps apparent paradox I would argue that this was certainly in part because they had some confidence that management's wishes would generally be negotiated rather than imposed by fiat. This confidence sprang to some extent from decisions taken by senior management, in order, as Burawoy might say, to manufacture consent. However, I shall argue that there was another side to this confidence and that it stemmed to some extent from the trust the workers had in their own, informal, negotiations, especially those they entered into with their supervisors. Incidents such as those that Nichols and Beynon interpreted as evidence of class warfare on the shop floor I see rather as sanctions imposed by the operators on anything they regarded as the improper performance of a managerial role.

The operators' ability to impose sanctions on supervisors exists largely due to the fact that their ability to coerce men has been very severely limited. This is no doubt in part due to the strategy of senior management, for, as we have seen (p. 65), Lazonick (1983) comments that in general it was found that attempts to coerce men by too stringent and too close supervision tended to be counter-productive. It is also certainly the case that in Britain unions have been able significantly to limit the disciplinary powers of management, and this has particularly curtailed the powers of supervisors. I shall also argue, however, that senior management curtailed the powers of supervisors without wholly understanding what the consequences would be; that in fact the consequences were beneficial for the company in that workers accepted managerial authority because its low-level representatives, being so powerless, had to seek, informally, the consent of the men. I shall argue, however, that senior management, not being omniscient or having sociological second sight, neither intended nor wholly understood the consequences they produced.

NOTES

1. The initial argument was put forward by Blauner (1964).
2. Nichols and Beynon (1977: ix) note that they make no reference to craftsmen because management made this a condition of allowing them to undertake their research. This is strange since it was never suggested to me that there was any problem about including these men in my study; but I did, of course, have to get the permission of the various shop-stewards concerned. Perhaps for some reason the then shop-stewards of the skilled trades objected to the idea of Nichols and Beynon's study. It would have been helpful, however, had they discussed the position of these men, even in general terms, in their analysis.

3
The cultural background of the ammonia plants

In order to be able to understand the conditions under which people had to attempt to wield managerial authority we need to look further at the culture of the ammonia plants at Riverside.

Since Nichols and Beynon (1977) stress that the locals were 'green', I must reiterate that although some of the men may have been industrially inexperienced they explicitly viewed themselves as being very resistant to any heavy-handed authoritarianism. The local men prided themselves particularly that they were egalitarian and that they were never obsequious in their relationships with management. The local unions may or may not have been militant. What seemed important to the men, those at least who came from the neighbourhood, was that in their area jobs had never been difficult to find, and that therefore, unlike those poor downtrodden northerners who had come with the company from its home base, they had never had to go cap in hand to beg anyone for work. They recounted with some glee stories about northern foremen, and even managers, who had arrived expecting to call the men by their Christian names and be addressed themselves as 'Mr' or even 'sir', and had found that they had to reconcile themselves to the fact that in this part of the world it was Christian-name terms for all;

these stories were part of the folklore of the works. It may of course have been that the works just happened to have been set up at a time when the legal status of the employee was changing sufficiently to permit such verbal equality, but this was not how the locals saw it. In their view it was simply that the local ethos had triumphed over the ill manners of the outsiders.

The process workers were, of course, not just a cross-section of the local labour force. They did not, in their background, have any common positive feature, except that they had been drawn from a variety of jobs because they had been attracted by the good pay. To this extent they were self-selected; and like the men on the Luton car assembly lines who were depicted in Goldthorpe *et al.* (1969: 56) they seemed often to have given up jobs they preferred in order to do the best for their families. Managerial selection procedures had, however, exercised considerable influence in selecting from among these local applicants. I have already made it clear that the work involved risks that could be avoided only by those who were prepared to do the work responsibly, and that certain of the tasks, notably that of control room operator, involved the assessment of complex information. Moreover, from management's viewpoint, training costs were high, since only after two to three years' training could an operator be trusted to work without special supervision. Men were rejected if it was thought that they would be unlikely to become responsible, successful operators who could cope psychologically and physically with the sense of constant danger and the stress of shift work. They were also rejected if it was thought unlikely that they would repay their initial training by staying in the job for some years at least. For this reason it was very seldom that an applicant skilled in any trade was taken on because it was assumed that he would leave the moment he had a chance of a job in that trade. In general, operators had been quite deliberately selected by the management because of their apparent qualities of intelligence and sense of responsibility; and for this latter reason men with obviously stable backgrounds were preferred.

The selection of men with a 'responsible' outlook is viewed by some analysts as in itself sinister, a manoeuvre to gather together workers who will be compliant and unwilling to do anything to risk their jobs for fear of harming their families. Nobody, of course, would deny the connection between financial obligations and attachment to a well-paying job. Nevertheless, in assessing the motives of management it must be wrong to omit the fact that ammonia production is potentially dangerous both to the men working in the plants and to the surrounding districts. This sense of potential danger, of lethal forces that carelessness might unleash, was something that surrounded me from the moment I started to work in the plants. The dangers were very real, and had the management not set out to recruit a responsible work-force they would have been guilty of a grave dereliction of duty.

It should also be noted, in the context of considering the task of exercising managerial authority amongst these operators, that the selection of men of this calibre did not necessarily make life easier. The operators were well informed and often astute in perceiving the hidden reasons for management actions. It was not, I thought, coincidental that the *Daily Telegraph* often featured (because its cross-word puzzles were popular) amongst the reading matter that they could legitimately bring in to while away their waiting times. If indeed management had set out to recruit a 'green' labour force then in my opinion the attempt had been a rather dismal failure.

A further factor that was relevant for those who had to exercise authority was that, as has been made clear, process operators were likely to feel very vulnerable if their jobs in these plants were threatened. An awareness of a threat that can be countered may lead to a deferential attitude; but if there is nothing that can be done to remove the threat one quite understandable reaction may be to say 'let us eat, drink and be merry'. A further reaction of those with very sound reasons for feeling anxious may be to exaggerate the threat and assume that many unrelated things are signs of impending catastrophe. Like anxious diviners searching the entrails of animals, these workers scrutinized management's every word and action.

However, one significant aspect of the plant culture was that operators were reasonably happy with their pay. For technological reasons continuous process work necessitates shift work for those who operate the machines. I was told of a USA ammonia plant run by day work only but it was stressed that it was built miles from habitation, and that safety considerations precluded any such system in Britain. Shift work means unsocial hours but higher pay than that earned by comparable day work; shift work that also involves special training leads to much higher pay. The great majority of process workers found their incomes rose dramatically on getting employment in the ammonia plants, even when previously they had held jobs of some responsibility. Two of the men had been managers of small retail shops and had enjoyed their work, but one assured me that when he had completed his initial ammonia training, his income had jumped to three times his previous salary, and other men had similar stories. One assured me he had never done a better day's work for himself in his life than when he had left his Welsh mining village and, coming to seek work in the city, had just casually asked for a job in the works, the first likely looking place he had seen on its outskirts. His job, he said, had not merely given his family a much better standard of living, but he had the time and the money to follow his hobby, industrial archaeology. Several men told me, spontaneously, that they had never, as boys, expected to achieve the kind of living standards their jobs with ChemCo had brought them.

Nevertheless shift work itself was the cause of considerable stress that brought disciplinary problems. The men received relatively high incomes, but once their pay had gone up they had taken on extra financial commitments that they felt unable to shed. Therefore, however much they might come to dislike night work, they could not quit. One man expressed as a grievance against the company the fact that he was trapped in his job because he could not get comparable pay elsewhere. His shift mates, who regarded him as both a bit greedy and a bit stupid, chuckled at him, but could understand how he felt. There were times when most of the men dreamed of being able to give up shift work, but knew that they could not afford to do so.

Nichols and Beynon (1977) stress this aspect of the shift workers' situation, and emphasize the amount of tiredness that this pattern of work entails (Nichols and Beynon 1977: 25–7). Gallie (1978) in turn, stresses that shift work associated with automation was the most important factor reducing job satisfaction in the refineries; and he comments with surprise that earlier writers on automated industries should have failed to have discussed the problem. Gallie also comments on a number of aspects of it that were continually brought to my attention. He notes particularly the strain incurred where the children have to be kept quiet in the day-time; the difficulty of getting enough sleep in a busy town whose inhabitants are geared to a day-time schedule of noise; often the impossibility of maintaining friendships with day workers who can never quite understand why a man who seems to have a lot of free time (because he may be off when they are going to work) cannot come round for a drink in the evening when invited, and seems often to resent friends who drop in uninvited (Gallie 1978: 88–9, 92–7).

Certainly, on the basis of my own experience I would argue that it is quite impossible to understand the attitudes of the ammonia operators to their jobs unless the problems of shift work are made very clear. I realized this by their reactions when, at the beginning of my research, I said I wanted to understand what shift work meant to those involved. It was so important to them that I found they immediately assumed that I had come to study shift work alone, and greeted the idea enthusiastically because they were sure outsiders simply had no understanding of what it entailed. Indeed, men were virtually queueing up to talk to me about it. Several times men used the same phrase to me: 'There are not only shift men, there are shift wives and shift children as well.'

To understand how this system of work affected people it is important to realize that what was being worked was the 'continental' system. This meant that instead of working a complete week or longer periods on particular shifts, there was a pattern of continuous rotation of hours of duty. If A shift started with the morning shift on a Monday, then they worked a morning shift also on Tuesday. On Wednesday and Thursday they worked the afternoon shift. On Friday and Saturday they worked the night shift, but they also worked on Sunday night because the rule was that whatever shift was worked on Friday had to be worked also for the next two days. After this A shift would then have two days off, and would return to work the following Wednesday morning. This rotation meant that the next weekend A shift would work the middle shift, from 2 p.m. to 10 p.m.; the third weekend they would work the morning shifts; and on the fourth weekend, because they would have Friday as their rest day, they would be completely free. They would then restart the cycle on the following Monday. The system depended on dividing each twenty-four hours into three blocks of unequal length, and having four shifts to rotate with one another.

It is a system that means that men work a seven-day week, not a five-day week like most people. It also means that while they appear to get two days off after their week's work like others, this is not what happens in practice. A man who comes off duty at 7 a.m. or 8 a.m., having worked the two or three previous nights, has to, or ought to, sleep during a large part of his first day off.

This means that usually he has only one clear day before his next seven-day work period begins, except every fourth week when he will get two clear days.

This pattern of shifts, common in British industry, leads to considerable tiredness. My subjective impression was that I could, with a fair degree of accuracy, pick out shift workers from day workers by the tired 'grey' faces of the former. Their work was seldom tiring in itself, but they suffered from lack of sleep, week in and week out. Certainly the men were very conscious of feeling tired. Nichols and Beynon (1977: 27) quote the story of a man who said that on one occasion when he was undisturbed he slept for twenty-four hours, and such stories are part of the common folklore, and entirely believable. There is probably no pattern of shift work that does not occasion some tiredness, but the 'continental' system, with its continual change of work to different times, makes it impossible for most men to become so adjusted that after a night shift they can reckon on sleeping for a proper length of time. Even if everything remains quiet, the body's normal physiology interrupts sleep. The man who comes off night work, goes home to a decent breakfast, and goes straight to bed, is almost bound to have to go to the lavatory after four or five hours, and for most this is the end of sleep for that day. I knew one man in his fifties who, having worked shifts all his life, was so completely adjusted that he always slept for seven or eight hours after night work. I also knew one younger man on Plant Y who, despite having been on shift work for years, still had a really healthy complexion. It was something I noticed that his mates remarked on and it was only later that I discovered he was notorious for sleeping on night shifts. On one occasion I overheard a group of men watching a former colleague walk past their window, and they commented on how much more sprightly his step was now that, just before retirement, he had been put for a spell on day work. Their remarks seemed a good indication that they were well aware of the physical toll exacted by shift work.

I have already commented on the trouble I found keeping awake and thinking sensibly on night shifts. The process workers were set the task not merely of keeping awake but of keeping alert. They had to be alert to calls on the tannoy, and to changes in the sounds of their machines; in the control room they had to watch the flickering of a multitude of dials and graph displays. This was a far more difficult task than working on, say, some night-running assembly line where enforced continual movement must make keeping awake a relatively easy task. On the ammonia plants there were stretches of the night when the operators had nothing physically to do, and to keep awake and alert in such circumstances calls for an enormous amount of discipline, partly self-imposed, but partly coming from supervisors, as we shall see.

It is worth-while to look in more detail at the problems shift work made for family relationships. Quite obviously it generated tiredness and tension in the men, and many were very conscious of the results this had for their families. They worried particularly that their children could not be expected to understand why their fathers were so often short-tempered and grumpy. They feared they must also seem unreliable, giving promises that went unfulfilled, because their duties at work had to take precedence.

Because of the potential danger of an ammonia plant left insufficiently attended, each process worker had to accept the obligation to stay at work until his relief on the next shift arrived; and if he did not arrive then a second shift would have to be worked. This was often not seen as an intolerable imposition since the second shift was paid for at overtime rates and was, therefore, often welcomed. Nevertheless the day came for every man when he had to choose between spending time at work and spending it with his family. A man might have promised to take his family out and then find at the last moment that there was great pressure put on him to stay on the plant. Men said ruefully that this usually seemed to happen when they had been working a Saturday morning shift. The chance of having a Saturday afternoon off was valued; men looked forward to it. If a man then found there was no relief for him at the last moment, or, for reasons that I shall discuss later, he found that great pressure was put on him to stay at work until 4 p.m., he was put into a very difficult situation. He would arrive home to be greeted by disappointment and recrimination from his children – surely if he had really tried he could have got someone else to have stayed in his place.

The social pressure on process operators not to let their mates at work down was, however, very strong. The strength of this pressure on them may be judged by the different patterns of time-keeping they showed as compared with maintenance men and other day workers. The system of 'clocking in' had recently been abolished throughout the site as a consequence of general company policy. As a result, so it was said, a lot of day workers had become very slack about time-keeping. It was quite different, however, with the process operators who were, especially on Plant X, meticulous. Indeed, as I have observed, many of these men got in well before the hour actually specified for their shifts, in order that their colleagues on the outgoing shift might have adequate time to discuss the running of their part of the plant and still leave, having had a shower and changed, before the official time of the changeover. This pattern of time-keeping obviously owed much to the way in which shift work was organized. The crucial factor was the rule that a man might not leave until his relief had arrived, and this had made it socially unacceptable to be late. In many cases it was considered the proper thing to do to get in with time to spare. This social presssure was at times strong enough to make the men put the interests of their mates before those of their families.

This came out most clearly when there was no absolute obligation to do extra work. For example, under certain circumstances a supervisor might ring up a man off duty in an effort to find someone willing to do the turn of an operator who had failed to turn up. This man then came under such moral pressure that he might agree to work, against the wishes of his wife. Again a man might be pressured to agree to come in to do, say, a week-end shift for someone who had a special reason for wanting the time off. I recall listening to a man being persuaded on a Wednesday night into promising to come in to work an extra Saturday afternoon shift to help out a friend; then I listened to him as he pondered how he was to break the fact to his wife, whom he had promised, only the night before, to take shopping then. He knew she would be very disappointed so he resolved to wait until after he had had his meal so that they did not have to eat while she was in a bad mood; then he would break the news to her and escape down to his allotment. It was a trivial incident but it illustrates the frequent occasions when, without anything very dramatic happening, a process operator had to choose between his work-mates and his family. The conflict was probably the greater because, as I have commented already, so many of the men had taken jobs as process operators precisely because they were family-oriented men.

It can be seen, therefore, that process work on the ammonia plants exerted distinct kinds of stimuli and stresses on the operators that did not result from the technology alone. They stemmed directly from this but also from the associated necessity of working shifts; from the formal refusal to classify operators as 'skilled' workers; and from their relatively high wages. The result, not surprisingly, was that men showed considerable ambivalence in their attitudes towards their work, and those of the same individual could vary considerably, depending on the circumstances of the moment. Men seemed, usually, to be very pleased with the standard of living made possible by their pay; nevertheless, they suffered a lot of stress and anxiety from the conflicting claims of work-mates and family, from the physical strain of shift work, and from nagging fear that their lives would be shattered if the works shut down.

As for the actual work itself, nobody could pretend the working environment was other than noisy, smelly, and potentially dangerous. The operators' actual tasks were seldom arduous and their reactions to them were very varied. One man, probably the worst operator I met, who had a very poor reputation among his mates for ham-fisted carelessness, found everything he did a most tedious bore. On the other hand there were a few men who enjoyed much of what they did and said this was the most interesting employment they had ever had.

It is scarcely surprising that men also often seemed ambivalent in their attitudes towards the company. A few men, almost always the older ones, were always positive, 'loyal'. Their mates said they were 'like a stick of rock; break them in half and you'd find "ChemCo" stamped through the centre'. Other men were usually hostile. Most operators, however, would say in some contexts, and mean it, that the company was quite generous, but in other contexts they would bitterly blame the company for the stresses of their work. It was part of the operators' folklore that not so long ago ChemCo had really cared for its workers and had repaid loyalty with loyalty, almost like the proverbially paternalistic Japanese firm. Even the most loyal of the workers concluded sadly, however, that this was no longer the case. It seemed that the men's loyalty was linked inextricably to confidence that the company would be loyal to them, and that this confidence was inevitably eroded by 'efficiency' drives and the concern of management with marginal labour costs already described. Much of what I shall have to say relates to this fact.

Since labour costs concerned management so much and the question of wages was so crucial for the relationships between management and worker, and between worker and worker, it will be useful at this stage to give an outline of the system of payment.

Basically it is much like that which Gallie (1978: 65) describes for the British oil refineries. All the Riverside craftsmen who had served their apprenticeship had been placed on a single basic grade with a single salary. One higher grade did exist for the man who, because of the nature of his work or because of the times at which he worked, could not be supervised; he was, therefore, paid extra for being 'self-supervised', but such men were exceptional amongst the tradesmen. A number of different grades, however, still existed for the operators, and these were ranked hierarchically. Hence the differences between the process and maintenance men seem to have been due in part to technical reasons and in part to what may be called socio-political factors. The time-served tradesman was, by union definition, deemed fully able to do everything proper to his craft. Moreover the skilled trades' unions were sufficiently strong to prevent management from exercising control through the use of different payments to different men. However, there were still significant differences in the tasks of operators, and since they did their learning on the job their union had to recognize that they did not all have the same expertise. Nevertheless, just as in the refineries, management, like the unions although for other reasons, was sympathetic to moves to eradicate the distinctions between grades. Technological change was continuous, so that what was wanted was flexibility, a willingness of men to lend a hand rather than a 'rigid adherence to a specific set of operations' (Gallie 1978: 219); a co-operative team was needed and this was not produced by stressing differences between work roles.

The simplicity of the pattern of payments thus created seems to have had rather different results in the ammonia plants from those that Gallie found among the British oil refineries. It had not, at Riverside, eradicated strife between the workers over their wages. Moreover although here, as in the refineries, disputes led to the intervention of shop-stewards, it did not seem that this necessarily increased their authority with their members, although this is something that Gallie (1978: 173) found in his study. Grade simplification at Riverside had been brought about by technological change and manpower reorganization and these had provided opportunities for the intervention of stewards. But as men still disagreed among themselves over details this sometimes created such a potent cause of friction between the different constituents of a shop steward that his task of fairly representing all his members could be difficult. Gallie (1978: 65) argues that the simplified grading system had kept out of British refineries some of the causes of jealousy he found among French workers. He also thinks it crucial that productivity bargaining had given the elected shop-stewards 'important independent powers' (Gallie 1978: 176) in certain areas, so that they exercised a major influence in the relationship between management and unions. However, in the ammonia plants the new system did not eliminate friction and involved the shop-stewards in the jealousies that resulted.

The simplification of the grades in Riverside had failed to lead to the elimination of differences in the pay-packets of individual workers and subgroups formally on the same grade. This was because there were very variable opportunities for working overtime between the men of different subgroups, and even within the same subgroup different individuals might exploit their nominally identical opportunities quite differently. Differential overtime chances quite altered the actual relationships within and between grades, and between the subgroups composing a grade. These differences commonly gave rise to rivalry and tension. Further, the simplified grading system in itself led to jealousies between groups and subgroups, as I shall show.

Gallie is perfectly correct to argue that no individual British operator could seek a rise for himself as an individual (unless of course he were able to achieve promotion) and that his efforts had to be directed to raising the level of his whole group. One group's rise, however, is it seems, necessarily perceived as being effected not so much at the company's expense as at the expense of the subgroup immediately senior, whose 'differentials' are thereby eroded. This move is a symbolic challenge to its formerly accepted status and leads either to a frantic attempt by the seniors to raise their grade in turn, or, if this is difficult, it leads to bitter hostility against the junior, upwardly mobile, subgroup. So much was this kind of friction a part of the culture that there was a special word for it – 'ani', short for animosity. Ani was not restricted to situations where there were jealousies about overtime and re-grading, but these provided a perfect seed-bed for its generation. At its most malevolent it occurred where differences in chances of overtime were so great that accepted differentials between different grades of workers either disappeared or were indeed reversed in financial terms.

Ani, in its most obvious and bitter form, showed itself in the relationships described between ammonia workers and maintenance men. Because one basic grade had been established for craftsmen, many very experienced men were still on the grade given to newly qualified apprentices. The older men, frustrated, seemed to feel that self-respect demanded that at least craftsmen should be on a higher grade than even the most senior process worker and led opposition to any up-grading proposed for them. Grading had become the main symbol of status; equal grades for process and maintenance would have destroyed all that an apprenticeship stood for. Tradesmen, however, could do little about the fact that their wage packets were often smaller than those of process workers, who had extra pay for working shifts, and much better chances of working overtime. As we saw formerly, a few maintenance men had worked shifts and some did overtime and this had occasioned jealousy within their ranks; but the recent loss of such opportunities led most craftsmen to feel bitter towards the operators, who reciprocated the sentiment.

Ani also, inevitably, affected relationships between different grades on the process side. This was true even where there was no question of the elimination of formal grade distinctions. For example, there is an important difference between the supervisor, who is formally on the lowest rung of the managerial grades, and the senior operator, who as the title implies, is at the top of the ordinary operator grade. Under a new company policy, however, the senior operators on Plant X had been acting periodically as 'deputies' for supervisors. As I shall describe, on this plant a serious quarrel had subsequently divided them because the Plant X senior operators had put in a consequent claim for regrading, and their understanding of the politics of the works had led them into the tactical manoeuvre of claiming pay equality with the supervisors rather than with the craftsmen, their other possible alternative. When I did my research the senior operators had had their claim substantially rejected, but between senior operators and supervisors on Plant X ani still rankled. This was not the end of the story. It seemed that two factors had spurred the senior operators to make their re-grading attempt. They thought that a chance of up-grading had been presented to them when they were asked to act as deputies to the supervisors. More than anything else, however, they had wanted to re-establish the seniority they had formerly enjoyed in relation to the control room operators on Plant X. These men, who were immediately their juniors, had themselves put forward a claim to be up-graded because they sometimes deputized for senior operators, and had been largely successful. This too had led to a sense of rivalry.

The simplified grading system, as it works in practice, therefore does not eliminate friction between workers over pay; moreover, these disputes, while they provided the occasions for the intervention of shop-stewards, presented them with no very easy task to accomplish. Disputes involving questions of ranking as between senior operators and supervisors and senior operators and maintenance men involve different unions and therefore different shop-stewards. This may make relationships between different stewards difficult but presents perhaps a not intolerable difficulty. In so far as the question of re-grading involved men at different levels of the ordinary operator hierarchy, however, the unfortuntate shop-steward found himself involved in a dispute in which his own constituents were on different sides. Inevitably the strain of such a situation could be considerable.

Finally, in this examination of the basic culture of the plants it is essential to consider the question of overtime. Apparently, in analysing the differences between French and British refineries, Gallie (1978) did not find it necessary to discuss details of overtime working because overtime for maintenance men had been eliminated by new productivity agreements, and it seems not to have been an issue with the process operators. The omission of the topic by Nichols and Beynon (1977), however, is odd since concern with overtime is an important and very general factor influencing attitudes at Riverside. (For example, the men on the bagging plant, whose heavy labours without the aid of new technology are so deplored in *Living with Capitalism*, enjoyed very high overtime levels and for fear of losing them went on strike when the new technology was introduced.) The question of overtime was certainly very important on the ammonia plants. Indeed, in many instances it was quite impossible to understand tensions and quarrels between workers and management and worker and worker without knowing how disputes related overtly or covertly to issues of overtime. For this reason it seems essential to end this chapter with a very detailed description of the reasons that overtime was so common, and why so much importance had come to be attached to attempts by the management to eliminate it, and by the workers to cling on to it. The issues were far more complex than they appeared to be at first sight.

Today 'overtime' has become something of a dirty word, a practice that both management and unions are united in wishing to eliminate. The former see it as grossly expensive, the latter assume that if it were eradicated more jobs would be created. Yet at all continuous process chemical works a certain amount of overtime will probably always be essential if permanent over-manning is to be avoided. Gallie (1978: 100) comments:

> 'It is extremely difficult to establish criteria for assessing the technically necessary level of manning for running the shifts. This is due to the highly irregular pattern of work. When the units are running smoothly, the work load is relatively light. The moment, however, that the units are in crisis, the work load escalates. If the units are manned in such a way as to keep to a reasonable level the degrees of work pressure on people at moments of crisis, then it is virtually certain that in periods of normal running there will be a substantial manning surplus. Conversely, if the units are manned so that people will be kept reasonably busy during normal running, then the operators are under very severe pressure in times of crisis. There is then no single, ideal level of manning that will cover the two extremes of operating conditions.'

Gallie (1978: 101) notes the connection between problems over manning levels and the necessity of working overtime. If manning levels are kept to a minimum then any failure of an operator to turn up means another man must work overtime. He notes the drawbacks of the system, the fact that inevitably it means either that people stay on at the end of their shift to cover absences, or that they come out to the refinery on one of their rest days. Either way he saw it as disruptive and a source of grievance. I had already made it clear that there were occasions when the necessity of working overtime was experienced as an imposition. Nevertheless, the possibility of being able to boost earnings was also regarded as a precious possession of the process operators, which they valued, and for which they were much envied.

Overtime is not necessarily against a firm's interests; nor are those who do overtime necessarily doing another man out of a job. Overtime working may be a perfectly rational way of coping with technical difficulties that make unpredictable demands on a labour force; and leniency regarding overtime may provide one way in which a management can cope with the problems of adapting a national wage agreement to the conditions of a local labour market. When Riverside was first opened both these factors encouraged reliance on overtime.

The works is in a relatively affluent region in which, back in the 1960s, a lot of employers were competing for good men. The situation here was very different from that in the home base of the company. There it was the main and best employer and it had no difficulty in keeping the stable labour force that is so desirable for a continuous process firm. Riverside management found, on the contrary, that it had an unacceptably high level of turnover amongst its employees, particularly among the craftsmen, but at one stage amongst the process workers also. The local management could do nothing to alter the basic pay rates since these were determined by the company at a national level. The only effective strategy for keeping men was, therefore, to be lenient in permitting them to work overtime, thus raising the actual level of their wages.

Further, when the ammonia plants were first opened, they experienced a great number of technical problems. Today the plants are regarded as rather old-fashioned; their problems have for the most part been dealt with and usually they run smoothly. This was not the case in earlier years when the plants were not merely new but experimental (the first one on the site was the first plant in the world to make ammonia in one single continuous process from basic feed stocks to the final ammonia gas). Moreover the first feed stock was not natural gas but naphtha, a much more difficult, indeed dangerous, source of hydrogen that caused a lot of stoppages, all of which led to surges in the demand for manpower.

The great days of the setting up of the plants have in a sense become mythical, and it would be difficult at this stage to determine how much overtime work men then did, or what was the degree of compulsion exercised over them. The flavour of these tales of the heroic past came out in stories told by a fitter's mate (a fitter's helper who has never served an apprenticeship) who had been employed at the works from the beginning. He boasted about the early days: then men knew how to work, they really worked, not like today; then they had worked twelve-hour shifts and a great deal of overtime; in those days no sooner had he got back from work than a taxi would arrive, sent by the company, to bring him back again because he was needed; the taxi drivers got to know him so well that they did not have to be told his address, for his name was sufficient! The young fitter with whom he worked could not possibly have known of these events except from hearsay, but he was so well imbued with the folklore that he kept up a kind of chorus supporting the older man, stressing the enormous efforts the workers had put into the setting up of the plants, their pride in their achievements, and their willingness to work hard and do all this overtime in the company's interests.

In much more recent years technical trouble in the plant had still been the occasion for great pressure to be put on men to work overtime if it were essential to cope with a breakdown. A young supervisor told of a fairly recent occasion when he had planned to have his first real week-end break for some time, sailing with his wife and sons. They were preparing to leave by 6.30 a.m. on the Saturday morning, with the boat hitched up to the car, when at 6.20 a taxi arrived to take him to the works. He thought that his plant manager, knowing his plans, had not telephoned him for fear that, guessing what was up, he might have let the phone ring and scurried off. As it was, of course, he got into the taxi; his wife had understood, but he said his sons were furious that he should have gone off and left them.

Even when nothing went wrong with the plants there were still regular occasions when overtime was worked. Sometimes overtime was worked because it had been virtually built into the payments system by the union negotiators, although nobody admitted it formally. The negotiators, instead of going for an addition to the basic pay award, asked rather for some small reduction in hours, which was known really to concern money rather than time. This was because the extra 'leisure' hours would in fact be worked, but at overtime rates. Overtime had also been customarily worked to cover gaps created by the absence of men, whether due to sickness or to holidays. Although there was room for disagreement between management and workers over the 'right' level of manning for a shift, no one thought it was practicable to demand that a shift should be so fully manned that overtime was never needed.

Moreover, it has to be stressed that the men on the shifts were normally very pleased to have the chance of extra work, especially when they were thinking about the bills for their own holidays. It was undoubtedly union policy to try to press for the manning levels on shifts to be kept up so that 'normal' absences did not make it necessary to work overtime, but it did not seem to be a policy that appealed to the operators generally. There had, therefore, seldom been problems between management and labour about the men being asked to do extra work. This situation had changed when I did my research, but the cause of friction was not that the men were being asked to do extra work but that they were no longer being allowed to do their customary overtime, because of the new concern of management with marginal labour costs. Indeed, it will become apparent that a great deal of friction between management and men was quite directly related to management attempts to cut down on the hours of overtime that men thought they had a right to work. Because the issue of overtime working was so socially important, it is essential at this point to explain carefully just what it entailed.

The most common form of overtime was occasioned by a man failing to turn up for work; then his opposite number on the earlier shift stayed on to do the second shift at overtime rates. This was called 'doing a doubler'. It involved a very long stretch of time at work but it was more or less physically tolerable because so much of a shift was normally spent resting, waiting to go into action.

Certain limits had been set to the length of time a man might work. If we examine the most common form of 'doubler', that caused by a man's failure to turn up for his night shift, we find that, normally, someone on the afternoon shift (2 p.m. to 10 p.m.) had to work on until 7 a.m. or 8 a.m. the next morning (depending on the custom of the plant). This involved a stretch of work of eighteen hours, which was considered acceptable, but only if the man then had at least eight hours away from the plant. This rule, however, in fact made it impossible for the operator to turn up for his next regular shift if it were still the 2 p.m. one, for this did not give him his eight-hour break. The consequential difficulties involved further overtime. Company and union agreed that the operator, necessarily late for his next shift, should not be penalized, and his pay was not docked for late arrival. However, the man's absence still had to be covered, so often the company paid a man on the morning shift to stay for an extra one or two hours. It was this rule that sometimes caused problems on a Saturday afternoon. Absentees were common on Friday night: if any man on the Friday afternoon shift worked a doubler on that night then he was not allowed to come in at the start of the Saturday afternoon shift, and someone from the morning had to stay on. Significantly, great pressure was put on operators by their fellows to tolerate the loss of this cherished free afternoon rather than make a fuss and limit another's overtime.

The one kind of doubler that was usually forbidden, although it was occasionally allowed on Plant Y, was for a man who had been on a night shift to continue to work on a morning shift. A man who had just worked overnight was regarded as being drained mentally and physically. This particular doubler was called a 'killer', and a man dead on his feet could scarcely be expected to work safely, let alone efficiently.

Management was aware that it was not a good thing to expect men to do the long stretches at work involved in any kind of doubler. There was indeed a way of avoiding doublers where an absence could be forseen because, for example, a man was known to be ill, or someone was on holiday. The alternative to doublers was, however, not popular with the men and they were not prepared to co-operate. The alternative was simple. If cover were needed for a night shift then a morning shift man could stay on from 2 p.m., when he should have left, until 8 p.m., giving him a twelve-hour stint of work, with six hours of overtime. The afternoon shift operator, in turn, could be told not to report for work until 8 p.m. and he too would have a twelve-hour work period. This man, however, would quite understandably regard himself as having been very ill-used, for instead of an afternoon shift he had to work a night shift, and all he got in return was overtime for two hours. Such an arrangement would have been resented as a great imposition. Yet it was not possible for management, who understood this perfectly well, to reward the man by paying him above the normal rate, for it could not be said that he was working a doubler. It had become his ordinary shift and, therefore, an abnormal payment would have led to jealousy. It is perfectly understandable that over the years the men should have campaigned to be allowed to work doublers rather than work the twelve-hour shift system.

Formerly, the most significant occasion when overtime had been worked had been certain extra 'leisure' hours that had been won by union negotiators some years before my visit. There had been an agreed 'reduction in hours' of two and a half hours per week. These had been aggregated so that each operator was nominally entitled to take off one shift in his normal monthly cycle. In practice, however, each man had worked his Extra Shift Off (ESO) at special overtime rates. This was because the ESO counted formally as part of the men's holiday period, and work done at such a time qualified for premium payments. Moreover at an earlier time a man's request to take an ESO as actual leave was regarded rather unfavourably by plant management since it had been felt that to work it posed the fewest problems for scheduling the manning of shifts. In practice, because of the high rates paid, it was in fact very rare indeed for a man to want such leave. By the time I did my research, however, such a great change had come about that the ESO had become a matter of bitter dispute between management and the work-force. The new management policy was to insist that the ESO be taken as leave; the men had responded in such a way that whilst they complied, the ESOs had become, for reasons I shall detail later, even more expensive for management than they had been previously; they had given rise to the payment that the men knew fondly as the 'golden nugget'.

There was no 'golden nugget' for the maintenance men; indeed, their chances of working overtime had recently been severely curtailed, and although this was in part due to their own decisions, it seemed to have led them to feel increased bitterness for the process operators. In the normal way the manning levels required for any maintenance job could be fairly accurately assessed so that the scope for unexpected overtime was limited; the reduced demands of the recession also meant that management no longer felt necessarily obliged, if machinery broke down, to organize overnight and week-end repairs. The skilled unions had successfully campaigned against their members working overtime unless it was really essential, and there had also been disputes that had led to special bans on overtime working.

So far as I could discover the facts, it seemed that amongst the craftsmen many individuals were not personally greatly disturbed at the reduction of overtime opportunities – they had possibilities, if they wished, of earning cash doing outside jobs. Of the electricians, for example, who met regularly to share out what overtime was available, I was told that, of the twenty-five men involved, only ten wanted regular overtime. Seven never wanted it at all, and the remaining eight worked for particular targets as and when they felt like it. As a group, however, they were as one in resenting the fact that there seemed to be little effective restriction on the amount of overtime the operators could work, and this resentment seemed common to most tradesmen. In particular, the fitters were furious that some of their members, who had previously been attached to shifts, and had earned the special allowances both for their 'unsocial hours' and for 'self-supervision' during these hours, had recently been returned to day work only, as the result of changes in management policy. Most of their anger was directed against the management, but at a group level (by no means necessarily in the case of individuals), ani influenced their relationships with the operators.

This then is the basic outline of the culture of the plants, against which I want to examine the issue of managerial control. The plants were units within which men were influenced by national institutional factors, by the immediate characteristics of the technology, and by the very nature of a continuous process operation. The plants were also arenas within which management interacted with workers, and workers of different grades, and different 'castes', interacted with one another.

One further point remains to be added about the relationships of process operators and the tradesmen. Each operator was attached to a particular plant that was the focus of all his social relationships. The tradesmen, by the very nature of their work, moved between plants. I found the socially perceptive maintenance man a mine of information about the 'habits and customs' of the different plants. Also, despite the inter-group friction that existed, the individual maintenance man, chatting with the operators on the plants carried gossip and opinions round the works. To the operators they remained outsiders, but they were very influential outsiders.

4
The meaning of authority:
an overview

Managerial authority is a topic about which there are conflicting ideas. Analysing the ammonia plants I shall assume for the moment that any authority delegated from the top is managerial authority, no matter who exercises it; I shall seek to justify this view later. In this context I will simply look at the linked concepts of authority and power.

Power is linked to might; authority to the concepts of consent and legitimacy. Gallie (1978) argues that management's power was limited by the fact that unions had considerable areas of power. Stewards could use union solidarity to veto management plants (Gallie 1978: 175); in general this same solidarity gave the unions 'a high level of potential power to coerce management' (p. 292); British management had 'conceded substantial rights of negotiation to the trade unions' (p. 303); British unions, having 'secured a highly dependable base' could 'effectively threaten management with severe economic losses if it failed to take into account their views' (p. 313). A significant positive consequence of all this for British management was that having granted the work-force 'a higher degree of participation', management was given 'a greater degree of legitimacy' (p. 307). Against all this, Nichols and

Beynon (1977), following Braverman's ideas, depict Riverside as a work-place within which unions had little or no independent power, and the men increasingly demonstrated their rejection of managerial authority by taking hostile counter-action on their own behalf; increasingly, it is asserted, they denied legitimacy to management (see especially Nichols and Benyon 1977: 166).

These arguments seem opposed, but I suggest there is reason to accept some part of each. Like Gallie, I found that managerial power had been eroded and that unions were in some areas powerful; it also appeared that management authority was accepted. It did not seem, however, that this 'legitimacy' of management rested exclusively on the high degree of participation in certain kinds of decision-making allowed to the unions. Rather the link was less direct and, ironically it seemed, related to the fact that men did indeed sometimes take action independent of the unions that was against management. My thesis, however, is that the restrictions placed on managerial power by the unions' rights led to authority being negotiated directly between those exercising it and the men. Although a constant theme of this essay will be that these negotiations sometimes included hostility to individual superiors, I finally argue this did not constitute rejection of managerial authority; rather its 'legitimacy' was linked to this negotiation process.

Riverside management at the top still had power and could impose its ideas on others in major respects. This was shown by the case of the 'shift-fitters'. Until shortly before I arrived at the works, maintenance on the plants had been done in two ways. During the normal working day teams of tradesmen had been available; but to carry out immediately necessary repairs each shift on each of the two ammonia plants had had attached to it one shift-fitter. This man knew the machines of his particular plant intimately, and could often deal swiftly with trouble arising in the course of his shift. Inevitably, however, these fitters spent a large part of their time simply waiting for things to go wrong and they were thus often, and obviously, idle. It was therefore decided, at senior managerial level, to reorganize the system, to rationalize it and to have one shift-fitter to service several plants. This change was effected by senior managerial edict. Objections from a number of different levels, stressing hardship to particular men and raising the issue of the relative cost, and ultimate efficiency, of the changed working pattern, were overruled.

There was thus no question about the ability of managerial power to effect a major reorganization in working practice. At the same time the limitations on this power were equally apparent. Informed gossip insisted that management would very much have liked to have retained in the new, small, shift-fitter team some men who, it was agreed, were outstandingly good fitters. It was, however, entirely beyond management's power to do so because at this point it confronted acknowledged union power. As Gallie (1978) makes abundantly clear, British union policy had successfully opposed the right of management to reward particular men because of particular skill. The fitters' union had insisted that the four men most senior by length of service be retained on the team. Chosen on this basis, the group contained only one of the really highly skilled men, but it did include an older man who, it was claimed, was past doing even a modestly competent job. ('I wouldn't trust him to put a washer on my tap at home,' as one of the operators said.) It followed that the best men had had their pay substantially cut, since they lost both their shift and 'self-supervision' allowances. There was simply no way by which management could pay them more than the character known to his friends for his lack of skill as 'Tommy Teflon, the non-stick welder'. The consequence was that the works lost the services of the best fitter in the group, who, I was told, had had to take a cut in pay of £29 a week; thinking of his mortgage and three young children he had promptly got himself a better job with another firm.

Thus, in this one incident both the power and powerlessness of management were demonstrated. It seemed significant that the men so unquestioningly accepted union control in situations such as this that management alone was blamed for what happened. 'They' must have known from the beginning what the consequences of the reorganization would be and therefore management must be held responsible for what followed.

The fitters, not surprisingly, attempted to take collective action against the new management policy, but here they ran into the problem of maintaining a united front. While the old shift-fitter system had existed, so I was told, ani bedevilled the relationships between the day-fitters and the shift-fitters, and it was only because the self-esteem of all the fitters suffered under this new policy, and because of their resentment that it was they rather than the operators who were losing out, that they took common action at all. For a while, however, all the fitters did agree to ban overtime. Nevertheless, before many weeks had passed one of the demoted fitters, socially always a loner, in an emergency agreed to do some overtime. Immediately the common front of the fitters fell apart, and those offered overtime jobs did them.

Thus it might seem that not only was managerial power still very great at the top, but that the divisions in the work-force meant that policies could be forced through without incurring serious costs. I doubt if such exercises of power were costless even at this level. It will become apparent, for example, that this incident led a lot of people who were not normally ill-disposed to management to question its wisdom and, in part, its legitimacy; and many argued that the policy was still bringing hidden costs in its train. Nevertheless, the shift-fitter system had been reorganized, and the new system may have brought economic benefits. What is quite clear, however, is that except at the top level, decisions simply could not be forced through in this way against the opposition of those affected. There had to be a large measure of tacit agreement at least if a new policy were to be successful; indeed, this agreement was necessary if normal everyday decisions were to be properly carried out. In fact I shall argue that the way the plants ran depended on management performance at very low levels in the hierarchy; that at these levels power was extremely limited. Indeed, it was so limited that despite all that Frederick Taylor may have written at the beginning of this century on the elimination by 'scientific management' of any need to rely on the 'good will' of the work-force, and despite Braverman's assertions about Taylor's overwhelming influence on capitalist industrial practice, one vital ingredient to managerial success was still this 'good will'.

In what follows I shall concentrate attention on very low level 'managerial' action, looking at the way those at the bottom of the hierarchy coped with exercising such authority as had been delegated to them. I shall be concerned not so much with what people said about management and whether or not they verbally 'accepted management's right to manage', but with how they actually did their jobs. I was continually struck by the difference between what people said and what they did. While some men talked about supporting management, but actually did poor work, others spoke as if they were highly antagonistic to management yet threw themselves into their jobs. We must, therefore, examine different levels of work actually done within the plants in order to look at how the relationships involved influenced the way in which commands, instructions, and advice were given and received. In order to do this systematically it will be necessary to run through the different, formally acknowledged roles associated with the plants. (What I say will refer to Plant X unless otherwise specified.)

Formerly there had been a hierarchical series of operator grades, and passage from one to the other was achieved relatively slowly. A man, on starting work on the plant, was taught his job in relation to only one section of it. From there progression was gradually upwards to different sections until eventually, if he earned the trust of his superiors, he might rise to the job of control room operator, which was a highly esteemed position. Then it was possible for a man to become assistant foreman, with the hope of rising to foreman (now called the supervisor), who has charge of a shift on a plant. From that point the fortunate man might advance to become 'shift manager', whose job was to exercise overall operational command over a particular shift throughout the entire site. (He had final say, for example, over the starting up of any large machine on any plant, since the surge in the demand for electricity that such a start-up causes might, if not properly co-ordinated with other demands, lead to serious electrical faults.) For the very few the pinnacle of achievement was available, that of plant manager, the man responsible for the performance of an entire plant, and the key figure linking the plant and higher management.

This situation had been altered by a combination of pressure from management and pressure from the unions. Because of technical changes and the concern with marginal labour costs that have already been mentioned, senior management was striving both to reduce the element of specific grading, in order to increase general flexibility, and to reduce the numbers at supervisory level. At the same time there was pressure from the unions to up-grade the men at the bottom of the hierarchy. As a result, as we have seen, there was on the craft side one standard grade, 'craftsmen' (those who have served their apprenticeship) and one higher offshoot, 'craftsmen who are self-supervised'. The process workers' career ladder still had a few rungs but these were clustered together in the middle of the ladder. Those rungs left at the top were becoming increasingly narrow and slippery.

The restructuring of grades at the lower end of the scale has meant that almost without exception all men within about five years of their first appointment are graded as 'team operators', fully competent in all spheres of work within the plant, including that of the control room. (I met only one man, who, because he hated control room work, had remained on the grade below that of the fully trained operator, despite long service.) The incentive for restructuring arises from the way pay is negotiated: wages are set at company level; there could be no wage rise for a Riverside grade alone; but if men proved 'work alteration' then the impossible became achievable. Thus, once plant operators received basic control room training they claimed they should be paid for their knowledge and not have to wait until they were formally appointed as control room operators. In effect, supported by the stewards, they removed the differential payment between the ordinary trained operator and the control room operator. After that the abolition of the formal distinction was easy. Attitudes to the change were instructive.

When the control room had been a grade on its own, above that of the ordinary operator, it could be reached only by those who were recommended for promotion by the supervisors. Most of these men deplored the changed position. They said, and I think they believed it, that not only the efficiency but the very safety of the plant might depend on decisions made by the control room operator and on the instructions he gave to the other operators. Significantly, they interpreted the change as due to union power, which, they thought, was directed against any manifestation of hierarchy, however trivial. They saw the alteration, therefore, not as being effected by management's initiative but as an illustration of the weakness of senior management, pusillanimously willing to sacrifice even safety in order to placate the union bosses. Possibly, however, the supervisors may here have been antagonistic to the change because it removed one of the props of their power with the men when it removed the supervisors' influence on the promotion of an operator. Moreover, senior managers may not have been weak. The inclusion of the control room job within the sphere of normal operator tasks was obviously a step on the road to the flexibility that was desired by management; and any possible risks were reduced by the technological developments that had made the plants so much safer.

As a result of this change in the status of the control room work the normal work unit consisted of a shift team of four or five operators, who ranked equally under one 'senior operator'.

Between them they rotated the work on the different sections of the plant, being responsible for checking the different areas of machinery, partly on their own initiative and partly on the instructions of the man who was currently working in the control room. (On Plant X there was also a special job that had to be done away from the plant itself, for it was responsible for the weighbridge where road and rail tankers were loaded with 'water-white', the ammonia in liquid form sold from the works.) The 'senior operator', like the 'responsible operator' that Gallie (1978: 221) discusses in the context of the British refineries, is both a full member of the shift team, and takes a lot of responsibility for organizing the division of work among the shift. Before the changes that had been introduced by the productivity agreement of the 1960s, this man had been called the assistant foreman, but the new title quite deliberately severed the clear link in rank between the senior operator and the foreman's successor, the supervisor. As promotion for a senior operator is much less certain than it was for the old assistant foreman, his links with his team continue to be socially very strong.

As we have seen, the supervisor has formal managerial status, but he is always appointed from the ranks of the operators. In the past foremen seem to have had considerable 'hiring and firing' power over their shifts, and had their position strongly supported by their plant managers, but now supervisors complained bitterly that senior management often failed to back them, and was harsh and disloyal in its treatment of them, as shown particularly by the fact that plans were afoot to reduce the numbers of supervisors.[1] It is obvious that in so far as support for supervisors' disciplinary actions had been reduced, it must have become more difficult for them to exercise control. Less obviously, however, the general loss of prospects of promotion for the work-force, also seemed to have made the supervisors' position more difficult.

Supervisors felt they had lost face through management 'attacks' on their powers. First their numbers had been cut. Objectively, the ammonia plants had quite a high supervisory ratio; they were more like the French refineries, that Gallie (1978: 222) noted had high levels (one supervisor to every five to nine operators) than they were like the British refineries (characterized by ratios of one supervisor to every fourteen to eighteen operators). The ammonia plants, compared with other British models, must have seemed to senior management to be top heavy, and in need of 'decentralization'; but this meant the transference of responsibilities to the operators, which thus hit the supervisors. Further 'flexibility' in the plants, desirable as it may be, entails the loss of grades and therefore of promotional prospects for the operators. Gallie (1978: 217) notes this as having led to frustration among French operators and precisely the same thing was happening in the ammonia plants. Loss of promotional prospects not only meant frustrated men but deprived the supervisors of quite an important 'carrot' in their dealings with them for promotion had normally depended on supervisors' references.

The loss of the chance to reward good employees with promotion was the more important because to a large extent the stick as well as the carrot had been taken out of management's hands; this was especially significant at the lowest levels of the managerial hierarchy. It has to be stressed that despite fears for the future of the works, nobody feared the sack for his behaviour as an individual. Even the worst offences likely to be uncovered by the supervisor, offences such as sleeping on night shifts or drunkenness on duty, were not necessarily followed by dismissals, at least according to gossip. The unions were unlikely to support, before the industrial tribunal, a man guilty of a serious breach of safety regulations but in all other cases union support was almost automatic, and against that support it was so difficult for the company to succeed that supervisors were not encouraged to be tough. Supervisors had lost power, therefore, either to threaten punishment, or to promise rewards by advancing the careers of their juniors.

To illustrate the consequences of the loss of the chances of promotion I will take the, inevitably extreme, cases of a maintenance man and an operator both in early middle-age and both with qualities that in other periods would probably have marked them out for advancement. Men to whom a small measure of authority had been delegated were clearly not going to have an easy ride in dealing with such individuals. I include a tradesman because process supervisors, and senior operators in some circumstances, and indeed even very occasionally control room men, were expected to deal not only with process operators, but with the skilled men also. Thus it is important to realize that in doing their work they had sometimes to exert their 'managerial authority' not only over operators but over the craftsmen. What would have been a hard task at the best of times could clearly become very difficult indeed when the people concerned were frustrated.

Ian, an electrician, had been with the company for the last five years. He had an excellent reputation amongst the process operators for the high quality of his work, which was significant because the friction between 'process' and 'trades' meant that operators were usually harshly critical of the standards of maintenance men. I found Ian not only highly intelligent but also socially perceptive and had reason to value the insights he gave me into the differing characteristics of the various plants on the site that he visited in the course of his work. Twice he had been a shop-steward but each time he had resigned. The first occasion was at one of his former places of employment where he had become disillusioned with his members. He had taken the initiative in negotiating for them an improved retirement scheme, only to find in the end that the men refused to make the small extra payments 'since they might not be alive in ten years' time'. On the second occasion he had become a steward at Riverside, but he had resigned shortly afterwards because he thought the other stewards were too interested in the perks the management offered them, and because he thought his own refusal to take advantage of them was getting him a reputation as a trouble-maker with one of the managers. (Others I knew regarded him highly.)

Ian was consciously frustrated, and he knew why. He said he was on the same grade that he could have been on as a 23-year-old who had only recently completed his apprenticeship. Ian knew he was very able; that he could size up a social attitude very quickly and that he could influence the men. He did not especially want more money but he would have loved more responsibility; he said explicitly that had there been any capacity in which he could have used his talents for the company he would have been happy to have done so. As it was he felt classed as a boy in perpetuity, shut in a dead-end job by a combination, as he recognized, of company and union policy. Positions for supervisors amongst the electricians were so limited that his chances of promotion seemed nil. He was becoming conscious of a thorough dislike of the works, which he found increasingly noisy and stinking of ammonia. He delightedly brought me *New Statesman* articles that were highly critical of the top management of the company. He was scathing about some of the process supervisors. Although he was no longer a shop-steward it was apparent that he was very influential with the men, mainly through crystallizing their grievances against management policy. Even although Ian was a card-carrying Liberal, and in no sense politically a left-winger, this did not make him any easier to handle for he was seldom in a mood to tolerate fools gladly. Only the best process supervisors and senior operators enjoyed working with him.

Amongst the operators, the clearest example of an able man frustrated by the absence of any prospect of promotion was Richard on Plant Y. He was one of the masters of the *Daily Telegraph* crossword puzzle which he was usually quick in solving. He bought the paper mainly to get the crossword, and for its financial news, but his only quarrel with its politics was that it was somewhat too liberal over the issues of race and capital punishment. He did not anticipate promotion, although he was convinced he had unusual qualifications for it since he had actually taken a chance to study chemical plant management at the local polytechnic, and, conquering his initial panic, he had entered and passed the exam. It had not helped him. Had he not feared that a job abroad, in Kuwait say, might lead to divorce he would have taken a post as a plant manager. He said he had several times applied for such jobs when he had seen them advertised, always choosing those where the interviews were in London or some interesting part of the country. He would take time off from work and get his fare and his hotel bill paid, and often come back with his self-esteem bolstered by the knowledge that the job was his if he wanted it. As it was, the job he kept from year to year bored him, and the only amusement he got out of it was beating the system. For example, if he happened to want to do a lot of overtime, as he did during part of my visit because he had bought a new car, it pleased him to be able to foil any rules about restricting overtime, and to be able to get his extra hours in more quickly than anyone else on his plant. It showed he was smarter. Richard was full of stories about the absurdities and nefarious doings of particular local managers – stories that were obviously highly embellished but funny. He was not, however, a cheerful man; on the contrary he was the gloomiest prophet I met when it came to discussing the future of the works. He was convinced that the date of the site's final closure had already been decided. Several times I heard him say firmly: 'The date's already there in somebody's file – they're just not telling us.' He talked at length about the nature of the world market in ammonia to justify his pessimism, but it seemed closely linked to his frustrations at the way his career was blocked. It would be quite impossible to understand the way in which formally delegated managerial authority was exercised in relation to this shift without understanding the position of this individual in the team.

At work Richard was a highly competent operator who knew he could do his job 'with one hand tied behind his back'. Socially he was the leading man on his shift and rather dominated the man who was formally its senior operator. It was under Richard's influence that they had become something of a group of gourmets who spent a lot of their spare time during the evenings and nights in cooking unusually delicious meals. Richard said, and the rest concurred, that their supervisor was 'as good as gold' which meant he would give them no trouble. They were undoubtedly right because although a technically competent man he was nearing retirement, and his mind seemed more on his hobby that was about to become his main activity than it was on stirring up any trouble with his shift. Richard and the other men had him, and knew they had him, literally and figuratively eating out of their hands; usually he stayed out of their way, and unless out on the plant would be amiably in his office waiting for the meals they carried across to him there.

In considering the way in which a plant functioned socially as well as technically, it is instructive to consider the impact of all this on the way in which, on Richard's shift, responsibilities were handled below the level of the supervisor. Formally, although he was now only *primus inter pares*, the control room operator of course gave instructions to operators on the shift. However, there were two young men in the team, and they were clearly made to feel that whether or not they were on control room duty, they were effectively the juniors. They might give instructions, but Richard and the senior operator responded only if and when they thought it necessary. They did not ignore calls when it would have been dangerous to do so – they were very competent men – but it was clear that they thought that seniority in years and experience were more important than the particular role assigned to them; it was up to any youngster to acknowledge their status. I watched a young man on this shift complain to the supervisor about an instrument on the control panel he was monitoring. He said it was always going wrong, ringing the alarm bell without cause, and the only way he could stop it was to get one of the other operators (usually busy cooking in the mess) to go down to adjust a particular piece of machinery. Often, he said, the man he asked would not go and the maddening alarm bell went on ringing; if he repeated his call for something to be done the others just got angry with him. The supervisor blandly told him that *he* should get angry with *them*, that it was his job to tell them what to do. The young control room operator said nothing but looked incredulous – an expression that the supervisor studiously ignored, walking away.

Other types of individuals could, of course, be difficult for a man with authority to deal with. A second case that I saw of disregard for a control room operator's instructions was that of a man who was certainly not in an obvious sense frustrated by lack of promotion; indeed, he was the man who had effectively refused it because he had refused to do control room work, apparently because he hated the idea of subjecting himself to hours of confinement within that room 'doing nothing but watching dials'. This man, Basil on Plant Y, had chosen to forgo the extra pay control room work would have given him, but he seemed unreconciled to accepting the idea that the man at those controls was his senior and had the right to instruct him. Basil, it seemed, set out to be as awkward as he could and above all enjoyed making his 'senior' lose his temper. His ploys were various, but mainly centred on ignoring instructions until the last possible moment. I was told by a very astute observer that in fact Basil kept a sharp eye on what was happening and never actually let things go wrong; but before he took any action he managed to give the control man some very bad moments. His favourite piece of mischief was to sit in the control room, ignoring any instructions, but ready, if the supervisor or plant manager should walk in, to leap to his feet saying that the control operator was an idiot not to have spotted sooner the fact that a reading showed that an adjustment on the plant was needed. A supervisor who knew perfectly well what was going on told me that when he had been in charge of Basil's shift he had quietly advised his other operators that they should give any instructions to Basil over the tannoy system, even when he was sitting beside them in the control room, for the only way for them to defend themselves was to make every instruction public.

These cases of Basil and of Richard were interesting because they seemed exceptional. It was not really difficult to get away with less than prompt responses to calls from the control room, and yet most men for the most part obeyed immediately and without question. Men seemed willingly to obey functionally necessary instructions from their fellows despite their lack of real power. They did this because, certainly in practice, they accepted that the plant ought to run with proper efficiency. In effect they accepted the legitimacy of managerial authority directed to this end. To illustrate this it is necessary to look in some detail at the plants in action.

Control room work was vital for the efficient running of the plant and the safety of the shift. The man in charge was at the nerve centre of the plant. The supervisor was normally near by but something might happen while he was called away. In an emergency, therefore, the control operator's ability to take the right action and give the right orders might spell the difference between a minor problem and disaster. In the normal course of events his judgement could make a great difference to the efficiency with which the plant ran. This may seem surprising, but despite all the automatic monitoring devices, there was still much scope for individual decisions about the settings of the controls. The plants were not uninfluenced by the natural environment. Because they used an enormous intake of air, fluctuations in external temperatures and atmospheric pressures required adjustment to the controls. Supervisors had an ultimate responsibility for plant productivity, but the men on Plant X had won a considerable degree of freedom to work in the control room without being continually checked, and a fussy supervisor who surreptitiously twiddled the knobs was known to earn the men's contempt. On most shifts, efficiency depended to a considerable extent on the ordinary man.

The operators' freedom in the control room was such that even to my eyes it was apparent that there were considerable differences in the dedication of different men. Sitting in the control room I found at one extreme a man who was enthusiastic about his job and talked about it at length. I might think it boring, he said, but he could make it as fascinating as a computer game; by adjusting his dials carefully he could have the satisfaction of knowing that under him the plant ran more efficiently than it had been doing for the man he had relieved. At the other extreme another operator at first left me with feelings of guilt because so long as I was there he seemed to devote his entire attention to talking to me about anything other than the job in hand, apparently leaving the plant to run itself unless an alarm bell actually rang. My guilt feelings evaporated when I realized his lack of attention was quite unconnected with my presence. Since his manifest lack of concern was not counterbalanced by any particular technical expertise (he could not even be relied on to test the fire alarm efficiently, which I think I could have coped with) I could understand the concern others felt when he was on the job. Had he been more sensitive, his mates' jibes would have hurt him, but as it was he was impervious. Gossip said he cared only about a private business he ran, and that he did a job at the works merely to provide 'cover' for tax purposes.

With such variations in the performance of the control operator's role it is understandable that there should have been some variations in the men's response to his instructions. Nevertheless, it was normal for these to be obeyed promptly, and men habitually left food and drink to get cold if they were called out from the control room. At one level the instructions they were given were normally seen as important data that they needed if they were to do their jobs properly. Therefore, although they did not regard the control operator as in any way their senior, they were normally content to obey him. Indeed, on most shifts it seemed that any initial slackness on the part of an operator new to the job would quickly have been dealt with by criticism from others on the team, and a man's failure to respond properly was picked out as *the* characteristic indicative of a really unsuitable recruit. In other ways also the shift team disciplined its members and maintained efficiency.

A Plant X shift team commonly imposed certain sanctions on members whose conduct displeased them. Quite apart from 'witty' remarks at the expense of a man coming in late for his shift, certain other forms of behaviour were sufficiently frowned on to give rise to adverse comment. I saw this in the case of a man who started to operate an overtime fiddle on Plant X where it was not accepted, although it would scarcely have caused raised eyebrows on Plant Y. The key to the fiddle was the rule that all employees were entitled to take up to three days off without having to produce a medical certificate. Formerly this had been a privilege extended only to 'staff' grades, but changes in legislation meant that it now applied universally. This, combined with overtime 'doublers', had produced what was known as 'the easy three'. I saw Fred take 'the easy three' on his most conveniently ordered week, when he worked the afternoon shifts on Wednesday and Thursday, and should have followed that by working a 'weekend of nights'. On Wednesday and Thursday Fred volunteered to work doublers for the night shift to cover for a sick man on the next shift. By Friday Fred was really tired, and as his mates predicted, on Friday night he 'phoned in sick' and had a night in bed. His 'sickness' continued over the Saturday and Sunday nights, during which period his mates said they knew he was working as an extra barman at a hotel owned by a friend. In all they thought he must have done rather well financially since his regular pay was not affected, and he earned in addition overtime rates for two shifts, and whatever he got, untaxed of course, for his two nights working in the bar. Fred did all this because he had just those commitments that, in theory, should have made him the helpless plaything of the capitalist system, that is, he was newly married and had heavy mortgage repayments on an equally new house. His shift mates understood his problems and had been prepared to help him up to a point. They were older men; two of them had their children nearly off their hands, and the third had careful, economical tastes. None was very anxious to do a lot of overtime, and they had been content to let Fred take almost all the overtime opportunities that were offered. Their attitude was beginning to change, however, because they said he was getting 'greedy', mucking them around in his chasing after quick money.

No one felt any moral indignation that Fred was defrauding the company – the 'easy three' situation was felt to be blatantly putting temptation in men's way, and it was 'their' own fault if men took advantage of it. What irritated Fred's mates was that his behaviour was forcing more work on them, and forcing them also into having to rely on men from other shifts to help out; something that was never as satisfactory as working with a proper team, since every group did things slightly differently. They said they understood Fred's situation, but they had all been through it and none of them had ever so consistently claimed sick leave. Fred's relationship with his mates was tense, and small incidents now led to periods when he was not on speaking terms with one or other of them. I was told that his supervisor had told him privately that everyone knew what was going on. His mates thought that Fred was both ambitious and had the makings of an extremely good operator, really interested in his job, and that he would probably settle down and do his proper night shifts. They were encouraging him in this direction by their readiness to take the mickey out of him.

Control over the Plant X shift was not of course left to such informal sanctions imposed by other operators for despite everything there were still the elements of a formal hierarchy affecting the shifts; and most immediately all shifts had their own senior operator formally appointed by management. These men were not 'staff', but they had a wide range of responsibilities. Daily details in the life of the shift were in practice usually left to the senior operator to organize.

It was the senior operator's responsibility to say who should work where on the plant; to work out a fair job rota that normally was accepted without question. A senior operator allocating jobs usually sounded quite decisive, but there was common agreement about what constituted a fair sharing out of tasks, and it was seldom that an operator felt it necessary to exercise his right to appeal to a supervisor, his right if he thought he were being unfairly treated.

In the eyes of his shift the senior operator's standing was considerable because it was he who commonly represented the process side of the plant in its dealings with the rest of the works. Throughout the year senior operators normally filled out and signed the job sheets of maintenance men doing work on the plant, a task fraught with tension because, as we have seen, the senior operator had a grade lower than that of the craftsmen. This was, however, an important part of the senior operator's routine, and it was very significant because this was the reason that on Plant X they were given a room on the plant as an office, which was something of considerable symbolic importance. Periodically, during the 'shut-down', the senior operator's responsibilities were even more apparent. At this time, I was told, when the plant manager and the supervisor were often called away from the plant itself, it was the senior operator who was formally in charge of the plant and had to deal with the swarms of maintenance men and contractors' men. At this time, therefore, it seems that the senior operator had particular prestige. However, the senior operator's position, standing as it did between the team operators on the one hand and the supervisors on the other, had its own tensions that were internal to the process men. These problems had been exacerbated by the pay-grade system that I have already outlined.

First there was the problem of the relationship between the senior operator and the rest of his shift. The team operators on Plant X had originally been one grade behind the senior operator, but they had changed this by their latest claim put in to the Management Review Committee. In this they said that their position had altered from what it had been; they were now men fully capable of doing any job on the plant and they had claimed that their new flexibility should be paid for by the company. On these grounds they demanded to be up-graded one step, and this necessarily meant they were attacking the senior operators' differentials. The senior operators objected in vain. The union, following its general policy, supported those seeking up-grading, and the company wanted to reward a willingness to be flexible. In the eyes of many the senior operators were thought to have suffered demotion.

The senior operators' response was a counterattack in which they tried to re-establish their position by a claim that would have raised them again, lifting them to the level of the supervisors. The effect of this claim was to make a rift between senior operators and supervisors. Between these two grades there is an important status distinction since the supervisor is formally on the lowest rung of the managerial grades, and his position is marked out not only by the fact that he is paid monthly rather than weekly but because supervisors have a salary graded on the managerial scale instead of having a wage graded on the scale used for ordinary workers. There were, therefore, obvious problems for the senior operators in trying to claim parity with supervisors, but rightly or wrongly, the former thought this was the only possible path to success. As senior operators were graded with 'self-supervised' craftsmen they thought that on 'political' grounds it would be fruitless to claim a higher grade in their own league. Senior operators simply disbelieved the management's claim that grades are allocated on entirely objective criteria without any consideration for 'political' issues. They knew that had they been successful in any claim the company would have been immediately faced by furious skilled trades wrathfully demanding to be up-graded, and they could not see how management could disregard that prospect. Therefore, since they sometimes deputized for supervisors, leading operators tried to claim parity of payment. They hoped in this way to slip unnoticed by the tradesmen, by not mentioning the latter's pay scale but talking instead about the 'injustice' of the company's policy of paying them at the supervisor's rate only for those shifts on which they actually deputized for a supervisor. The principle had been accepted in other contexts that the ability to do a senior job should be paid for even when a man was doing lower grade work; senior operators therefore, they argued, deserved the supervisor's rate. They knew, of course, that their chances of winning this argument were very slight, and that the supervisors would be furious, but the gambit was worth trying given the assumed impossibility of ever successfully claiming more than craftsmen.

Of course the Plant X supervisors were bitterly hostile. They had indeed been hostile to the very idea that senior operators might deputize for them for, as I shall explain, this was seen as a potential threat to the ability of a supervisor to earn overtime, and might ultimately lead to a reduction in the number of supervisors. The subsequent claim to parity of grading was literally to add insult to injury. When I did my research the senior operators had had their claim substantially rejected but between senior operators and supervisors 'ani' still rankled.

Between senior operators and team operators resentment also lingered. Not only had the senior men lost out initially, but in their struggle for parity with supervisors there had been further causes for irritation. Team operators had resented the attempt of senior operators to get their differentials back again, and it seemed that there had also been trouble as a consequence of the wording of the claim made by the senior operators in their attempt to raise their pay to that of the supervisors. They said that they, like supervisors, 'instructed' operators and the word 'instruct' was used in the double sense of 'telling how' and 'ordering' their inferiors to do things.

To the team operators it had seemed, apparently, that the senior operators were making a new assertion of authority. The supervisors had no power to make this claim good and they found it difficult to cope with the operators' response, which in a minor way was one of passive disobedience. Previously the right of the senior operator to instruct had been an entirely unwritten rule, and operators had been willing to help out whenever asked, and willing also to do as they were told. Once the word had been written and was seen to be part of a new claim, a common reaction had been for the men to cease to take any responsibility for themselves. The plant manager was thought to have accepted in a preliminary way the written submission of the senior operators in which they used the word 'instruct'. (He seems to have accepted it in the sense that he was prepared to hand it to the Management Review Committee, and did not reject it out of hand.) The senior operators, so the supervisors said, had promptly started bossing the men around, confident that their orders would now be backed by management, and the men had responded by doing nothing unless they were actually told to do it. I do not necessarily take the supervisors' account wholly at its face value, for as we have seen there were reasons for a certain animosity between them and the senior operators. Moreover, any elite tends to believe that those just below them have no idea how to treat underlings. Nevertheless, the stories seemed inherently probable. Informal instruction by the senior operator to his men, that had seemed perfectly acceptable in the context of relationships based on social exchange within a small shift would be very likely to seem intolerable when asserted as a formal right without any reference to the view of the men who were allegedly the 'instructees'. The implied assumption that their goodwill was irrelevant would have courted trouble.

The relationships that existed between Plant X senior operators and supervisors can tell us something more about the nature, extent, and limitations of managerial powers on the plants. We have seen already that there was strain between these grades, due to the senior operators' attempts to erode the differentials separating them, and that linked up with this was the question of senior operators deputizing for supervisors. This was inherently a contentious issue because of the way it was linked to management policy. In the drive to reduce the amount of overtime that was worked, one specific aim was to reduce the overtime that supervisors could earn, and one way of doing this was to persuade the senior operators to deputize for them. What happened is significant for the question of authority and consent.

Formerly the rule had been that if a supervisor were away, he could be covered only by another supervisor, and it was this rule that senior management wanted to change. During the holiday period this rule had generated quite a lot of overtime for supervisors and they valued this particularly because normally supervisors so meticulously turned up for work that they gave one another very little chance to work overtime. As we have seen, one of the ammonia plants, Y, had refused to have anything to do with the deputizing scheme, but on plant X it had been decided to test it for a trial period on a limited way. It was agreed that in the absence of a supervisor, his shift's senior operator might deputize for him. This, however, was only if the shift were so fully manned that the senior operator's regular work could be covered by another man from the same shift. Thus the amount of deputizing possible was very limited.

The senior operators would not agree to any pattern of deputizing that was more flexible because they knew that that would really antagonize the supervisors; its effect would be virtually to eliminate any chance supervisors might have to work overtime in the future. It seemed to me that the senior operators would have liked to have done more deputizing work; and the plant manager, trying to effect senior management policy, would very much have liked to have pushed through a more flexible agreement. The senior operators, however, felt their position would become very difficult indeed if they were further to antagonize the supervisors. Consequently, although they would have found it difficult to have avoided accepting any agreement made between the senior operators and the plant manager, the supervisors' known wishes played a very active part in structuring that agreement.

We began this section by looking at an example of the alteration of established practice by the decree of senior management. We end with an example in which management's ability to effect its wishes was clearly limited. Management had been able to decree that it would simply no longer employ the same number of fitters as it had done previously to do shift work at special rates. As I have indicated, this led to a great deal of trouble, and the freedom of management to take decisions was far from total, but nevertheless the structure of work was altered. The situation regarding the process men on the plants was somewhat different. In certain areas it had been conceded that working practices involving men with different statuses would not be changed without their agreement; there could be no management diktat. Modifications to established practice had to come, if at all, from assent voted by those involved on each plant separately; this was part of the result of the changes made when the 'new' productivity agreements were made in the 1970s. It is precisely this limitation on management power within the plants that makes the study of the supervisors' position so important. Supervisors represented the lowest echelon of management, but their powers in practice were so minimal that they could operate effectively only if they gained the consent of their men to their authority. This is the situation that I want now to explore carefully. Enough has been said already to indicate that any authority supervisors on Plant X possessed had to be exercised in a situation that was particularly fraught with tensions; they could not expect an easy ride. This makes the more remarkable the amount of influence that some of them at least were able to exert.

NOTE

1. Nichols and Beynon (1977: 47–8) refer to this discontent of supervisors in the context of suggesting that the only supervisors to survive in the future would be those so clearly on management's side that the gulf between workers and management (including supervisors) would become increasingly wide. They are not concerned with whether or not such a situation would lead to a deterioration in general productivity, although there is a general assumption that it would lead to greater hostility.

5

Managerial authority and the supervisors' role

We have seen that process supervisors are men promoted from
the ranks of the operators to the lowest rung on the 'staff' ladder.
They, like managers, are paid on a monthly rather than a weekly
basis, and this symbolizes their aggregation to the managerial side
of the company. Ideally, from the company's viewpoint, they
should identify with managers. The kind of power they wield is
thought to be more akin to that of other managers than it is to that
of senior operators. The latter are simply the first among equals,
but the supervisors are formally superior. They are functionally
equivalent to the old foremen, and I want, in this section to
examine very closely the extent of their power, and the nature and
basis of any authority they wield. I also want to take up certain
issues raised by Nichols and Beynon (1977). They seek to show
that the Riverside supervisors, previously very loyal to their
company, began to lose that loyalty because of the way they had
been treated. I am not concerned to dispute the broad outlines of
this argument but to examine a paradox. The supervisors I knew
often disagreed with the policy of senior management and
criticized the company but they were apparently devoted to their
work. Yet Nichols and Beynon suggest that the work of the

supervisors was primarily to act as the eyes and ears of management, and to whisper the arguments of managers into men's ears. What, therefore, is the real nature of the supervisor's job? How was it that despite feeling let down by ChemCo they still seemed to take a pride in it?

Riverside supervisors are depicted in *Living with Capitalism* as the agents of capital, opposed to the workers. Their main tasks are said to be to pass inside information about the plants to their superiors and to keep tabs on their men. By the early 1970s there had, it seemed, been a further development of their role in that they had a new and truly capitalistic function: like other managers, the supervisor was to be concerned with accounting, with watching the profit and loss made by the shift he was running and by his plant. All supervisors were, however, even then themselves under threat from the company's new drive for efficiency (Nichols and Beynon 1977: 46–7). To Nichols and Beynon, concerned to show up the ruthlessness of capital, it is essentially ironical that it should be the supervisors, the betrayers of the working class, the 'understrappers' of capitalism, and the most loyal servants of the company, who should be those the company had come to regard as most expendable in its new drive to accumulate capital. To these authors, it seems, it is significant for the future of capitalism that, shocked and dismayed, the supervisors seemed to be about to seek the protection of a union for themselves, for 'capital's need to accumulate makes it but a poor respector of its petty servants' (Nichols and Beynon 1977: 51–2). It was assumed that this discovery would fundamentally alter supervisors' attitudes.

As Nichols and Beynon (1977) depict the situation at Riverside in the early 1970s, the supervisors were 'in for a shock' (p. 45). The company's intention was to change the structure and practice of the supervisors in order to fit them in with the alterations being made in the way management in general was being organized. Since the concept of self-supervision was being introduced for many workers, both maintenance men and those on process shift teams, the ranks of the supervisors were to be 'slashed', and numbers are said to have already fallen by 30 per cent between 1965 and 1973. The old hierarchy of foremen had disappeared; where there had been senior foremen, foremen, and assistant foremen, there was now only the foremen's successor, the supervisor. (Nichols and Beynon do not note the existence of the senior operator.)

The theme of the chapter on 'Foremen' in *Living with Capitalism* is that, like the ordinary worker, the supervisors had been 'conned' by management. In the interests of 'capital accumulation' they faced an 'economising logic' in which fewer people had to do more work and face tighter bureaucratic control in order to cut labour costs. The supervisors found themselves starkly confronted by the fact that they were sellers of labour power, itself ever more closely costed and evaluated by capital's criteria. The threats of redundancy and the pressure on supervisors to accept early retirement were said to be 'driving them into the worker-like reaction of trade unionism' (Nichols and Beynon 1977: 46–7).

Attempting to avoid the danger of over-generalization, Nichols and Beynon say that there are actually two types of supervisors, the *traditional foremen*, then said to comprise the great majority of Riverside's supervisors, and the *management men*, 'just half a dozen out of forty-odd foremen' (Nichols and Beynon 1977: 48).

'Management men' differed from the other supervisors: they were self-confidently competent in their bureaucratic tasks that involved paperwork, checking absenteeism, labour turnover and lateness records; they professed a liberal attitude to the workers; above all they thought of their plants as tiny corporations in which they were the employers. It seems, indeed, that although they may not have been uncritical of the company, they certainly identified with capitalism. They were truly the agents of capital. Real managers valued their judgement. Supervisors did the little jobs managers themselves could not do. They chatted up the shop-stewards and assessed their strength. They privately advised men how to get together to get rid of an ' "awkard" West Indian' by making complaints about him. They hinted that a co-operative worker who wanted a job on a different plant could have it if he were prepared to become a compliant shop-steward. There was no doubt whose side they were on (Nichols and Beynon 1977: 48–50). The epitome of this type of supervisor was Alan. He was very bright and much concerned with personal success; although formerly a socialist and a shop-steward he was now concerned only about promotion. He had a 'large, detached, expensively furnished house and a small boat to go with it' (p. 51).

The 'traditional foremen' were very different. They disliked the new bureaucratic methods, although they seem to have valued the fact that there was 'no difficulty now in amassing material to "throw the book" at troublesome workers'. They felt, however, that 'to be a good foreman is to be a "good bastard" '. Given the choice 'these men would much sooner exercise control by way of tricks and bluffs and shouts . . . Through the tricks and the bluffs and the shouting these men still found "satisfaction" in their work', but they felt let down by the changes that had been made, the loss of the old status distinctions, the former benefits of being a 'trusty', and the old security that came from the former policy the company had pursued of never sacking or demoting a supervisor. There was no question, even in the 1970s of a man being sacked, but it was no longer uncommon for an inefficient supervisor to be pressured into taking early retirement (Nichols and Beynon 1977: 52–9).

Nichols and Beynon stress the problems involved in being a supervisor during the time they did their research. A supervisor might have to change from plant to plant because of some reorganization, and could find it very difficult, if he had no solid technical background, to learn the new job. If he were unsuccessful he would be made conscious that the men despised him. If he were really incompetent he would become so frightened of his responsibilities that he would be glad to quit. Moreover they say that 'During the three years that we visited the site the foremen were subjected to innumerable indignities' that seriously reduced the advantages of their position (Nichols and Beynon 1977: 60). For them 'capitalist rationality' meant a change in the 'character' of the company and in the culture of the factory (p. 63). It was ironic that 'the managerial strategy of increasing profitability . . . has led to the disaffection of the one group whose involvement was unquestionable. What these men now want is not "involvement" but a union.' They had always had a 'Foreman's Association' but now they were looking for an organization that could give them greater protection. It is implied that they were in dire need of such protection for now the traditional foremen were on their way out, and that even the management men amongst the supervisors were living in cloud cuckoo land. 'The "modern managers" of this "modern factory" are revamping the image and style of the labour of superintendance; planning ahead they don't want to make provision "for any more of this type of supervision" ' (Nichols and Beynon 1977: 66).

Nearly ten years later I am not concerned to follow in detail the lines of argument here outlined. It would be pointless, for example, to argue about the existence of two types of supervisors. I suspect that that dichotomy may have involved an over-generalization verging on stereotyping, but it is possible to argue that many differences in the 1980s might be accounted for by the fact that the new breed of supervisor had become the dominant type. The issue of whether or not to join an ordinary union rather than the foreman's association seemed to have been resolved by most supervisors joining both. It was seldom a matter of sufficient importance for men to raise it spontaneously. It is, however, important to note that the fact that supervisors were members of a union did not seem to have created any very significant difference in attitudes in so far as most seemed very 'involved' in their jobs. This was despite the fact that they faced a lot of problems. In the 1980s senior management, desperately concerned to cut all possible costs in order to keep an old-fashioned works in production, still had, as one target for cost-cutting, the supervisors' salaries. Tension was, therefore, still considerable in the relationship of supervisor with management. Just how did the supervisor do the job on the lowest rung of management? What powers did he have? What, indeed, was his job? I shall argue that their powers were very limited indeed, that they therefore had to base their position on consent; and that it was in this respect that their job was most interesting theoretically; if legitimacy is based on consent, super-visors who had to rely on that consent played a major part in making managerial authority legitimate. But did senior manage-ment understand this?

Supervisors' powers were limited, as we have seen, by their loss of both carrot and stick. Moreover, as no one believed that management even wanted to back them strongly, their prestige had suffered. Indeed, in 1981, relationships between the supervisors and the senior managers were obviously strained. Only in the last resort could supervisors expect to be backed in disciplinary action; that is, if a man had disobeyed a direct and proper order. The threat of such action was, however, hardly ever in anyone's mind. Only in the rarest cases did men obey a supervisor because this threat hung over them. Yet, despite all this, most of the supervisors I knew were enthusiastically work-centred, and most carried a real measure of authority with their men. I shall argue, first, that supervisors were often motivated by a kind of loyalty to their plant itself that, *pace* Nichols and Beynon, was independent of any feeling they had for the company or capitalism; and, second, they wanted the respect of their peers, the other supervisors. In turn, their men co-operated with them willingly if they earned respect through their work, and through demonstrating that they had, for the most part, the interests of their men at heart. A supervisor could do little with his men if they did not trust him; he depended on their goodwill, and had little power to force compliance.

At this point, before going on to discuss the evidence for the supervisor's 'work centredness', it will be useful to make two things very clear: that supervisors had lost most of their former trust in senior management; and that it was not difficult for a supervisor to get away with doing less than a first-rate job. To this end we shall examine in more detail the reasons why supervisors were disillusioned, and then look at a case of less than enthusiastic supervision.

Much that was happening in 1981 fits in with what Nichols and Beynon depict for the 1970s. Supervisors had lost the old foreman's proverbial trust that they would be well treated by the company. Indeed, they saw themselves, rightly or wrongly, as a group of men who, because they earned a little more than operators, had become the target for a major economy drive. They believed that their numbers were to be reduced and their work given to senior operators. Where it was impossible to replace supervisors they thought their privileges were to be reduced, and indeed they thought their sense of duty was to be exploited so that they would end up, in practice, with fewer privileges than were given to the men they supervised. Already they felt they had effectively lost most of the symbols of high status that the old foremen had enjoyed. They had formerly been marked out from the ordinary worker because they had great job security, lenient treatment if they were sick, and good pension rights, but now everyone shared these benefits. Moreover, supervisors felt themselves in certain respects to be actually disadvantaged in regard to earning overtime and choosing their holidays. On Plant X they had agreed (some felt they had been 'conned' into agreeing) to accept the principle, as 'staff men', of *noblesse oblige*. That is they accepted that they ought to try to avoid asking the company to pay them at overtime rates and, as a linked obligation, they had agreed that they should, within certain limits, select their holidays at times that would avoid generating a great deal of overtime, even if this inconvenienced themselves and their families. Ordinary operators were not expected to take any account of such factors and were free to choose their holidays when it suited them.

On Plant X the question of supervisors' overtime was central to several current issues. Whether or not senior operators should be allowed to deputize for supervisors was seen to be 'really' about overtime, and it seemed clear that the pressure being put on the supervisors to agree to the practice was phrased in terms of what they *ought* to do as staff men. They were also told that if they were asked to do a relief shift for an absent supervisor, they *ought* not to ask for overtime payment. Instead, it was said, they should do the extra work at the normal rate and in return simply take time off, a so-called 'lieu day', at a time when their absence would be convenient to the company, in the sense that it would generate little overtime. This particular requirement led to a lot of resentment because, in practice, it seemed to mean that they had to work extra shifts at week-ends, and take their 'lieu' days in the middle of the week. The problem here was not simply that most people like to have free week-ends but that some supervisors had young children; they were already concerned that shift work meant that they saw too little of them in any case, and a 'lieu day' taken when the youngsters were at school was no real compensation for week-end working. If they had to work these shifts then the only acceptable return was, they felt, the high payments under overtime rates. It was some indication of the extent to which supervisors had bowed to management pressure that, on Plant X, I was told, the average supervisor worked only half the overtime hours put in by the average operator. Nevertheless the supervisors clearly resented the fact that they should be kept on a tighter rein than their men.

It is useful to look at the result of the fact that supervisors were less free than their men to select holiday periods. The men had an almost free choice, and the company, for the moment, simply accepted that this would generate overtime (although as we have seen plans were well advanced for introducing a new shift pattern which, whatever its stated advantages to the men, was seen by them as having as its purpose the severe limitation of overtime in the holiday season). Supervisors were explicitly bound to fix their own holidays only after their men had chosen theirs, and then the supervisors were expected to choose their time off when not too many of their shift were away, in order to keep overtime to a minimum. Grudgingly, the supervisors had accepted this obligation, but their resentment at having to do so had increased their opposition to accepting that senior operators might deputize for them. What annoyed the supervisors was that it looked as if the senior operators were likely to gain some of the financial advantages of being supervisors while still having, as members of the operators' team, the men's right to a free choice of holidays. Indeed, as part of a surreptitious campaign to persuade the senior operators not to deputize for them, the supervisors whispered that if they did they would probably lose this freedom of holiday choice. Moreover, the intensity of the feelings sparked off by this question of the holiday periods was shown by the quarrels the matter sometimes generated between supervisors with school-age children, as each sought to claim a period within the school holidays.

The other major respect in which supervisors felt that the privileges of their job were being reduced related, as we have seen, to their prospects of promotion. Once shift managers had been recruited from supervisors and some of those I knew had even started training for this level, in the sense that occasionally they deputized for an absent shift manager. Recent changes in company policy, however, appeared finally to have blocked the possibility of such promotion. Moreover, the threat of a reduction in ordinary level supervisors' posts was now taken very seriously indeed.

The threat of a reduction in the numbers of supervisors' posts was not one that any supervisor took lightly, even if he were quite confident that his own career was safe. This may have been because most supervisors seemed to be bound very closely to other supervisors. Of course, as individuals they might be incompatible, or in some way rivals. Nevertheless, to most of these men the other supervisors constituted a very important 'reference group'. Separated in some ways from their men, and doubtful of their status as real managers, supervisors paid an enormous amount of attention to the behaviour and opinions of other supervisors and looked to them for support, especially of course to those supervisors attached to the same plant. It will be useful, therefore, to look at two cases in which supervisors seemed particularly worried about company plans to cut their posts.

The first case related to management's wish to cut one supervisor's post on Plant X. On this plant there were six supervisors in all, of whom four worked over the four shifts, and two were officially 'on days'. In practice, one of these men was primarily a relief supervisor; he worked with any shift whose supervisor had to be away and this might of course include night shifts. The other supervisor did work exclusively in the day; he was in charge of operations connected with the despatch of ammonia by road and rail tanker. Although this might go on round the clock, the 'weighbridge supervisor' worked only from 8 a.m. to 4 p.m. and this gave the post considerable significance. Supervisory duties were rotated. No supervisor stayed with one shift for longer than three years; and the two supervisors currently not attached to any one shift normally divided the tasks of the relief and weighbridge supervisor between them, a spell of duty on one of these jobs lasting about six months. It was known that management regarded the weighbridge supervisor's job as unnecessary and therefore wanted to eliminate it. It was believed that the plan was to axe it as soon as the next ammonia supervisor retired. This would, in fact, be a man on Plant Y, and the rumour was that at this point one of the Plant X supervisors would be transferred there. This would leave five supervisors on Plant X, and instead of having one man as a relief supervisor, each of the five would then be attached, so it was said, to one of the new five shifts that management planned to bring in to replace the current four-shift system. Plant X supervisors bitterly opposed the idea of such changes, and their reasons are instructive.

These reasons, however, were not put forward explicitly to senior management. One covert reason for opposition to the plan was simply the existence of strong plant loyalty that made any supervisor shudder at the thought that he might have to be the one to move to Plant Y. A very much more serious objection was that the weighbridge job represented for all of them the only possible way out if, through illness or just tiredness, they needed a break from shift work. The problem for the supervisors was the dearth of posts at their level that were not attached to shifts. They knew how great was the strain of shift work and were worried that they might not continue to be able to stand the pace until retirement. The weighbridge job gave each in turn a respite from shifts, and was a job that, if necessary, could fairly easily be made available to a man who had been sick. This gave the weighbridge post a value far exceeding that of one extra position, and its proposed elimination was the cause of considerable anxiety. Nevertheless, so I was told, this fact, which was the main objection to the proposal, was not put forward officially in any of the arguments for the retention of the post, because they thought it would not be regarded as valid by a management who, the supervisors thought, had no appreciation of the strains of shift work. Instead, the supervisors put forward arguments that some of them at any rate did not really believe; they asserted the absolute functional necessity of having a supervisor on day work at the weighbridge. This argument was not expected to succeed, and the supervisors gloomily predicted the loss of this post.

The second case was far more complex and posed a much more radical threat to the whole supervisory structure of the ammonia plants. The background involved the attempt of Plant X supervisors to improve their position relative to all those who had been pushing them from below and removing their differentials; once more the ploy involved an attempt to get a wage increase by getting a job up-graded. The basic ambition was to move the job of ammonia supervisor from grade 9 to grade 10 on the management pay scale. They found out that supervisors at one of ChemCo's new ammonia plants elsewhere had been raised to grade 10, and the Plant X men convinced themselves that their job was comparable. I was told they had arranged to look at the supposedly confidential document submitted by their successful colleagues. The Plant X supervisors told me they had then submitted a description of their own job to the Management Review Committee that was practically identical. If the higher pay scale was given elsewhere then surely, they argued, they deserved no less.

The company appear to have countered by indicating that there was a serious objection; at least I was told that unofficially it had been pointed out that there were 'political' objections. Formerly ammonia supervisors generally had been paid more than others, but this had been changed to give every supervisor the same scale, and if ammonia supervisors at Riverside were now to be up-graded then every other supervisor at the works, even if his job did involve less responsibility, would immediately demand an identical grade. It was thus impossible to concede the up-grading claim. In fact all the ammonia supervisors believed this assessment of the situation to be sound and did not regard it as a mere management ploy. Indeed one of them, describing the attitude of the other supervisors, mimed the posture of runners starting a race.

A possible way out of this unfortunate situation had been, so I was told, suggested by management. It was pointed out that the successful ammonia supervisors had in fact been regarded not as 'supervisors' at all but as 'superintendents': the key to advancement must therefore lie in devising some scheme that would enable the Riverside ammonia supervisors in their turn to qualify as *superintendents*. It was suggested that there was, as it happened, one way in which this might be achieved, thus making it possible for the company to give them a higher salary without finding itself locked in any comparability wrangle. The way suggested was for the supervisors to agree to the administrative merger of Plant X and Plant Y. If this happened, each supervisor would then be in charge of both plants during his shifts and, since he could obviously not be in two places at once, whenever the supervisor was in one plant the senior operator on the other plant would deputize for him. The supervisor would however retain an ultimate responsibility for that other plant. Thus a double responsibility would be his and a higher grade would obviously be merited.

For ammonia supervisors generally, however, this scheme suggested real disadvantages despite offering them some benefits. The major disadvantage was that the overall number of supervisors on the two ammonia plants would be cut right down to five men, just one for each of the proposed future five shifts. Nevertheless no supervisor would lose his job. Two supervisors were shortly due for retirement, and it was promised that three of the most senior supervisors would be promoted to the grade of shift manager. In the short term the proposed package had looked quite attractive to the Plant X supervisors, especially as they were confident that the new shift managers would be chosen from their ranks. Looking only a little way ahead, however, it seemed apparent that this scheme had great disadvantages. To have agreed to the package would have meant that quite quickly ammonia supervisors would have been cut from eleven men to five, and there was no guarantee that the five posts of shift manager would, in the future, be reserved for former ammonia supervisors. Moreover, acceptance would mean the virtual ending of any chance that a supervisor might ever work at overtime rates: the provision for deputizing by senior operators for supervisors was so built into the package that in practice there would always have been a (cheaper) senior operator ready to step in whenever a supervisor could not work. Finally there was what some supervisors seemed genuinely to think was a very serious disadvantage, the reduction of safety in the plants.

Supervisors really did not think that senior operators had either the skill or the experience in technical matters to cope with emergencies; nor, they thought, did senior operators have the necessary authority with their men to enable them to get the degree of obedience that might be essential if the occasional real danger were to be avoided. Supervisors said that the scheme could have been put safely into operation only if it could somehow have been guaranteed that real emergencies would not occur simultaneously on both plants. Since this was obviously not possible, there was genuine concern at the prospect of a plant in real trouble being unable to call on the supervisor for help because he was already fully occupied in dealing with an emergency on the other plant.

The proposed scheme was eventually turned down by the Plant X supervisors (they were the ones primarily involved since their claim for up-grading had provided the occasion for this counter-suggestion). They found sufficient merit in the ideas to toy with them for a short while, but eventually they decided that the disadvantages outweighed the good points. This rejection was made despite the fact that their plant manager had, I was told, advised them to accept it, arguing that in the end it would prove to be in their long-term, as well as their short-term interests. The supervisors respected their plant manager's knowledge of the management plans, but in this case they thought his advice might not have been disinterested. They thought that his reputation with senior management and, therefore, his career prospects, would have been advanced if he could have got their agreement to the scheme. To explain their rejection formally they chose to present that reason that was publicly the most acceptable, the fact that, in their opinion, the scheme took inadequate account of safety factors. Unofficially their other, unexpressed reasons also weighed heavily with them.

The company's reactions to this rejection were very significant in this present context of considering the power and powerlessness of management. The plan had been either abandoned or shelved. There seemed to be absolutely no thought that the management could there and then have forced through the scheme in the absence of prior agreement. On the other hand the company then totally rejected the supervisors' claims for up-grading. This had been accepted as inevitable, but other events had taken place that the supervisors interpreted as deliberate punishment that they had not anticipated; the punishment was meted out not by Riverside's management but by the company at a high level. The ammonia supervisors had assumed that all shift managers at Riverside would necessarily have been appointed from among their number, because of their level of technical competence. In the event, however, what happened was that, after the rejection of the scheme outlined, the posts of shift manager were given to men from other works belonging to the company (and certainly some senior Riverside managers thought their works had been unfairly treated, in a way that was bound to bring a lot of discontent). The Riverside supervisors characteristically focused their complaint on the question of safety. Three men from elsewhere were appointed. One of these was acceptable because his technical competence was clear; the other two, however, had had no previous experience of ammonia production and were therefore considered incapable of really understanding the job to which they were appointed, their training for it being regarded as wholly inadequate. It was instructive that a certain *schadenfreude* was detectable in the reactions of one or two of the Plant Y supervisors, who themselves were not thought to have had much chance of becoming shift supervisors. They said, virtuously, that the works ought to play its part in making posts available for those relatively senior men who might otherwise have been forced into early retirement. These sentiments were, I suspect, primarily a symptom of the hostility that the Plant Y supervisors felt for those on Plant X: they were blamed for having, even for a moment, toyed with the idea of joint supervision of the two plants, and the fact that they had done so was ascribed to their greedy selfishness, in that they were known to have calculated that under the package they would have got the plum jobs.

In the general context of the relationship between supervisors and senior managers there was a final twist that sometimes made supervisors particularly bitter. Occasionally, those who had put in a bid to be upgraded had found themselves worse off at the end of an unsuccessful period of negotiation than they had been at the beginning. When, as part of the review procedure, descriptions of jobs were submitted to the Management Review Committee, they were naturally couched in terms that were thought most likely to achieve up-grading. Occasionally, in order to place themselves in the best possible light, men had given an outline of how they would, in the future, be prepared to work if their up-grading request were granted. I was told, however, that sometimes, although the particular request was not granted, they nevertheless found themselves bound in the future to follow that pattern of work they had claimed would be perfectly possible. This had happened in past negotiations between the supervisors and management. Specifically I was told that there used to be seven, not six, supervisors on Plant X. Just before one supervisor had been due to retire they had at that time submitted, on their plant manager's advice, an up-grading proposal in which they showed how they would be able to run the plant with just six supervisors. In the event their request had not been granted but they were told that since they said they could operate perfectly well with only six supervisors that was how they would henceforth have to work. They admitted to me that this was a perfectly adequate number, but they felt they had been unfairly caught, and it rankled.

Another somewhat similar case was possibly in process while I was doing my research. In the course of making their current claim they had been asked to describe afresh for management the details of their work as supervisors, and their debate centred on how they should handle the matter of overtime. Their plant manager had reportedly advised them that it would help their bid for up-grading if they were to suggest that they would not claim for any overtime at all, but would instead be satisfied with a small consolidated weekly rise (£8 was mentioned). The plant manager was said to have argued that they would be likely to lose their opportunities for overtime in any case in the near future, and that they might as well make a virtue of necessity. Certainly I overheard him mention to a small group of supervisors that while their current re-assessment claim was pending they would be wise, over the next couple of months, to restrict the amount of overtime they claimed. One of the supervisors, Cassandra-like, warned the others that they would make a great error if they followed the advice to ask for a consolidated payment instead of overtime; they would be unsuccessful in their general claim, he said, but would be held to have agreed to work without asking for any overtime at all. I am not sure what the final outcome of the assessment was. I am certain, however, that if these forebodings proved correct, not merely would there be resentment against senior management in general, but the plant manager would be held to have 'conned' his supervisors. He may have given his advice with no concern except for the well-being of his supervisors, but it was clear to me that if it proved wrong he would have been held to have misled them deliberately in order to have furthered his own reputation as one who could manipulate his men in the company's interests. That the possibility of a genuine error on his part would not have been considered suggests that, even in the case of supervisors, a knife-edge existed between trust and distrust in dealing with management. If straight dealing was not proved by events then duplicity was assumed.

I think it is obvious, therefore, from all this that I was studying the ammonia plants at a time when the supervisors, especially those on Plant X, were aggrieved as a group, and rather hostile to management in general. Moreover the broad outline of the treatment they had received was known and their men were well aware that the supervisors' pride and prospects had been hurt. In these circumstances why indeed had they not, as Nichols and Beynon seemed to have assumed would happen, lost their enthusiasm for their work? I shall argue that there is clear evidence that they were rather work-centred and that this must suggest that they perceived in it some other object than that of being the management's dutiful lackeys – indeed, that they were able to find in it some reward despite all the experiences that made them disillusioned about their place in the company. Meeting the challenge of being a good supervisor to some extent gave some men intrinsic satisfaction. But this raises a second question – if they lacked both power and the obvious moral support of senior management, how could they in fact be successful as supervisors? What, indeed, counted as success? Whose opinions of their performance really mattered?

Nichols and Beynon call their new type of supervisor the 'agent of capital' because, they say, he was like a manager in his concern that his plant should be profitable. I would say that some of the supervisors I knew were apparently even more concerned than some managers that 'their' particular plant should earn its keep in economic terms, for the good reason that supervisors, like operators, had careers that were tied very largely to particular plants, and certainly to the Riverside works. Managers might, in sociological jargon, be 'spiralists', moving round different works belonging to the company as they pursued an upward career, but the supervisors expected their careers to end where they had begun, at Riverside. This was understood by the men, and it was one reason that it was easier for a supervisor to earn their trust than it was for a plant manager to do so. However, this alone was not enough. At the very least, to win any prestige a supervisor had to be able to run his plant during his shift with technical competence. Those he had to impress with his prowess were not so much managers who were his seniors, for what was the point when promotion was impossible no matter what his technical ability? In practice the opinions that mattered most to him were those of his men, and of his fellow supervisors.

The importance of a supervisor's technical competence lies in the fact that he had the ultimate responsibility during his shift for making any major decisions affecting production. The control room operator is responsible for making limited, routine decisions, but anything of more major significance had to be decided on both plants by the supervisors. As an illustration of this, and of the extent to which a supervisor had freedom to act or not to act without incurring his plant manager's interference, I will describe a very aberrant case. This was that of a supervisor with a reputation amongst his colleagues for being rather idle who, by refusing to bestir himself, wasted a great deal of company money in a very short time, and earned the contempt of an operator. The case also makes the important point, to which I referred earlier, that supervisors had considerable freedom not to give of their best in their work if they chose not to do so.

One afternoon a fairly serious fault developed on Plant X; it meant that the operation of one section had to be curtailed, although there was no actual shut-down. There were conflicting accounts as to how long the repair job was going to take, and the control room operator, who was good at his job, anxiously watched his instruments. He had to decide whether it might be sensible to make a major cut in the amount of natural gas feed stock he was taking in, since the reduced production of one section of the plant meant that he was having to vent into the atmosphere a significant proportion of the hydrogen that was being extracted from the feed stock. It was harmless to the environment, but it was a very costly waste; yet to have cut down the rate at which the feed stock was taken in would have necessitated a large number of other adjustments to the plant. Before normal production could then have been resumed, everything would have needed readjustment, and this would have taken time. In consequence he was having to balance in his mind the cost of the wasted hydrogen against the cost of the ultimate loss of production. Everything really hinged on how long the repairs would take.

After a while an electrician came through the control room, and in response to a question told the operator that it would be at least another two hours before the job could be finished. At once the operator called another man to watch his dials while he slipped out to tell his supervisor the news and to ask permission to start cutting down on the gas intake. This would have meant that the supervisor would have had to leave his office (and, I think, a commentary on a test match to which he was listening on his transistor), to come to the control room to concentrate on what was going on and to be ready with advice if this were needed. Even my limited experience led me to expect that he would have come immediately, probably with a word of praise for his operator for his good thinking and wit in having extracted vital information from a maintenance man. Instead, lolling back in his chair, Jack, the supervisor, asked the name of the electrician concerned. Finding it was a man with a distinctly poor reputation (both work-shy and rash) he remarked that the story was probably all wrong. Without taking any steps to check it himself, he said that no changes were to be made in the intake levels and remained in his office. In fact it was nearer to four hours before the repairs were finally completed and the waste of expensively produced hydrogen was ended.

The operator went back fuming to his control room. I had expected him to say 'Isn't Jack lazy,' or words to that effect. Instead he said: 'There you are! They say they're interested in cutting costs, but look at this – they're wasting thousands in a single afternoon.' He was, of course, right. What interested me, however, was the way on this occasion that he referred to his supervisor. It was rare, on Plant X where this incident occurred, for a man to refer to his supervisor by anything other than his Christian name; yet on this occasion he was lumped together with the rest of management as 'they'. The clue here is that one of the stereotypes of The Manager amongst the men is that he is as careless about real waste as he is nit-picking in his attitude to any little perks the men may have. Disgust at the supervisor's behaviour had, as it were, so increased the distance between them that the supervisor was pushed out of the inner circle into the world of the incomprehensible 'them'.

It must not be thought from this incident that no checks were kept on supervisors by their plant managers, but conditions were such that there was room for considerable variation in performance, and it was often difficult to prove that a supervisor was really at fault. There were, if things were running smoothly, clear ideas as to what constituted proper production, and a supervisor whose shift failed to attain them would be noted, and he might be criticized by his manager. Even the newest manager would know if normal production were not being maintained and would want to know why. If it was a supervisor's fault there was a kind of code for telling him obliquely. For example, a supervisor, James, complaining that his new plant manager was very unperceptive mentioned as an illustration that this man had come in earlier in the week and wanted to know why the previous night's production was low; the supervisor told him '*I* don't know, *I* wasn't on,' but the manager was so thick he had not got the message and remained puzzled. Only later, when another manager had come in, did the young man understand the situation. Having been asked the same question, the second manager took one look at the record sheet and, seeing the name of the supervisor, said: 'Oh well, look who was on!'.

The man thus referred to was, in fact, a supervisor with a generally very poor reputation. Most believed him to be technically incompetent and not good at handling his operators. He would never have been picked for further promotion, but this was no longer a sanction. It is significant also for the present argument that there was virtually nothing that could be done to get rid of him unless some very obvious and very serious dereliction of duty could be proved against him. In other words, if a supervisor for any reason remained insensitive to the opinions of either his superiors or his peers, there were no effective sanctions against even repeatedly displayed poor performances.

The incident of the wasted hydrogen, however, is significant because it illustrates how difficult it would be to make any irrefutable criticism of a supervisor when a loss of production is associated, as it most often is, with some technical fault. For the reasons I have given there would have been a case for saying that the supervisor had not been improperly idle. It was not his fault that there was no automatic flow of information between a maintenance team and a supervisor. A supervisor could develop informal contacts with its members to the point where he would be kept in touch with how their work was going – but such links depended on individual initiative. As there was no obligation on a repair team to keep the process side properly informed, and the 'structural' tensions between the two often made the maintenance men unco-operative, who could blame a supervisor if he were kept in the dark? Moreover, in this hydrogen incident everyone knew the poor reputation of the electrician who was the source of the news. Had Jack been challenged he would have had plenty of legitimate excuses to offer. His shift was not deceived, but, so far as I know, his conduct was never criticized by his manager. I would guess that a lazy supervisor could generally have found such excuses for idleness.

What is really remarkable, therefore, is that this example of a supervisor's indolence was, in my experience, most unusual. Supervisors could often have got away with work that was less than their best, and I have indicated how much reason they thought they had to be disgruntled with the treatment they had received from the company. Nevertheless I was continually impressed with the fact that supervisors were generally keen. They were enthusiastic and well-informed when talking about their work and they were concerned with efficient production. It was surely paradoxical that men who had had their careers blocked, and were in many cases thoroughly disillusioned, should have been so anxious to do a good job.

As I shall argue that the job they did was in fact more crucial than management commonly realized, and success in it often depended on their doing things that could not have been demanded of them, it is important to look in some detail at what they actually did. The best way to begin to do this is to follow a supervisor at work on his shift.

On Plant X the morning shift begins at 8 a.m. and the supervisor normally appeared by 7.45 at the latest, in order to go over any technical problems that might have cropped up on the previous shift. He would discuss these with the night supervisor he was relieving, and allow this man to get away by 8 o'clock. The new supervisor seeks information relating to any possible technical problem that he may need for his own shift. As we shall see, there were various difficulties that might arise, from the trivial to the serious, but for the moment we will suppose that when the supervisor takes over the shift no great technical problem confronts him.

When a supervisor took over a morning shift and nothing serious was reported to him, the first major event of the day was a meeting designed to bring together representatives of all the groups of men associated with the plant. Before it took place, at

9 a.m., the supervisor would have a quick look round the plant to make sure that all his men had arrived and that everything was going smoothly. Then he might relax briefly, and wait for the outsiders to arrive. This meeting, that may last from five minutes to half an hour, brought together the process supervisor and the supervisors of the most important trades (fitters, electricians, and instrument artificers) connected with the plant, the plant manager normally taking the chair. Significantly, if the plant manager could not do so, the process supervisor acted as chairman as he was then formally in charge of the plant.

Usually the morning meeting dealt with technical problems that were routine and its business was simply that of exchanging information amongst the relevant supervisors so that each might ensure that any necessary work, such as the checking of some minor electrical fault, or the testing of an instrument suspected of giving a wrong reading, was efficiently allocated amongst the men. When any question arose of really serious trouble, then a technical expert, such as an engineer manager, was usually asked to come over to discuss the problem.

After the morning meeting the supervisor inspected any new fault that had been discussed. On Plant Y supervisors performed routine practical tasks, but as we have seen, on Plant X, by a decision of some years' standing, supervisors did not normally operate any part of the plant themselves. This had been a decision taken to ensure that the operators should play vital roles in the plant's running, and both supervisors and men took pride in the fact that the ordinary operator was trusted with such tasks. On this plant the supervisor's job was essentially to check and advise, and the best supervisor was thought to be the one who interfered as little as possible, but was always on hand when he was needed, ready with calm inaction to indicate to an operator that he was handling everything well, or, if necessary, ready to make immediate, knowledgeable suggestions and, of course, ready in an emergency to take immediate and decisive action.

It was obvious that the efficiency with which a plant was run depended to a considerable extent on the kind of relationships between the people concerned, and that these were matters of individual negotiation. Even the plant manager could not directly control the schedules of maintenance tasks to be done for these were worked out by the trades supervisors, and they in their turn were responsible for the details of these not to the plant manager but to their own technical managers. The plant manager, therefore, could not give a direct order to a trades supervisor, but had to make requests; and the response to these depended on the pattern of negotiations between the individuals concerned. Again I have to stress that the kind of relationship that existed between the process and maintenance sides of a plant had a very great influence on its efficiency; this relationship could not be determined by any rule book, but was in fact dependent on a highly complex network of interpersonal relationships. I was surprised, for example, that the current fitter supervisor dealing with Plant X was thought to be remarkably co-operative just because he would, as normal practice, agree to alter the daily schedules of his men to take immediate account of matters brought up at the morning meeting. Some of the other trades supervisors would, I was told, do this only in cases of really serious emergency.

The most common serious fault which might demand the attention of the supervisor seemed to be the suspicion of damage to a valve on one of the huge gas compressors. To repeat what was said earlier, each has a series of valves controlling the flow of the increasingly compressed gas from one section of the machine to the next. These very expensive valves are very vulnerable to water because of the impossibility of compressing water. It is very easy for water to enter the compressor and damage the valve. If early signs of damage to a valve are not spotted, and pieces of metal actually break away from it there is a kind of domino effect. Therefore the slightest change in the sound of a valve was a matter for urgent consultation between the operator, who should be alert to such noise alterations, and the supervisor. His job was to judge which was the valve responsible, and to take the decision as to whether or not the machine should be stopped. It might seem a relatively simple thing to determine the source of the trouble, but in fact it was often extremely difficult. The general level of machinery noise was very high; parts of the compressors were physically very difficult to reach, for as with some cars, the designers of Plant X in particular seemed to have had no regard for the needs of maintenance. Sounds echoed off other pieces of machinery and it took considerable dedication to the task, and experience, to be able to make the right initial assessment of the source of the trouble. Having decided that something was wrong and located it, the supervisor had then to decide the probable extent of the damage and whether or not it would be safe to continue running the compressor. Obviously it was better to shut a machine right down than to risk great damage, but it might be perfectly possible to continue running it, perhaps on reduced speed, at least for a while. Sometimes it was possible to do small repairs while only a part of the machine was shut down. To shut a compressor down entirely was a serious matter for it could result in the shutting down of the whole plant, with a consequent major loss of production. A nervous supervisor might shut down too soon; a rash one might keep going too long and leave a trail of damage; the cool and skilful man kept his machines running as long as possible but had the judgement to shut them down before serious damage resulted.

If such valve trouble occurred there was one more occasion for a supervisor to exercise his skill and ingenuity, this time of a social kind. I have just commented on the fact that it was the supervisor's job to decide which valve was giving trouble and act accordingly. However, he did not do the repair work, for that had to be done by the fitters. He had, therefore, to call in a maintenance man and tell him what was wrong. But here lay the difficulty, for he had somehow to do this without offending the fitter's professional sensitivity. It was an article of faith with every skilled man that no process worker, even a supervisor, could form any reasonable judgement about any technical matter whatever. This was so important an issue that it had been agreed between unions and management that no process supervisor might 'instruct' a skilled man on a technical point. What did or did not amount to such 'instruction' depended, it seemed, on the kinds of relationship a supervisor was able to develop with maintenance men. If they privately respected a supervisor's judgement, and if he went about matters the right way, then they would listen to him (for after all he spent his entire working life listening to the sounds of his plant, and this knowledge might more than compensate for any lack of basic technical training). If, for whatever reasons, his relationships with maintenance men were poor, then if he said valve N was faulty, the fitter would almost certainly dismantle a different one to start with, thus prolonging the period of complete or partial shut-down. It was clear, from the reactions of Joe, the most co-operative and friendly of the fitters (who had formerly been the shift-fitter on Plant X, and often dropped in to see his old friends there), that he could scarcely bring himself to admit that the process supervisor could possibly know what he was talking about when he said which valve was faulty. At most Joe would admit that the supervisor might, just possibly, be right about the general area that was giving trouble. If this was Joe's attitude other fitters were convinced that process supervisors could never help them.

How process supervisors dealt with this problem of the maintenance men was instructive. There were really two problems: that of getting quick attention if they thought some machine was developing a serious fault, and that of getting the maintenance man to listen to their opinions when he eventually arrived. A supervisor who was not confident in his own technical competence would leave the problem entirely to maintenance staff, and blame them for any delays. Most supervisors tried to develop relationships that were sufficiently friendly to ensure reasonably quick service; and if, in fact, they thought they could pinpoint a faulty valve better than the average fitter, who was not really familiar with the plant, they tried hard to be tactful, and would carefully say to the fitter something like 'I am not instructing you, I am merely trying to help you by telling you where I think the fault is.' One supervisor, James, conveyed the impression that he had solved both problems by rather strong-arm tactics. He said that if he decided that, for example, a valve was going wrong and that he needed help quickly, he would ring up the fitters and say, 'I am not instructing you, but I have a fault in a valve. I think it is in No. 24. If you would like to come over within the next half hour you can hear the noise yourself, because the machine will be running. After that I shall switch it off because I fear it will cause damage; and I shall not allow it to be turned on again.' The point of all this was that, by company rules, the process supervisor was fully entitled, as the man in charge of the plant, to make the decisions about which machines might or might not be run with safety. If he decided a machine was to be shut down, no fitter could countermand that order, and if it were silent then the fitter would have to go systematically through every valve until he found the troublesome one. The last thing James wanted was a long shut-down, but he gambled that the fitter himself would not want such a tedious job.

The background to the success that it seemed James had achieved in getting swift and co-operative service from the various maintenance groups has to be understood if we are to understand why such peremptory tactics did not misfire. In the first place no one doubted that James was technically very competent. Second, James had quite deliberately set himself out to cultivate the maintenance men. We have seen already that it was perfectly possible for a process supervisor to be left substantially in the dark about any repairs being carried out on his plant. Maintenance men were under no obligation to communicate with him. James, and two of the other supervisors, set out to improve what they regarded as an unsatisfactory situation. They could do nothing formally but informally they saw to it that when their shifts were on, any skilled man coming on to the plant knew that he only had to put his head into the supervisor's office to be welcomed at once with offers of tea, and with gossip and banter. Of course, the tradesmen had their formal 'tea breaks' and should not have stopped for more, but to the supervisor the link was crucial. Once the tradesmen got into the habit of dropping in to see the supervisor every time the plant had to be visited just for a mug of tea and a chat, the supervisor was well on the way to getting detailed information about technical problems, and prompt attention when he was in trouble. A more 'correct' supervisor would be left frustrated and ignorant.

That process supervisors exerted a clear influence on the efficiency of the maintenance service that a plant received under their charge was shown by the way in which this service varied quite markedly, depending on the identity of the supervisor. For example, an untactful supervisor had in the past tried to take a strong line against maintenance men he considered to be dilatory by making official complaints to his plant manager. The result was that it seemed extraordinarily difficult to repair electrical faults that occurred while he was on duty; often it was only when his shift had finished and the next had taken over that the job was done. It might be said that he had tried to use his formal powers as a supervisor instead of informal influence, and that he had failed dismally.

A supervisor's technical ability concerned his operators just as much as it did the tradesmen. Throughout every shift the supervisor should be on hand, and his men should be able to rely on his being fully alert to possible technical problems. The supervisor was expected personally to investigate any fresh report an operator might make of a gas leak, or of overheating bearings, or of a valve that had started 'knocking'. He had to gauge the extent of the problem and decide if any outside help should be requested from 'maintenance', for clearly not every problem could wait until the next day's morning meeting. I noted that supervisors, even more than the men, were always listening and watching for trouble. Above the constant roar of the machinery they would notice the extra hiss of air that might mean that a valve somewhere was blowing gas to the atmosphere. I have heard a conversation between supervisors stopped by a sound that I could hear only when they told me what to listen for – the just audible noise of a fitter wielding his hammer. Similarly, the sudden dimming of the lights, indicating a surge in the demand for electricity, seemed to make them hold their breath while they waited to see whether it meant trouble on their plant, or just a headache for the shift manager because it was due to some fault on another plant. The men on a shift were very ready to assess the technical skill of a supervisor and if they trusted him at this level they were the more ready to trust him generally.

The supervisors' concern with their technical competence emerged very early in my research, when I began to study Plant X. I found that supervisors were often telling me stories about technical crises in its history, and especially various accounts of how the speaker, or a colleague, had on occasions kept production going by saving the plant from being shut down, that is from 'tripping', a term derived from the use of the 'trip switch' to stop machinery in an emergency. These were not stories thought up simply to impress me for some were clearly old chestnuts to anyone else who heard them, and it seemed, often enough, that the speaker was delighted to have found a new listener. Sometimes, when the story teller left the room I would be asked some such question as 'Has he told you yet the one about the time he . . .? No? Oh, don't worry, he will!'

In retelling these stories the supervisors were, of course, less concerned with relating accounts about how production was kept up than they were with impressing others with their own technical expertise, courage, and quick-wittedness. For example, there was a story about why Tom had originally grown his beard. Originally he had done it when his face was still recovering from burns he had suffered when he had rushed to relight the furnace immediately it had gone out. The rule book method would have allowed everything to get cold, and would have led to a real shut-down; instead Tom had used the unorthodox, but effective, method of applying a lighted oily rag to the gas jets while they were still red hot. Unluckily, that day there had been an unusual blow-back, and he had been badly burned. Other supervisors thought highly of

Tom, not because he had saved the company a few hundred pounds – or because he had done anything rash, his accident was regarded as just bad luck. He had done something that competent supervisors had done many times and the blow-back was seen as something so unusual as hardly to be anticipated. Tom was an example because his accident had not changed him – he was still regarded as technically highly competent, he was still unruffled by emergencies, and he was still ready to step in and, if necessary, take unorthodox measures to keep the plant going. The story illustrated Tom's moral character, which was really measured by the repeated instances men could quote when Tom had demonstrated that he could swiftly sum up a situation and determine what had to be done. The story of how he came by his beard was merely the most dramatic of the tales about him. There were many such stories relating to Tom and to other supervisors. What was apparent was that the supervisors' own self-perception was very much bound up with their ability, or their lack of ability, to keep the plant functioning when, by the book, it should have shut down.

I must stress that it seemed that senior management normally knew nothing about such unorthodox practices and therefore certainly did not condone the taking of risks. Indeed, senior management only entered these stories I was told to threaten punishment that added to the risks that the supervisors took. It is important to note that these unorthodox strategies were presented to me as being, as it were, the private property of the supervisors, special knowledge that made all the difference between being an insider and being an outsider. Because of this it is indeed possible that the secret nature of the knowledge was even exaggerated. Nevertheless, the point is that, as these stories are presented (and many of them refer to the heroic past when the plant ran on naphtha and was much more dangerous than it is at present), the prestige of the individual supervisor, and above all his standing with his peers, was explicitly related to his ability to cope with potentially dangerous situations on the plant and to keep it running when, by all normal standards, it should have come to an ignominious halt.

The importance attached to a proper grasp of this private technical knowledge was well illustrated by the explanation given to me as to why one supervisor, Bill, had remained socially an outsider and, allegedly, a technically incompetent one. He was said to have barred himself at the beginning of his career from all access to this knowledge, which is, essentially, orally handed on and not part of the official plant manual that sets out how each piece of machinery should be operated. Now this manual was, in fact, largely the work of the supervisors themselves. Although it might carry the name of the plant manager who edited it, the sections were actually written by the supervisors and periodically were updated by them. The manual was, therefore, not something that was totally unconnected with plant practice. Nevertheless, some of the most important bits of information, about unorthodox but effective short cuts, were not committed to paper. Apparently Bill's difficulties with the other men on the plant started when an attempt was made to teach him this oral knowledge. Bill would deny this for he alleged that all the trouble stemmed from the fact that he had been a supervisor on a different plant, unconnected with ammonia, and when it closed down he was transferred and appointed an ammonia supervisor over the head of Martin, then an assistant foreman, who had expected the supervisor's job to be his. With a fine lack of sensitivity, the then plant manager had put Martin in charge of Bill's training in the technicalities of ammonia. Bill said that Martin and the other supervisors had never treated him fairly since then. Martin said frankly that of course he had been jealous of Bill to start with, but would long ago have forgotten all about it. After all, he said, they were all perfectly happy with another of the plant supervisors who had also been transferred from a non-ammonia plant. But what had transformed passing resentment into lasting animosity was that when he had tried loyally to teach Bill all he knew, including the unorthodox bits, Bill had been very suspicious because he could not find it all in the Manual, and had gone to the plant manager to complain that Martin was giving him false information! After that, Martin said, no one ever again passed the covert knowledge on to Bill. Certainly the others seemed to regard him as an outsider, barred by his own folly from this valuable, indeed essential, insider's information. Without it he could not possibly be as technically effective as the other supervisors.

The importance attached to the technical competence that gave a supervisor the ability to keep a plant running, despite defects in machinery, was very neatly shown to me one evening in a wholly different context. James, in the course of discussing plant safety with me, decided to take the advice of his plant manager and use a new 'dial a safety tip' service that the company had just started at its central works for the ammonia supervisors from all its different works. James was horrified at what he heard when he rang the number. The tip was supposedly based on a real-life incident in which trouble at an ammonia plant had occurred because the man in charge of the control room was not sufficiently familiar with the lay-out to be able to find the master trip switch for the plant in a hurry; when a compressor developed a serious fault he had pressed only the fire alarm as he ran away. The moral apparently intended was that supervisors should see that the control room operator could find the trip switch even in the dark. James was appalled not by the idiocy of mistaking the switches but by the level of general incompetence it revealed. 'We wouldn't have stopped the machine to repair that fault; and if we had done we wouldn't have tripped the plant; and if we had done we wouldn't have run – there was everything to do to shut the plant down properly.' Later I heard him discussing the story with other supervisors and they were almost incredulous. On the facts presented about the technical problem that had arisen they agreed with James that they would have been thoroughly ashamed to have behaved as those in the story apparently had done, and one by one the supervisors dialled the service to hear the extraordinary tale for themselves.

I saw something of the technical concern and the technical ability of the supervisors when a serious fault developed on Plant X over a week-end when the plant manager was on holiday and the engineering manager normally responsible for ammonia maintenance was ill. This left the fitter supervisor and the process supervisors to try to cope with the problem themselves; and their relationship was one of total co-operation. The fault that developed was serious and unusual because it involved a leak in the arsenic catalyst, and it was not easy either to determine its cause, or to know how to deal with it. The plant had to be run at a reduced rate, and it was clear that unless it could be dealt with rapidly the whole plant would have to shut down. For shift after shift the supervisors gave the matter their concentrated attention and the subject dominated all their conversations. At last they thought they knew what the cause was, and Dick, the fitter supervisor, contacted the emergency service of a specialist London firm to discuss with them the best way of capping the leak, and to get them to send someone to help. When Monday morning came and they were able to show the returning managers what they had done they were quietly very pleased with themselves. James said nonchalantly to the plant manager, 'You see, we got your plant back on for you' but did not go on to detail the very real effort that had been put into solving the problem. It seemed to be much more a matter of personal satisfaction and pride than it was a concern to show senior management what clever boys they, the supervisors, had been.

It was, of course, really essential that all the supervisors should have some basic technical expertise because from 4 p.m. until 9 a.m. the next morning plant supervisors had effective control of the plants, and everyone who worked on them was aware of the extent to which their safe and efficient running depended on these men. The plant manager was, in a sense, always there in the background. Between 9 a.m. and 4 o'clock in the afternoon, he was usually somewhere in the works and easily contactable. After that, although he left the works, he had an obligation always to make it possible for the supervisor to reach him by telephone, whatever time of night it might be, if an emergency arose. In fact, however, most supervisors seemed extremely reluctant to ring the plant manager at home, not because he would be irritated but because to them it seemed an admission of failure unless a real crisis justified such an action. I was told by the Plant X supervisors that their plant manager, who had been with them three years, had been telephoned at home only seven or eight times in that period. This is the more noteworthy because he was a man for whose technical expertise they all had particular regard, so that the temptation to ring him if things got difficult must have been very great. Effectively, therefore, most of the time, from late afternoon onwards, the supervisor made all the decisions about running the plant. It is true that during this period there was always a 'shift supervisor' in charge of the whole works. It was the duty of the plant supervisor to keep him informed of anything likely to necessitate major changes in the plant's energy demands. It was, however, purely a matter of chance as to whether or not the shift supervisor had any experience that would enable him to help an ammonia plant supervisor with a technical problem. It was certainly no part of his official duty to do so, although in one case, where a shift supervisor was a former ammonia supervisor with a good reputation, informal consultation with him was much valued. It was entirely up to the supervisor to decide, if any technical problem did arise, whether or not to contact the plant manager – the shift supervisor had no standing in that context. In the case of the leaking arsenic catalyst the shift supervisor was kept informed of developments but could do nothing to help.

I have tried to illustrate the fact that supervisors, to be successful, needed to be technically competent; that those who were seemed to take a pride in the fact that they had to exercise technical judgement, and that this might be a major factor in determining whether production was kept up or lost. A supervisor's general reputation with his peers depended very much on his technical reputation amongst them. However, a supervisor also had to exercise social judgement, for an important element in the situation was also always the supervisor's social relations with others.

The social competence of the plant supervisor was judged primarily by his success or failure in keeping up the basic discipline of a shift that determined its general level of efficiency; the acid test here was its performance at night. It was, of course, against the rules for anyone to sleep at work. Officially anyone caught sleeping, in the sense of having been found hidden away and bedded down, but not the man who has just dozed off in the mess, was liable to immediate dismissal. In practice most shifts, most of the time, seemed to have observed the no sleeping rule quite strictly. There were variations, however, and I learned ultimately, that James, the supervisor of the shift that offered to let me begin my work by studying its activities, was the only man totally confident that I would never catch any of his men having even a brief nap.

The different ways that supervisors behaved in relation to the crucial matter of sleeping on night shifts is instructive. Martin, a supervisor who generally got on very well with his men but was well known to be an overtly strict disciplinarian, made regular, obvious, checks through the night of all the most likely nooks and crannies into which a man might creep. The last thing he wanted to do was to catch a man sleeping, but his activity simply meant that nobody tried it on. 'My' supervisor's tactics were entirely different. What he did, apparently to the scandal of some of the older supervisors, was to play cards with his men. He did this on quiet nights, when men were most likely to want to go to sleep, but he did not allow anyone to play for money (gambling was against company rules). His aim was quite explicitly to keep his men alert and to make sure that nobody *wanted* to slink off into a quiet corner. They always played the same game, 'beat the lady'. This was a useful game because it involved all those not actually working on the plant. They played in the control room, and the supervisor could quietly ensure that the instruments were being properly monitored and any warning signs promptly heeded. Only four men could actually play at the same time, but the game gripped even those just watching for it could be won only by skill and not by luck alone. Interest remained high, even if it seemed that one man held a very lucky hand, because it was possible for those who knew they could not win to gang up to ensure the victory of someone other than the lucky one. This supervisor was concerned to keep his team alert not because he had some unusually strong desire to add to ChemCo's profits, but because he thought, quite explicitly, that a dozy shift was a shift in danger, and that to keep the men wide awake was entirely in their best interests. He tried to do it without rousing their resentment because he believed that if he did that it was bound to have repercussions on their work.

At the other end of the scale was a shift that had a poor reputation for alertness. Martin told me he had been horrified, when he took it over on relief duty one night, to hear one of the operators calmly say he was going to take a nap, and to see him put his head down on the mess table. The blame was placed entirely at the door of this shift's supervisor. Martin said that he had been on that operator's shift for a total of six years (unusually, they had changed shifts together) and in all that time the man had never been seen to doze off, even unintentionally; the only explanation for his change in behaviour had to be the slackness of his supervisor, who was suspected by his colleagues of allowing himself to take naps.

It was accepted that if the supervisor were slack then the men might make little effort to keep awake, but that if the supervisor himself were alert then the men were likely themselves to be strict. It was recognized that some men found it particularly difficult to stay awake. One man was notorious for his sleepiness, and he was the butt of jokes because in an effort one night to keep himself awake he had stood up, leaning against a wall and reading – and even then he had dozed, so I was told, subsiding gently to the ground still clutching his book. No man would make such an effort for a self-indulgent supervisor. By example, therefore, by thought, and by tact, a supervisor could keep an efficient shift, or he might not bother, and his shift would become thoroughly slack. What was true of the discipline on night shifts seemed to be also true, although less obviously so, on the other shifts.

One point that is very significant for the general argument here is that in the story of the sleeping operator told me by Martin as the relief supervisor, it was clear that what happens on a shift depends very much on the state of 'negotiations' between the men and their own supervisor. The mere fact that the relief supervisor held a given place in the official works' hierarchy gave him little influence over men's behaviour. The sleeping operator obviously knew perfectly well what that supervisor's views on sleeping were, and in all probability was, in a sense, deliberately saying that things were different now on that shift. Obviously a supervisor's 'office' alone did not give him a right to interfere in the shift's behaviour. As we shall see, this attitude cropped up in relation to the control of overtime by another relief supervisor. Moreover, this general attitude was also given to me as the reason why Plant X, unlike the other plants at the works, started all morning shifts at 8 a.m. Formerly, it was said, the men's shift had changed at 7 o'clock, but the supervisors' morning shift began at 8 a.m. This, however, had led to an awkward overlap, since for the first hour, the men of the morning shift were supervised by a man with whom they had established no 'negotiating procedures' regarding behaviour. I was told there had been a real row when an operator, told to do something, had responded by saying to the supervisor: 'You're not my foreman, I don't have to do what you say!' The supervisors had then had a discussion and they and the men generally had agreed that while, formally, the night supervisor for the first hour of the day shift really did have the right to expect obedience, it would be better to avoid such contention in the future. It was decided therefore that the morning shift would not start work until 8 a.m., although they felt the last hour of the night shift to drag dreadfully. This change had occurred some time back, and some people now thought that the change had been made simply so that operators and supervisors could the more conveniently share car journeys from their homes into work. Older hands, however, insisted that although this was a very useful result of the change, the real reason initially was to avoid friction between operator and supervisor. I would say that it was done to avoid the difficulties that a supervisor faced in trying to exert his authority in the absence of developed understandings with the shift team.

It was obvious that supervisors took a lot of personal interest in their shift team. On these small shifts this was no doubt relatively easy, but it was also essential since if an operator became difficult, for whatever reason, it could make life extremely awkward for everyone else on the shift, and indeed, lower its efficiency. I was struck by the way in which the supervisors on Plant X took it for granted that they would know if a man had personal problems. I first realized this on an occasion when I listened to some supervisors discussing the annual reports they had to make about their operators. One said that it was a bit of a farce: if a man had previously been recommended for any kind of promotion there was always pressure subsequently on any supervisor writing a report about him to say that he was above average, for otherwise it would seem like an apparent criticism of the earlier supervisor. I butted in to say that surely it might happen that because of personal problems a man's performance might deteriorate. At once there was a chorus from the supervisors, saying that they would of course know all about such problems and these would have been taken into consideration.

My impression was that the supervisors took a lot of trouble to know and to understand the difficulties, usually marital, of the men under them. So far as possible they were lenient in their demands on men who had what were considered to be real problems. Moreover, the management encouraged this, for the supervisor was allowed, in a minor way, to grant special leave in emergencies – for example, if a man's wife left him and he did not know how to cope with the children. Supervisors were supposed to write confidential reports about such cases for the personnel department; but James, who doubted how secure such files were, said he sometimes refused to write anything, although he was always willing to say verbally why he had taken some particular action, and his firm stand had been reluctantly accepted. The Plant X manager, a wise man, had apparently accepted the confidentiality of the relationship between his supervisors and the operators. I was told about various occasions when he had asked why something had been done and had not persisted when the answer from the supervisor had been 'I would prefer not to say.'

The importance of close links between supervisors and men if a shift were to run smoothly was shown by stories I was told on Plant X about the ways in which trouble-makers were dealt with. By 'trouble-makers' I mean here not militants but the man who causes difficulties between shift mates. In such small groups this can be a serious problem.

One case was that of a man who, allegedly, was extremely awkward, and who set out to make trouble between other men on his shift just for the malicious amusement he got out of seeing them quarrelling. Apparently he found out that one man, A, was an extremely jealous husband, and he told him a story about having seen another man, B, on the same shift come out of his (A's) house. The story was true but, as the mischief-maker knew, B had been sent to deliver a message from the company. There was, however, a furious row, and suspicion was sown that the truth did not wholly eradicate. The supervisor reacted by taking the shop-steward into his confidence and then by giving the man every possible difficult job, until at last he was glad to ask for a transfer to another plant within the works.

A very recent case had concerned several of the supervisors on Plant X. They were disturbed because they found out that one of the men, Nick, had started to harass one of their few coloured immigrant operators. Nick had got several friends together and, claiming to be from the National Front, they took it in turns to ring the man up, threatening him and his family. The target of these attacks had, apparently, no idea that his shift mates were involved. In this case the supervisors took the plant manager into their confidence, but persuaded him that it would be much better for all concerned if he were to stifle his anger and allow them to handle the matter informally. They then took the ring-leader aside and told him just how, with the blessing of the shop-steward whom they had also consulted, they would make his life hell if all the harassment were not immediately ended. It was.

In both these instances we can see the concern to handle even serious matters informally, if possible. In the second case formal disciplinary action could have been taken, but then there would have been problems of proof, and the possibility that the immigrant would have become the target of a lot of resentment from the other operators. The supervisors were also trying to avoid any obvious confrontation between 'the operators' and 'management'. In the first case the supervisor would have found it almost impossible to use any formal disciplinary rules against the offender, although it was clearly in everyone's interests that the mischief should be stopped. In neither case could the supervisors dump the problem in the lap of the shop-steward, but in each case they could act only with his acquiescence; once the supervisors had got his 'go-ahead', the operators knew they could turn to no one to defend them and had to give way. If the supervisors had been acting against the shop-steward the situation would have been very different.

An illustration of the limited use to which a supervisor could put his formal powers was the case of the supervisor James, and the so-called 'killer shift'. This was the morning shift worked as an overtime 'doubler' by a man who had just worked through the night, and it got its name because everyone was aware that it put an enormous strain on any individual who tried to do it. On Plant X it had been prohibited as the result of a vote taken at a plant meeting, but it had been banned through the initiative that James had taken as the result of incidents that had arisen when he had tried to use his formal powers as a supervisor to prevent a man from working such overtime. James had made the abolition of the 'killer' the object of a personal campaign because he was horrified at its effects both on the man and on the efficiency and safety of the shift with such an individual working on it. Formally a supervisor had the right to ban from working overtime on his shift any man who had already done a previous shift if it seemed the man were so tired as to be unable to do a normally efficient job. James said he had twice stopped men from working a 'killer' when he had thought they were so tired that they were not merely likely to be inefficient but might be actually dangerous. In each case, however, the men of his own shift had at once seen it as an instance of a supervisor acting against the interests of the operators, and no other man would cover for the work that the exhausted man was supposed to have done. This was not a matter in which the men could expect their steward's support because the union was on the side of safety; it was simply the automatic response of the men to what they saw as a confrontation. Therefore, whatever the rules might say, the supervisor ran into great difficulties if he tried to apply the rule; he was really powerless to exercise the discretion that was formally his. James's way round the problem was to get the general agreement of the men at the plant meeting to a banning of the 'killer'. This had not been difficult because in principle the men were ready to agree that it should be prohibited; it was simply that, faced with a supervisor confronting an operator with the rule book, they had at once taken up the 'defence' of operators' rights. The way round had been to shift the basis of future action from the supervisor's formal rights to the men's free vote.

We can see more of the problems that beset a supervisor who relied too much on his formal powers by looking again at Basil, the operator who hated control room duty. We have seen that Basil specialized in flouting the control man's authority, but he was not always instantly obedient when asked to do something by his supervisor. In the end he would obey because that was his formal obligation, but it tended to be in his own good time. Quite recently Basil had been told by Jack, his supervisor, to go down to the tanker-loading bay, because a man was unexpectedly off sick and a change had to be made in the roster of duties. Basil was still sitting gossiping in the control room five minutes later. Normally it is probable that nothing would have been said, and that Basil would, in a leisurely way, have gone off to the tanker bay quite soon. On this occasion, however, the supervisor himself had to go off elsewhere and was handing the shift over to a relief supervisor James. I surmised that behaviour that would have been accepted within the shift suddenly seemed to Jack to be a public flouting of his authority that had to be checked if he were not to seem incompetent. He asked Basil sharply if he was or was not going. The challenge was down and Basil said he would not go. A shouting match started to develop, but James stepped in to say that he was now officially in charge of the shift, and that his colleague had better go or he would be late for his appointment. The relief supervisor then asked Basil quietly if he would go. As he still refused the supervisor turned to another operator and asked him to go. This man's first response was to say 'No', why should he, it was Basil's job. However James did what he said he always tried to avoid doing; he appealed personally to this man saying it would make life a lot easier if he would agree to go, and the man went off cheerfully enough. Having got over the immediate problem that an important job was being left uncovered, the supervisor then turned back to Basil. He said that obviously he would have to put in a report about the incident, as Basil knew, but perhaps he would like to come into the office to say why he had behaved as he had, so that his side of the story could go in. It turned out that James's hunch was correct and that Basil did feel that he had a genuine grievance. He would not light-heartedly have flouted his supervisor's legitimate order (as he habitually did that of the control room operator). Basil felt he had a long-standing grievance, believing that his supervisor disliked him and always picked on him to do the unexpected, unattractive job. He would have gone in the end, however, even on this day had his supervisor not barked an order at him demanding instant obedience. James put all this into his report, and by handling Basil in this way believed that he had taken the proper disciplinary action without having incurred Basil's lasting enmity.

There was a particular reason for the relief supervisor to handle Basil so sympathetically. Unlikely as it might seem, Basil was regarded by some of the supervisors as an excellent operator. Indeed, both James and Martin, independently on other occasions when I asked them, singled Basil out as the man they would most like to have with them if they were able to pick a shift team out of all the operators on the plant. The reason was that they were judging him not by his outward behaviour towards authority, but by the level of his skill at his work. Certainly they accepted that he did his best to tease 'those in authority over him'; nevertheless, he was singled out for high praise because it was believed that if a dangerous crisis arose on the plant, Basil could be trusted to know exactly what to do, and could be trusted to do it without having to be told, whatever the danger to himself. They had worked with him in the past when there had been many moments of crisis on the plant, and they had complete confidence in his abilities. In a context in which the plant had run so well and so smoothly in the last few years that the supervisors feared that the new recruits, and especially the new breed of control men, might simply lack the will and the experience to cope, Basil was valued as an old, knowledgeable hand on the plant, whose reliability in difficult situations made any lack of deference on his part seem of trivial importance.

To illustrate a number of aspects of the relationships of supervisors with their shifts I will take the case of the 'holiday overtime scandal'.

It is the duty of the senior operator to make out the holiday and overtime schedules for his men. The *formal* rule is that these should be scrutinized by the supervisor, for he normally has the ultimate responsibility for accepting or rejecting them. He should reject them if they were to go against the agreed procedures of the plant. By *custom*, however, so it was explained to me, the responsibility really lies with the senior operator since it would be very bad manners in a supervisor to appear to distrust his senior operator. It would be like carefully counting the change given you by a shop-keeper with whom you often played darts at the pub in the evening – it would be an impossible display of a lack of trust. Nevertheless, just as such a customer would be peripherally aware of what the change in his hand should look like to a casual glance, so an alert supervisor would know at once if there were something a little odd in the schedule presented to him. Open checking was, however, definitely 'out'.

This was the setting on Plant X when the supervisor, James, went on holiday for a week and his senior operator took to the relief supervisor, Martin, a schedule that allowed, in a future week, three of the men to take their ESOs (see p. 103) on consecutive days. The unsuspecting supervisor signed the schedule, and it was only later that he realized that, in effect, this was something of a rip-off. There were to be two men on holiday in the period concerned, with the result that a great deal of overtime would be generated. Yet this form of overtime had been specifically ruled out by an agreement made at a plant meeting that men were to choose their ESOs in a way that did not lead to exceptional overtime, and specifically that they were not to be booked on days when it was known in advance that two men were due to be absent.

On his return, James was very worried that what he regarded as a piece of sharp practice should have been perpetrated by his senior operator; he thought it a betrayal of trust that must mean that something was really upsetting this man. Of course everyone had been irritated by the new rules that forbade a man to work his own ESO, but James thought there must be something else behind the incident or such an unkind trick would not have been played on the relief supervisor, who had been made to look foolish and would be reprimanded by the plant manager. The trick was particularly mean because by the company's rules the supervisor ought to have checked, yet for the relief man to have done so would have been socially unacceptable since it would have signalled not merely distrust of the senior operator, but also a lack of confidence in James's ability to establish proper relationships with his men. James was so confident that his senior operator was normally 'straight' that he felt sure there must be some special reason for such double dealing.

James was also angry and he believed his plant manager was very annoyed. I heard him tell the manager that he was quite certain that the whole thing had been done deliberately, because the senior operator was far from stupid. James told the manager that it was important that in this case he should countermand the acceptance of the schedule by the relief supervisor (the plant manager had such powers although it was extremely rare for them to be used). James told him that such an action was essential if there were to be any chance that in the future the plant meeting's agreement on ESOs was to be kept.

Despite all this, when we were alone, James said that although he believed very strongly that for the good of the plant the manager should follow his advice, he himself felt that his whole relationship with his particular shift would be threatened if he did not now stand by the three members who were about to be carpeted by the manager. James said, in so many words, that unless they felt they could trust him he would get nowhere with them. Therefore, while they were sitting in the mess waiting for the manager to come back on to the plant, James slipped in for a long chat with them. Later he told me that he had told them the manager was furious, and that he thought the manager would be fully justified in preventing them taking these ESOs. He had then asked them what they were going to say in their defence. Apparently they told him they were going to say they were very sorry, but they had just not realized that two men were going to be away that week; and surely, they would say, the plant manager would never countermand his supervisor! James said he told them exactly what short work the manager would make of that nonsense. He had gone on to say that their only hope was for each to think up a special reason why it had been really important to him to have his ESO on the day he had chosen; and whatever happened, James said, they should stick to these stories and stick together.

While the plant manager was interviewing these men, James talked to me gloomily, predicting that the manager, although he would not believe one word of the stories he was told, would, nevertheless, appear to do so, and would agree to the men having their ESOs as planned. He would do this, James said, because he was very anxious not to offend any of the senior operators. The manager was about to have a crucial meeting with them at which he was going to try to get them finally to agree to 'deputize' for supervisors (something to which, in fact, James was very opposed). Because this was such a contentious issue, James said it would look very well on the manager's record if he could get such agreement before he was transferred to a new post he was due to take up shortly.

When the manager came back into the supervisors' office, it was, indeed, to say that the whole thing seemed to be the result of unfortunate coincidences – an eighteenth birthday party and sudden news of visits by far-flung relatives. He had decided in the circumstances it would be hard on the men to refuse any of their requests for these ESOs and he would, therefore, allow the arrangements to stand. James said nothing until the manager went out, but then he exploded with irritation, saying that it was all right for the manager, he was going, but the supervisors were going to have to live with the precedent he had allowed to be created. The plant meeting had agreed, and it was written down, that in order to cut excessive overtime, ESOs could *not* be taken when a shift had two men off. Nobody liked the ruling but it had been accepted; but now it would be impossible to stick to it as every shift would insist that what one could do all could do.

A few days later, when I was in the mess drinking tea with the men involved, I discovered that James had been right in thinking the senior operator did what he did for a purpose. He told me that he and his friends had put in the dubious schedule quite deliberately, for two reasons. First, they had just seen a sudden chance to buck the system, to defeat the new rule that they disliked. Second, however, they had seen a chance to punish the relief supervisor for actions of which they disapproved. Martin was generally liked, it was true, and he had done nothing against them personally, but they thought he needed to be taught a lesson because they considered he had behaved badly to the senior operator on his own shift over the question of deputizing. He was appearing to co-operate with the new scheme by allowing his senior operator to stand in for him, but he was making sure that this man could deputize only on those shifts, weekend nights, that everyone was anxious to avoid. (This assertion was true for the supervisor himself commented to me that everyone had to start by doing this and he himself was willing to learn the shift supervisor's job by doing such shifts.) Thus, the men on James's shift had seen a chance to earn easy overtime pay and take the mickey out of a supervisor who, they thought, needed to be reminded that he should be fair. It had been too good a chance to miss.

This series of incidents seemed to illustrate most of the points about the social aspects of a supervisor's role that I came to think important. They showed the significance of formal, 'structural' relationships, but also they showed the extent to which the smooth functioning of the plant depended on the existence of good informal relationships developed by individuals and on the existence of a consensus about permitted and unpermitted behaviour. These incidents were also significant because they demonstrate why it was that the supervisors felt strongly that the proper running of the plant depended on them. Senior management might imagine that the situation was different and that it was the plant manager who was the crucial figure, with the interest of the plant really at heart. The supervisors, however, saw themselves as the residents, who necessarily were more concerned than anyone else about what happened. Plant managers came and went and most were thought to see the plant merely as a stepping stone to higher things, but supervisors had nowhere else to go, so of course they cared about it.

Supervisors' loyalty to their plants existed independently of their attitude to management. This was shown very clearly in the case of the disputes surrounding the change in the shift-fitter system, which, it will be remembered, had been altered by the fiat of senior management, leaving many people unhappy. By 'loyalty' I mean here a real concern that the plant should keep up its level of production and should produce economically, in order that it should continue to provide jobs for all those currently employed there. Since they did not expect ChemCo to keep it open if it ran at a loss the supervisors wanted the plant to make a profit, and to this end they were anxious to stop anything they regarded as excessively wasteful. Had they believed the old shift-fitter organization to have come into this category they would have accepted that change was necessary; and I think it is obvious, given the rivalry between 'trades' and 'process', that the process supervisors would not have deceived themselves because of any sentimental sorrow for the poor fitters. Mere fellow-feeling and brotherly love would have been unlikely to have led supervisors into the, for them, unusual situation of denouncing senior management for its treatment of the craftsmen and siding with them. Their reasons were instructive.

To make the issues clear, it will be helpful to go over the details of the system. Plant X and Plant Y each had had a shift-fitter team, that is, they had had one fitter attached to each of their four shifts; such a fitter probably worked only three hours out of every shift (on official work, that is, because sometimes they may have done work on operators' cars, but here it has to be remembered that since they came to work at odd hours and with very little help from public transport, the operators were excessively dependent on having cars that were reliable). Each shift-fitter team also generated quite a lot of overtime, since the rule had been that the absence of one of them could be covered only by the presence of another shift-fitter, and no fall-back had been allowed on to the ordinary day fitters. Clearly, to senior management, it had seemed perfectly reasonable to suggest that it would be a sensible economy to organize a single fitter team to service the plants. That collectively the fitters might then be expected perhaps to put in about eighteen hours' work during the twenty-four hours for which they were actually paid to be on hand did not seem to mean that they would be unreasonably overworked.

There was, of course, a snag, of which senior management were fully aware: both ammonia plants might develop serious faults (so-called 'limitation' faults) at the same time; as one fitter would be unable to deal with both plants simultaneously then it was indeed probable that one would have its production limited. However, the history of faults on the plants suggested this was not a very likely occurrence; the demand for fertilizer, while steady and not depressed, was being satisfied by current production, and there were no unsatisfied customers. Therefore, so the reasoning of senior management went, it was obviously sensible to make a considerable saving on labour costs rather than retain in existence a very expensive shift-fitter system that had been designed to maintain a very high production level.

Supervisors and operators on the ammonia plants took a fundamentally different view, not because they thought that the works should produce more fertilizer than it could sell, but because some of the most thoughtful believed that if an effort had been put into marketing ammonia itself, rather than the end product of fertilizer, then they could have sold, at a profit, all that they could have produced. They dismissed as feeble the management response that as the basic purpose of the works was to produce ammonia for the sake of producing fertilizer, it was not in the business of encouraging the ammonia plants to 'go it alone'. Those on the ammonia plants could see no reason why the output of ammonia should be restricted to that required by their own fertilizer plant. The works already 'exported' some ammonia in tankers to other works and other firms. From their reading of the technical journals, and from their conversations with some of the managers, it was believed that the company could have derived a substantial profit from every tonne of ammonia produced (The figure mention was £50 per tonne, when they could make from 400 to 500 tonnes per day.) Surely, they reasoned, it would make good business sense to keep production up. Despite the recession, there was no doubt that they were able to sell all they produced.

It was against this background that the supervisors argued that although the old shift-fitter system was a bit extravagant, if the change in it really hindered production, then surely management action was short-sighted. The people blamed were a somewhat mysterious group, 'The Accountants'. They were condemned not for trying to make things more efficient but for being blind to the real costs of the 'savings' that they made. These savings were almost always thought to be those that seemed obvious, those that the accountants found it easy to add up and quantify, so that they 'looked very good on paper'. The accountants, through indolence and stupidity, were supposed not to bother, or to be unable, to add up all the hidden costs of reduced production, occasioned both by small delays caused on the one hand by unavoidable extra delays in repairs, and by the loss of goodwill on the part of the fitters. The fact that such costs were difficult or impossible to quantify did not mean that they were not real. Senior management could have known about them if only they had been willing to listen to what the supervisors tried to tell them.

I want to explore further the supervisors' reactions to the changes made in the shift-fitter system, partly because it was obviously something about which they felt deeply, but also because their reactions are relevant to some of the arguments of Gallie (1978) and of Nichols and Beynon (1977). One of the questions Gallie tried to answer was how far the workers he studied were 'integrated' within the capitalist system (Gallie 1978: 3) and it seems that he based his answer on the extent to which those he studied 'accepted' management's authority. One of the things I want to argue is that we should be very careful before we assume that 'acceptance' means that those who do accept it think they must therefore be dutifully obedient. I think that I have said enough in relation to the supervisors' (and indeed the operators') concern with profitability to make the point that they appeared to be pretty well integrated within capitalism; this did not prevent them from believing that they knew better than management how the plants could be most profitably run.[1] The corollary, of course, is that resistance to particular plans of management, or the plans of particular managers, should not lead to the assumption that those concerned are somehow necessarily 'against the system', or just motivated by some short-sighted vision of their own best interests. The latter view is sometimes taken by management, and the former is also sometimes held by management; and from a very different political standpoint seems also to be the view of Nichols and Beynon (1977). Let us, therefore, look carefully at the attitudes of supervisors to management's policy of reorganizing the shift-fitters.

The supervisors thought the new scheme was bad partly because it had led, they said, to so much bitterness on the part of the fitters that break-down times were increasing to the point where, if the total loss of production had been added up, it would have been seen to have been more important than management was prepared to admit. They were concerned not with major break-downs but with the many occasions when a few hours of full production were lost. I heard many stories about this, but I will just quote a case I observed. I was sitting in the mess on Plant X, chatting to the supervisor Martin and Joe, the former shift-fitter, was in and was drinking tea with some of the operators who were also in the mess. It was a Sunday morning and all was quiet. Then there was a telephone message saying that the fitter was needed on Plant Y, to take out a valve that was giving trouble. Joe's response was to say, 'Well, I'll go over, but they needn't think I'm going to do anything without a rigger to help me!' Martin, said, banteringly, 'Oh, come off it, you often did jobs like that for us by yourself when you were our shift-fitter.' Joe's answer was, 'I may have done, but I'm not doing it now.' The supervisor persisted. 'Oh, come on, Joe, you could swing it out with a tripod,' but Joe stubbornly insisted, 'I must have a man to help me.' The supervisor replied, 'Well, use one of their lads, then. You used to do that here.' But Joe ended the exchange by saying, 'Not any longer – the rule book says I'm to have a rigger; I'm sticking to the rule book now.' Since no rigger was available until Monday morning Plant Y had to limp along on reduced production for nearly twenty-four hours. This exchange was the more significant just because Joe was a very friendly and well-disposed man who, because he was getting towards retirement age and had been feeling the strains of shift work, was personally pleased rather than otherwise to have been changed on to day work. It had meant a cut in his wages, but he welcomed the fact that he could now have most week-ends off. (This particular Sunday was for him a special case of overtime in the holiday period.) Joe would probably still have put himself out for special supervisor friends on Plant X. Among the fitters generally, however, there was now a very large element of working to rule that gave rise to costs that, so far as I know, had not been quantified.

The supervisors' arguments could be summarized quite simply. There had been eight shift-fitters, each of whom had suffered, through their altered work patterns, a cut in wages of about £3,000 a year, which had been cushioned by lump sum payments of about £1,500 and some extra money in the first year. As they saw it, savings of this order might seem a good idea to the management but, as one of them put it, the plant had only to be shut down for ten hours instead of one hour and many of the apparent savings must surely have been wiped out. They thought that with the degree of working to rule encountered amongst the fitters, and with other hidden rises in maintenance costs that were thought to be linked with attempts to reduce maintenance overtime, the most optimistic view of real savings made by management must be that they were absolutely minimal.

The genuineness of this view seemed vouched for by the reaction of a process supervisor, when I told him that I had been puzzled by the fact that Dick, the fitter supervisor, had apparently changed his mind about the re-organization issue. When I had first spoken to him, he, like the process supervisors, had argued strongly that management was mistaken in its action and that the unnecessary delays in repairing faults were 'galling'. However, when I spoke to him several weeks later about the matter, he gave me the straight management view. Had Dick, I asked, decided I was some sort of management spy? The process supervisor said this was certainly not the problem. The trouble was that poor Dick was feeling so fed up with the way his manager had treated him that for the moment he had given up bothering about his job. As we saw, Dick had used a lot of initiative in helping to solve the problem of the leak in the arsenic catalyst. When the crisis was over a senior engineer manager had, in Dick's presence, congratulated Dick's own manager (who had been off sick at the time of the trouble) on his smart job in finding a solution to the problem, and the man had simply smiled modestly. Dick was furious, but, I was told, he would feel better when he had had his holiday!

Supervisors were similarly critical of the way in which management economizing in regard to overtime had, in their opinion, occasioned large, unexamined costs through delays to repairs. By comparison, they thought the saving on wages had been small. In effect they charged that the pattern of costs here was being 'laundered' in order to 'look good on paper'. To make it appear that the works was really pruning its labour costs by cutting out overtime, real costs were being sent up by the way in which servicing was actually being done. So here the stories were of extra delays of ten days or more in getting important machines back in working order. In one particular case there was a story, that seemed well-founded, of electric motors which could have been repaired perfectly well at the works being sent out to an independent firm for servicing. The actual extra cost was alleged to be £1,000 per motor, and the only advantage was a book-keeping one of the elimination of a whole category of overtime payments.

Maintenance and process supervisors alike expressed anxiety that because of short-sighted cost-cutting, the plants were being so inadequately serviced that before long the repair bills for break-downs would be serious. Moreover, maintenance supervisors were becoming very concerned about what they saw as the poor quality of the outside contractors who always had to be brought in to help in the periodic overhauls of the plants. It was asserted that most contractors were real cowboys (and the first kind of gossip to which I was admitted, when I began to get to know people, related to the manifold and monstrous fiddles worked by the cowboy contractors and their men). The few good contractors, it was said, kept their men only by allowing them, legitimately, to earn very high wages, and they did this by ensuring that they could get a lot of easy overtime. Now, in its cost-cutting zeal, management had said that the contractors were not to be allowed to work overtime. The consequence was that the good firms simply refused to come and the cowboys were flooding in, with potentially disastrous consequences. Those supervisors with long memories said that a decade earlier ChemCo had tried similar economies and learned the hard way that it simply did not pay. Now that generation of engineer managers had gone and the new ones thought they could economize. They would find the consequent real expenses phenomenal.

It was possible to find the odd supervisor who was happy to go along with the new arrangements. A Plant Y supervisor said of senior management, 'If that's the way they want it, then why worry? The worst that can happen is that the plant will trip.' But he was the elderly supervisor I have already mentioned, who, on the verge of retirement, had given up bothering about his job and was 'as good as gold' in the hands of the 'gourmet' shift. By contrast, James, who was dedicated to his work, and especially concerned with the technical problems of keeping his plant running well and efficiently, repeatedly condemned all the new changes in conversation with me and with others he met in my presence. In doing this he heartily condemned the managers who had initiated the changes.

It seemed particularly significant that the supervisors spoke with real resentment and hostility about the behaviour of managers when, a few months before my study began, they had taken a tough line in the face of a rumbling labour dispute elsewhere on the works, and had threatened to 'throw the switch' on all the plants. The supervisors' reaction was significant because in general their complaint was always that the management were too weak in the face of the unions, and that, indeed, they had somehow 'given up managing'. The explanation of the apparent paradox seemed to be not the implication that in a recession the management held the whip hand, but that this threat seemed a kind of blasphemy to the supervisors because they were so dedicated to keeping the plants running. The incident suggested that perhaps management did not really care, and the supervisors found this inherently shocking. As I have already indicated, to most of the supervisors I knew 'tripping the plant' carried implications of personal failure, even though they knew that sometimes the action was unavoidable. Their whole self-image seemed inextricably linked up with the plant they ran. They measured their skill and responsibility in relation to other supervisors at the works by contrasting the complexity of their job with others. Less important plants, whose supervisors, naturally, had lesser merit, could be wholly shut down and then put back 'on line' within a couple of hours. However, if ammonia plants were tripped and allowed to get cold, it might take up to forty-eight hours to start them up. They judged themselves in relation to other ammonia supervisors elsewhere by the belief that they, the Riverside men, were more skilled at keeping their plants running. Had not the incident of the recorded safety trip demonstrated that? The supervisors of each of the two Riverside plants were convinced that they, as a group, were really better than the men who ran the other plant, and each group sought to prove it to me by getting me to understand that really Plant X, or Plant Y, was the more complex and important. For management to talk light-heartedly to these men about 'throwing the switch' on the plants was simply proof that managers had a wrong sense of values.

This distrust of management raises the question of the relationship of the supervisors with their plant manager. Clearly the plant manager had a certain formally defined position in the hierarchy, but it seemed that, in this case too, his effectiveness depended to a considerable extent on his prestige, and on the trust felt for him. Whether his superiors considered him 'effective' or not of course depended in a large part on the degree of success he had in carrying out their wishes in bringing about changes in working patterns. Effectiveness in their eyes must have been much more difficult to achieve than in earlier periods for plant managers had in some ways been set almost impossible tasks: they were required to get acceptance at their plant meetings of changes that the men thought likely to involve both income losses and a worsening of the conditions under which they worked; and the relation between such sacrifices and the future well-being of the plant had not been convincingly demonstrated. How the plant manager was to achieve success seemed to have been left to him to determine. I am concerned to show how much his effectiveness really depended on the nature of the informal relationships he was able to establish with his supervisors. It was obvious, from listening to their conversation about the different plant managers under whom they had worked, that relationships varied very much from manager to manager.

A plant manager's prestige, like that of a supervisor, seemed to depend to a great extent on his technical ability and the width of his experience with similar plants. A manager who came to the plant with a real expertise in this field seemed sure of an enthusiastic welcome from his supervisors. They found it immensely reassuring to know that there would always be someone at the end of the telephone from whom they could expect help if they faced a serious technical problem. By contrast, the manager who was believed to be a technical ignoramus was regarded with genuine anxiety. This was an attitude revealed by a supervisor's comment on a new manager: 'Oh, if I have a real problem I will ring him up. Not that he knows anything, but it's always useful to have someone you can discuss things with. Even if he only asks silly questions it may help you to think things out!'

The best of technical knowledge, however, would not build up a manager's prestige if he showed resentment if supervisors sought his advice at awkward times. I have already suggested that supervisors hated to ring the plant manager at night because it indicated a personal failure to cope, and they were, therefore, very sensitive to any show of irritation on the manager's part if they did telephone him. Martin, for example, had never forgiven an earlier plant manager for such a display. Some years ago Martin had been extremely worried one night because one of his machines developed a leak in a valve, and it threatened to blow a plug out. This, he knew, would inevitably lead to a breakdown that would necessitate tripping the plant. Martin tried, unavailingly, to get advice from maintenance men on the site to discover whether an idea he had for plugging the leak would work, or would be dangerous. In desperation, about 2 a.m. he rang his plant manager, but before he could get his problem out he was asked 'why the hell' he was ringing at that hour. Martin put down the phone. Shortly afterwards, as he had not dared to apply his remedy, which he found later would have been successful, the plug was blown out, and he had to trip a section of the plant. Martin then felt justified, although it was still only about 3 a.m., in telephoning for advice to a senior engineer manager with whom he enjoyed good relationships as they were both keen rugby supporters. Martin put his problem, explaining why he could not go back to his plant manager. With the engineer's help Martin was able to effect such a quick start-up of the section that had gone down that he did not have to shut down the whole plant. Martin recalled with satisfaction that his plant manager had rung him about 5 a.m. to find out how he was getting on, and Martin was able to tell him tersely that the plant was normal. Martin liked to think that the engineer must have rung the plant manager and torn a strip off him. Afterwards his relations with Martin were never the same again. Martin said that he never again discussed any problem with him verbally: if anything had to be reported to the manager Martin wrote it down in the plant's log; but effectively they were not on speaking terms.

In the supervisors' rogues' gallery of awful plant manager types, the one that was apparently most dreaded was the 'whiz kid' who had recently got his degree but had no practical experience. At first I wondered whether this antagonism might not really stem from the fact that the supervisors, mostly older men, did not really accept the managerial hierarchy, and were basically unprepared to take orders from a much younger man. The whiz kind, it seemed, could do nothing right. The last such manager on Plant X was regarded as having been a walking disaster in every way. James said he was so ignorant technically, and so insensitive to his machines, that he thought they could be run flat out all the time if greater production were needed, and had not appreciated the strain this put on the equipment. Moreover, he was so inept that if he tried to negotiate with the union he would end up by having given away more than had originally been asked, and would not even realize what he had done. Significantly, the most dreaded of all a whiz kid's traits was that he could, quite unnecessarily and unintentionally, rub the operators up the wrong way; that could transform a normally co-operative group of men into a difficult bunch, and make life very hard for everyone.

It became apparent to me however, that in making these criticisms the supervisors were reacting to actual characteristics of actual men, and were not covertly rejecting a manager's authority simply because he was young. When one plant manager left during the course of my study, I was able to listen to an intense debate amongst the supervisors as to who was likely to be chosen to succeed, and their relative merits and demerits. One name put forward was that of a manager who had graduated relatively recently, and was not only young but looked even younger than he was. I expected the mere suggestion of his appointment to give rise to indignation, but on the contrary, the idea was greeted with some enthusiasm. Of course, he lacked experience, but they thought he was technically very competent. Socially he seemed acceptable because he had a pleasant, friendly manner, and he took the trouble to come round to the club house and play skittles and darts with them and the men there. The supervisors did not seem to imagine that they could manipulate him, for he was reckoned to be nobody's fool, but they thought they could have worked happily with him. The fact that these men would, apparently, have been perfectly prepared to accept, without resentment, direction from a man so much younger than themselves seems evidence of their willingness to accept, in principle, a manager's basic authority.

This did not mean that they were prepared to suffer fools gladly just because they held managerial status.

From my outsider's position it seemed apparent that the role of the plant manager was, socially, a particularly difficult one, because he not only had to reconcile men to the policies of senior management, which must have been difficult enough in itself, but he also had to deal with men who were themselves much divided by mutual jealousies. It is too simple to say that the divisions could enable the plant manager to 'divide and rule' for in themselves they could create difficulties for him. His authority was, of course, stronger than that of the supervisors, but even the plant manager's powers were limited enough to make it essential for him to carry opinion with him; and how could he do this if groups were at odds with one another?

The plant manager's problems were highlighted for me by the story of the supervisor and the fitter. We have seen how jealous skilled men are of their position relative to process supervisors, and how indignant they are at the idea that such a supervisor might 'instruct' them. Nevertheless, the process supervisor is undoubtedly responsible for the safety of all those on his plant. One day, on Plant X, a maintenance job had to be done on one of the catalysts, and when he looked over the work sheet that had been made out, the supervisor filled in the section that stipulated that protective clothing should be worn. It was said that most of the fitters would have accepted this as reasonable, but the individual concerned was an awkward customer who chose to make an issue of the matter, saying that the supervisor was 'instructing' him. The row actually blew up when the fitter arrived to start work, by which time there had been a shift change, and the supervisor who had entered the offending words had gone off duty. The plant manager was then faced with the problem of getting a necessary repair job done when the fitters, instigated by the first man, had decided that their collective dignity had been affronted. The manager capitulated, scratching out the 'instructions' and the job was done. The responsible supervisor, when he heard about it, was furious. He *was* responsible for the safety of the plant; he had merely indicated, quite properly, that certain protective clothing had to be worn before anyone might deal with that catalyst; the manager had no right to countermand what he had written. The dispute, I was told, dragged on in a desultory way for *two years* for now it was an issue of principle involving two unions. In the end, it was officially decided that on Plant X the process supervisor, or his deputy the senior operator, might give written 'advice' on protective clothing, but might not prohibit a maintenance job from being done (except in extreme circumstances) if the skilled man chose to ignore his advice. This agreement meant that the supervisor, having written his advice, would be legally covered; the skilled men had to pay attention to the new Health and Safety at Work legislation (a man may be prosecuted for injuring himself by reckless behaviour); nevertheless it was agreed that the skilled man might make the ultimate decision for himself. In this dispute it is worth pointing out that nobody doubted the importance of safety; nobody's financial interests were threatened. The only issue was the sensitive one of relative status, and the manager's handling of the problem left his relations with his supervisors strained.

A plant manager had to try to get along amicably with several small, conflicting groups, and this was never easy. To effect the changes that senior management wanted him to bring about he usually had to persuade rather than order, and to persuade he had first to listen sympathetically to particular viewpoints, and try to convey to the men concerned his sympathetic understanding of their case. It is, of course, perfectly possible to feel sympathy for certain aspects of both sides in a dispute. One of the problems for the manager, however, was that the men in these small, antagonistic, apparently closed groups, were not always so divided as they might appear. During the day they may feel so conscious of their public image as scarcely to be on speaking terms. At night, however, the tensions slacken, and often the men come together, discussing what the manager may have said, and each group tends to present managerial murmurings of understanding as whole-hearted support for a particular cause. In such circumstances it is difficult for a manager not to appear duplicitous.

What is true of the problems that beset the plant manager in dealing with groups within his plant is also true when he acts as the intermediary between his plant and senior management. This is a real conflict within the role of the plant manager. His position with his men, and therefore his ability to get any of their practices changed, depends on his ability to negotiate with them a relationship of sympathetic understanding. Without winning their trust he has no hope of being able to get their willing acquiescence to change. Nevertheless, to his bosses, too great a sympathy with the men on his plant may make a manager seem disloyal. I saw the problem when I attended a plant meeting at which the shift-fitter issue was discussed. I heard the plant manager say that he, like everyone else, was really grieved at the production problems that were being raised for the plant; that he, too, feared that perhaps inadequate attention was being paid to the hidden costs involved in the change. Nevertheless, he said, the change was, sadly, now an accomplished fact, and they would have to live with the result and try to make the best of it. With genuine delight the supervisor who was writing the minutes duly recorded, in all the detail he could remember the manager's expressions of support for the men's viewpoint, and said very little about his remarks on the need to work the new system. Now the minutes of the plant meetings are circulated through the works and copies go to senior management, and the plant manager must accept the minutes of the meeting as a true record before they are circulated. Thus a scandal arose among the supervisors, for when he checked the minutes the plant manager censored all reference to his own remarks! Everyone who was anyone was indignantly shown the mauled manuscript and the edited final version. Indeed, I counted it as a milestone in my research that I was able to say that I myself had seen those pages. It also showed me very clearly the social problems of being a successful plant manager!

I must now try to summarize some of the main points that I have been trying to make in this chapter. One of the most remarkable aspects of the relationship between the plant manager and his supervisors seemed to be that the manager often failed to realize how concerned supervisors were that the plant should be economically successful. Managers to whom I said that the supervisors seemed to me to be intensely interested in this were very surprised; and this was the case not only with managers who were somewhat removed from the plants. One plant manager, to whom I expressed these views after I had seen his supervisors battle with the arsenic leak, said, almost wistfully, 'Do you really think so? I wish I could think that!' The supervisors themselves sensed this attitude of management and it puzzled them. When a Plant Y supervisor asked me what I had learned in my first weeks on Plant X, and I spoke of this concern for the plant, and for production, he warmly agreed, and added, 'But this is what they [the managers] don't understand!'.

Why was the impression I received not also conveyed to management? The answer is, I think, twofold. In the first place the supervisors' attitudes were commonly implicit rather than explicit, even when they were talking amongst themselves: their personal identification with their plant was hidden in the stories about times when, against all the odds, some supervisor saved the plant from tripping. Second, if managers were, indeed, not omniscient, they may have fallen into the obvious trap of supposing that real loyalty would have shown itself in obedience; surely, if concern for a well-run, profitable plant really existed amongst the supervisors, it would manifest itself in some kind of ready compliance with management policies. Clearly it did not, and if managers made this assumption then even those most closely in touch with the supervisors might have concluded that they were not very anxious that the plants should be profitable to the company, for the evidence of the supervisors' resistance to senior management was clear. As I observed them, supervisors were far from deferential to managers personally, and they made sure that their constant and reiterated criticisms of management policy were heard by the managers. Moreover the supervisors resisted, in varying measure but sometimes with subtle skill and determination, the pressure of senior management to get them to cut some of the more obvious overtime costs. Any manager who believed in the rightness of senior management policy, and assumed that a concern for profitability must be linked to a willingness to co-operate with that policy, would be almost bound to think that supervisors just did not care. This was especially likely since many managers seemed to share a common prejudice that no one who had originally been 'on the shop floor' and so shared shop floor attitudes, could be expected really to understand that the future of the works depended upon its being profitable.

For all the reasons that have been outlined, I would argue, on the contrary, that the ammonia supervisors were profoundly anxious that the plants should be profitable, but that neither this fact nor their general acceptance of 'management's right to manage' led them to show that compliance that their seniors expected. Supervisors did not necessarily think that particular management policies were wise, nor that particular managers were wise; nor even that particular managers were always motivated by a desire to pursue the best interests of either the plants or the works. Moreover, as I heard them, supervisors were not always filled with either charity or understanding when they discussed the action of managers in the hearing of management. None of this meant that they were not intensely loyal to their plants. None of this stopped them from being deeply committed to their work. I think, however, that it did create a barrier between them and the senior managers. Burawoy (1979), it seems, would suspect that senior management must, somehow, not only have known of the dedication of the supervisors to their work but must actually have contrived the situation. I think that the evidence is simply against this, and that instead of attempting to capitalize on this fund of goodwill, senior managers had, instead, been attempting to build up and use the union shop-stewards as intermediaries with the men. How they set about this and what success they met with we will consider in the next chapter.

NOTE

1. Gallie (1978: ch. 5) discusses criticisms of management by refinery workers. White and Trevor (1983: 12) comment that much might be learned from a direct investigation of workers' perceptions of management methods.

6
Shop-stewards and the 'management of consent'

In this chapter I want to look at the position of the shop-steward in relation to his men on the one hand and management on the other; and I shall discuss the extent of his authority and influence in comparison with that of the supervisors. I quite deliberately avoid, for the most part, reference to the stewards currently on the plants at the time I did my research, because each plant had one steward only and it would be improper to go into much detail. It is, however, essential to examine material on stewards carefully. Current discussions on the role of senior management in gaining the co-operation of the work-force make it important to examine the extent to which there is deliberate manipulation of any men who are, in whatever ways, intermediaries; we shall also consider the extent to which any such manipulation succeeds in its aim, or has unintended consequences.

We examined in the beginning of this account two widely differing views on union, and therefore shop-steward, power within British industry. Gallie (1978) has argued that it is the power of unions in negotiation with management that has, in the widest sense, given the latter 'legitimacy' in the eyes of the men, because it is this that means that management has to enter into negotiations with those who represent the interest of the workers (see especially Gallie 1978: 313–15). Nichols and Beynon (1977: 147, 159–60), conversely, argue that shop-stewards at Riverside had no power to act for the men against management. My material lends support to the view that management were certainly trying to make friends among the stewards and influence them; but it also suggests that this was not the whole story. It seems that the Riverside management in the 1970s were very conscious of the new powers that the unions had, and that the management believed, on the grounds of both virtue and expediency, that attempts should be made to work with and not against the stewards. It seemed virtuous because stewards were elected by their members and, therefore, in a society committed to 'democracy', the authority of an elected steward must be more 'legitimate' than that of a supervisor, which rested on his position in the management hierarchy. It was expedient because on these grounds men could be told that they *ought* to accept arrangements made between the shop-stewards and the management. Whether the management was or was not machiavellian is not the issue here; I am, rather, concerned with whether or not such goodwill and consent as I found among the work-force was 'manufactured' by management. The answer to this question does not depend on the virtue of the strategies used but on their success. I shall argue that, lacking omniscience, management were barking up the wrong tree and that consent existed to a significant extent despite, rather than because of, management strategies.

Nichols and Beynon (1977) assume, like Braverman (1974), that trade unions in general are management's servants. It is taken for granted that the company had to control the stewards because the men could, had they combined, have frustrated management; they did not do this and it is, therefore, assumed that stewards were controlled. The management talked about union 'participation' in 'decision-making' but this, necessarily, was so limited as to be, to Nichols and Beynon, bogus. This is argued on general principles: 'participation', had it been real, might have involved union wishes being allowed to override considerations of profit or loss; since management reserved its right in the last resort to take decisions to keep costs down, it must uphold the hierarchic 'class' structure of the works, and thus exclude stewards from real participation (Nichols and Beynon 1977: 115, 176). Clearly, once 'participation' is defined in this way, it is obviously incompatible with the structure of a firm that has to operate in a market economy. In these circumstances Nichols and Beynon believe that union officials who negotiated with the company lacked any ultimate freedom, and by the very act of negotiation betrayed their members, for if they negotiated they necessarily accepted the basic capitalist position.

Nichols and Beynon (1977) present evidence to suggest that Riverside management was actively concerned to subvert the shop-stewards and were thoroughly successful. This success began with the choice of the steward for it is claimed that supervisors were used to search for 'compliant' men who might be persuaded to stand for election as stewards. Having got the right men elected they had to be suborned, and evidence of management success in this is found in the existence of friendly links between supervisor and steward, for these are, *ipso facto*, evidence of subversion; success here led to compliant workers. A remark by a supervisor to the effect that 'a good shop-steward [who] knows the procedure . . . is my friend. He's an asset' (Nichols and Beynon 1977: 115), immediately takes on sinister overtones for the only reason he could be an asset would be his willingness and ability to persuade his members that management's policies were right. In fact most shop-stewards are presented as having been rendered ineffective in their proper role (which is seen as total opposition to management) because they had been enmeshed in a network of friendly personal relations with managers. Only a small minority, it is suggested, remained outside and, therefore, were capable of taking action that was not in accordance with management's wishes. The question asked, in effect, of every situation that appears to favour the company is 'How has management brought this about?', and the impression is conveyed that everything that happened in relation to 'the union' was in fact engineered by management in its own interests. This comes out very clearly in relation to the account given of the attitude of the men towards their union. When the men are said to be distrustful of their stewards this distrust is explained as having been fostered by management to make the men lukewarm towards the union. Yet it is said almost immediately that 'The value [to management] of Trade Unionism is its [apparent] independence from Capital' and management are said to take steps to encourage men to trust the union (Nichols and Beynon 1977: 128–9). Any objection by the reader that such contradictory aims might be difficult to achieve is

stifled by the bland assertion that it is 'the function of management
. . . to manage contradictions to prevent the system from running
out of control' (p. 130). Management is indeed omnipotent.

In presenting my own material relevant to the use of stewards to
'manufacture consent' I shall begin with data that supports the
idea of attempted management manipulation of stewards; I shall
argue, however, that in my opinion management was far from
being wholly successful in its ultimate aim of securing consent
through the shop-stewards. Undoubtedly there was a period in the
1970s when the works' management were prepared to go to great
lengths to be indulgent to stewards as individuals. Moreover,
senior management seem to have been prepared to support shop-
stewards, whatever the cost to the authority of supervisors.
Nevertheless, the results were not, I think, what management
intended.

I found that the ordinary operators believed that shop-stewards
had for a considerable period of time been especially favoured by
management. Many examples were recounted of what was seen as
management's absurd leniency in relation to stewards. They were
said to be allowed to make outrageous claims for expenses and for
overtime; their claims to be allowed to take night-shifts off
because of union business were said to have been invariably
granted; and it was said that managers showed a deplorable
readiness to promote the steward above his more worthy fellows.
Moreover, there was in effect a charge that the management were
generally sycophantic (in the full OED sense of being 'servile,
abject and cringing') in relation to leading union officers. The most
blatant examples of management indulgence of stewards and
union officers referred to their treatment when attending conferences. General union meetings attended by delegates from all
the company's sites were notorious in this respect, but other get-
togethers were as bad.

One operator told me that he had had his eyes opened as to
what went on when, some years previously, he had gone as a
'safety rep', not a steward, to an exhibition on safety that was
attended primarily by stewards and union officials. He had been
told by his manager that he might claim expenses for his food, and
specifically for lunch he might claim up to £1.60, which at the time
was generous. So, finding himself at the exhibition in the company
of his union chairman he suggested at about midday that they
should go to eat at one of the cafeterias in the hall. The chairman,

however, telling him not to be so stupid, collected all their works' delegates and, to my informant's consternation, bundled them into a taxi and took them to the most expensive local hotel where they had a magnificent meal at £7.50 a head. Later, when he presented his expense account, fearful that he would have to foot the bill himself, the only reaction he got as it was accepted was a laugh and the remark: 'Oh, I see you had lunch with X,' the union chairman.

On another occasion, when this same operator had attended a safety conference arranged by the company, he noted that although the accommodation and all meals were paid for, the delegates were still allowed to get away with presenting expense accounts for food they could not possibly have eaten. The stewards were simply working a fiddle. A steward, taking advantage of the fact that the company allowed sandwiches to be charged to his expense account, would ask a waiter not for sandwiches but for a bill for sandwiches; the waiter was then given half the amount and the steward later claimed the full amount from the company. My informant had seen an even more extreme example of the management's willingness to indulge union officials at the last safety conference he had attended. As before, he had stayed at a good hotel at the company's expense, along with other safety representatives, including the union chairman; this time, however, the works manager had stayed at the same hotel with them. At night, after this manager had gone to his room, my informant said that as he was going to get some crisps from the bar, he had asked if anyone else wanted some. The chairman again told him not to be so stupid and, turning to a waiter, ordered a large quantity of turkey sandwiches. These he put down to a room number that was that of the works manager. Next morning, when the bill was presented, the manager, not surprisingly, said he had no recollection of having given any such order. The union chairman then broke in to say that that must have been because he had been too drunk to remember anything, and the manager had simply laughed and accepted the account. Even this was not the end of the story so far as this safety representative was concerned. Travelling home he was taken aback when the chairman went into a shop to buy presents for his wife and daughter that he said confidently he would put down on his expense account. But what was totally astonishing was that a few moments later the chairman said, 'Oh, I've forgotten the dog' and turned into a sweet shop to buy chocolate drops that he said would also go on the same account.

When my informant remonstrated with him, the chairman simply said, 'My dog's very fond of me and pines when I leave her – I must go back with a present'!

Supervisors often blamed management for refusing to support them over matters of discipline because, it was said, management preferred not to confront the unions and the stewards. As an extreme case one supervisor told me how a friend of his, a supervisor on a different plant, had under him a man who was a dreadful absentee. It was said that in a whole year this man had not worked a single regular night-shift, because he always claimed to be sick when he should have done one, so that he worked at nights only at overtime rates on someone else's shift. I was told that the supervisor had gone through all the proper procedures and had then demanded that the man be dismissed; the management, however, had been so reluctant to antagonize the unions that the man was not even suspended. On another occasion, according to this same supervisor, he had himself caught a man sleeping on his night-shift, when the man was not simply dozing but had actually bedded himself down in an obscure corner. This supervisor had demanded that the man be dismissed but the manager had accepted the man's cock and bull excuses and had actually turned round afterwards and had told the supervisor not to be so high-handed. Here again the inference was drawn that the manager did not want to offend the unions. I am somewhat sceptical of this last illustration because I know that the supervisor concerned, not having good informal relations with his shift, was in part excusing himself for not being able to get better results from his men; in effect he was saying it was all the management's fault for not backing him. Undoubtedly, however, he had convinced himself of his stories and expected other people to believe them. This was scarcely surprising since similar stories of the management's preference for backing 'the union' rather than the supervisors were common amongst all the men. For example, everyone believed that management had failed to uphold a supervisor who had summarily dismissed a process operator who had come on to a night-shift 'so drunk he was legless'. It was agreed that management had, up to a point, tried to support the supervisor by initially confirming the dismissal, but when the union had supported the man before an industrial tribunal, on the grounds that having come into work on previous occasions slightly the worse for drink without any action having been taken against him, he had grounds for thinking that management condoned his drunkenness, management had given way and agreed to allow him to come back.

Supervisors were certainly generally convinced that management was much less concerned to keep in with them than to earn the goodwill of the stewards. For example, a Plant Y supervisor, thinking to help the training of his new operators, designed a longish set of simple questions that he put to those men nearing the end of their training. He knew that it occasioned them a little anxiety but thought that when they actually came to the test most men gained real self-confidence by discovering to their own surprise how much they really knew about their work. However, one man who became a steward in the course of his training, when he was due to take this test complained to the works manager, and he, fearful of union trouble it was said, called the supervisor in and forbade him to give the test even to those men who would have liked to have taken it.

Another case was regarded as very revealing. I was told independently by two very reliable informants that it had been a long-standing company custom to invite men with twenty years' service to a celebratory dinner. Each came with his wife, and as his guests he brought his plant manager and his wife. It was clearly a rite of aggregation into the works' establishment. On the occasion in question, however, a Plant X supervisor who had been called in to the works manager's office to receive his invitation remarked that he would enjoy the dinner much more if, instead of having to have his plant manager as his guest, he might be allowed to invite another employee, a close friend, and his wife. To his consternation the answer was that it was an excellent idea, and instead of his plant manager his shop-steward should be invited. The supervisor's protests were roughly brushed aside – it was decided; every one with twenty years' service should come bringing his shop-steward, and invitations were issued accordingly. Matters apparently came to a head when the supervisor's wife met his shop-steward's wife in the supermarket and she boasted that from now on she and her husband would be going to the dinner every year, but that the supervisor's wife would go only once. The fat was in fire! The supervisor told the works manager that rather than take his shop-steward he would decline the invitation, and that others amongst the twenty-year invitees felt the same way. The works manager is said to have been furious and to have warned the supervisor that he would never get further promotion. Ultimately the situation was saved only when the shop-steward at the centre of the quarrel persuaded the other stewards that it would be a mistake for them to rouse so much resentment, and as a group they wrote declining their invitations.

Clearly, the management in general and the works manager in particular were, in the 1970s, trying to win over the union stewards and officials. In part it may just have been that in this the company was bowing to new legislation that increased union power. A supervisor told me that when he complained to the then works manager about a particular steward, he was told sharply, 'Don't you understand? They rule now.' Nevertheless it would certainly seem, simply on the basis of the examples I have just given, that there was more in it than merely a bowing to a formal change in the power structure. Certainly it is probable that some individual managers may have hoped to retain freedom of movement in the new situation by, in effect, buying over the union officers and stewards – 'corrupting' them would not be too strong in some cases. Ian, the electrician (see pp. 113–14), was justifiably suspicious when he found that, as a shop-steward, he was not only being invited out to dinner on Saturday nights, to 'discuss union business' with management, but was also invited to charge for his time at overtime rates. It seemed more sinister that he believed that he had been marked out as a trouble-maker when he refused to attend. But this was not, necessarily, the most important aspect of what management hoped to achieve.

Looking at all the evidence about management's attempts to deal with the unions in the 1970s, there is a clear case for saying that in the changed economic, legal, and social situation of that decade, a way was being sought that would enable a manager in the future to work not simply through the formally established channels of the official hierarchy, but rather through a man who would have genuine authority because he had been chosen by the operators themselves to represent them. Management seems to have felt that there was such a person, or, at least, that there was potentially such a person, in the shop-steward. The existence of such a belief amongst senior managers, while it helps to explain a great deal of what went on, does not mean that 'management' was necessarily successful in achieving its aims. If we accept, for the sake of argument, that managers were here engaged in seeking to 'manufacture consent' it does not follow that their strategies or their tactics really achieved that end. If they do not we are still left with the task of discovering on what consent, to the extent that it does exist, is based.

It would be wrong to suggest that only machiavellian motives activated managers in this situation; there seems to have been the idea that it would be morally preferable to work through shop-stewards, if this were possible. It was, of course, recognized that the relationship with the steward would have to be very different from the one that had existed between management and supervisor; it would have to be much more 'democratic' but this is what gave the idea its moral value. To be successful a manager would have to go out of his way to explain his actions, and to reason things out. It would obviously be difficult but if the manager could build up a good relationship with the steward it would be morally better than anything that had existed previously. Most managers fully accepted the general assumption that 'democracy' means governing with the consent of the governed and that this can be assured by a system of electing a 'representative'. However, with this word expediency reappears, for representatives are empowered to take decisions on behalf of their members, whilst delegates cannot do so. It was not by chance that on a number of occasions I heard plant managers say, in response to criticism by men of their shop-steward, 'He is your democratically elected *representative*.' This was an idea they were anxious to get over.

In the 1970s, when these changes were taking place, it seems to have been hoped that management might enter a new era of a really co-operative relationship with the men. Certainly at this period the policy of management was to try to change its relationship with the unions from one characterized by hostility or indifference to one based on consultation. As a matter of conscious policy, and not simply because of the new constraints of union power, union officials and stewards were allowed to take over many matters relating to discipline, and to become active in other spheres of decision-making at the plant level. Older supervisors say of this time that 'management gave up managing'. Some younger supervisors thought differently. Nichols and Beynon (1977), as we saw, think it inherently suspicious that a supervisor should refer to a good steward as his 'friend', but James, the most consciously left-wing of the supervisors I knew, saw the change as genuinely for the good. He spoke gleefully of the astonishment he had caused when he had attended a short course for junior managers from various local companies and had made it clear that he did not see the steward as someone essentially antagonistic to a firm's best interests. Apparently the wonder of his fellow students grew when he went on to say that he saw the steward as one who, in so far as he articulated the wishes of his men, played a role that any sensible manager should value. To James, and to the managers from whom he had acquired these views, such a recognition of the steward's role was not a Machiavellian plot but a step on the road to greater 'democracy' in the work-place. They did not imagine that it would lead to the workers' control of ammonia production, but they did see it as enlarging the area within which men could make decisions.

Here we have, therefore, a policy instituted by senior management with a mixture of motives but undoubtedly aimed at 'manufacturing consent'. I think, however, that the policy was bound to fail, and that in so far as consent existed it was due largely to the unintended consequences of other factors which were not understood. We shall return to this argument. For the moment I am simply arguing that the management, in so far as they were attempting to rule through the stewards, were trying, probably without realizing it, to apply the British colonial pattern of 'indirect rule' to an industrial situation, and I think the attempt failed for the very reason that indirect rule failed in Africa. Certainly it seemed that many of the problems that beset the chief under indirect rule beset the steward also, and were bound to do so.

The British in Nigeria had attempted to work through the 'native authorities', rather than directly through their own district officers. The idea of ruling through local chiefs appealed to the British authorities both because it cut the costs of administration, and because idealists saw it as morally preferable to a total reliance on a bureaucratic power structure that was quite alien to the people. Under indirect rule the civil service hierarchy stopped at the level of junior district officers. Below this the administration depended on the ability of these men to negotiate with the so-called 'natural rulers'. These chiefs were paid small salaries, but the fundamental idea was that they should really depend for their position on the genuine authority that must, it was thought, come to them just because they were indigenous, the 'natural' rulers. It was assumed that they were best fitted to represent their people to the colonial authorities, and in turn would be best able to persuade their people to follow the 'progressive' paths mapped out for their future. This was the theory. In practice government support often proved incompatible with the chiefs maintaining, or developing, good relationships with the people whom they were supposed to represent. In talking to them, therefore, the administration might be just as cut off from contact with popular opinion as were the French colonial authorities who simply appointed compliant local people as very junior civil servants. It is instructive to consider some of the reactions of the governed to indirect rule.

Far from being happy with these chiefs, the Nigerians often regarded them with considerable resentment: they were accused of being dictatorial, and of embezzling public funds. The antagonism was such that in some areas they were regularly accused of witchcraft; this occurred where there was no tradition of chiefship. There the idea that a leader might objectively consider the claims of a group other than his own small circle of kin was not accepted; yet a chief, expected to represent a wider area, had to do this. Moreover, the people were simply not used to the idea that they had any duty to comply with agreements such a 'chief' might make. So, out of resentment, they attacked his legitimacy, by making accusations of witchcraft that turned him into a moral outcast. In less extreme cases resentment was bred by the 'perks' given to chiefs, who often in consequence threw their weight around. This destroyed a chief's moral influence. Thus it was that those British administrators who believed that to consult the chiefs was better than to adopt the French system deluded themselves, for even those chiefs who were originally esteemed lost touch with their followers.

I would argue that Riverside management fell into the two main traps that had ensnared the colonial authorities in their attempts to develop the system of indirect rule. In the first place, it seems that relatively little attention was paid to the question of whether there really existed the basis of regarding the shop-steward as the 'legitimate' representative of his members. If he were going to have to convince others that they were bound by agreements he might make on their behalf a very special kind of authority was needed; arguably Riverside, like certain tribes, provided no foundation for such authority. The second error, it seemed to me, in management strategy was that in practice it tended to undermine any authority the steward might have.

Crucial to the success of this management strategy was the

development of a thoroughly accepted 'democratic' system in which a steward would be acknowledged by the men electing him to have such legitimacy that they would accept his authority; on this basis he would be able to represent them to management and would also be able to get them to accept any agreement he might make with management on their behalf. The strategy demanded, as we have seen, that the steward be accepted by the men as a representative, one able to take decisions without continually referring back to his constituents. But such a position assumes the presence of a number of factors that were, in fact, absent. It has been remarked (Jay 1967: 87) that there are two kinds of democracy: there is 'technical democracy, the democracy of the ballot box, sometimes called psephocracy', and there is democracy in a 'popular' sense that is something else 'a way of doing things, which consults people in advance and takes account of their views and wishes and ideas before making final decisions'.

The success of the management scheme depended, of course, in the first place on the constituents' willingness to recognize as valid the idea that they should vote for someone whose authority they ought afterwards to accept. But such validity depended on the steward acting 'democratically'; to be successful in influencing his men, he had to inspire trust that he was at least trying to act in the spirit of the popular sense of 'democracy'. I would argue that the very fact that management was determined to regard them as 'representatives', who by definition could commit their members to actions without seeking their consent, made it inherently unlikely that the stewards would behave democratically in the popular sense; therefore, they could not easily influence opinions. Consequently management began by hoping for more from the stewards than they could possibly deliver. Further, every step management took to win over the trust and friendship of the stewards by treating them generously was inherently likely to undermine the crucially necessary trust felt for a steward personally. And finally, other factors, added to suspicion about the generosity with which management treated them, could result in the erosion of the stewards' basic position by casting doubt on the legitimacy of their elections.

If management strategy was to establish good relationships with 'the men's representatives', who should then persuade their members to accept management policy, it was bound to fail for management's generosity to the stewards called up 'ani' against them. 'Ani', it will be remembered, is short for that animosity felt for anyone who is believed to be getting an unfair advantage; and 'unfair' may be simply defined on some occasions as 'anything I have not got' or as 'something that reduces the differential I enjoy'. Once this is recognized it can be seen that there were many occasions for wrath to be aroused against union officials, simply because they were believed to be especially favoured by management.

Of course, the more blatant examples of management indulgence of stewards caused particular resentment, but this was not the only thing that aroused indignation. True the operator who told me about events at the safety conferences he had attended was particularly indignant, not because he wanted the perks for himself but because he really disapproved of the behaviour he had witnessed. After he had finished talking to me I heard him muttering to himself: 'Chocky drops for the dog; chocky drops for the dog'! More generally, however, there seemed to be bitter resentment that stewards, especially the more influential ones, could claim overtime from the company for periods they spent on their rest days and even their ESOs, working (or, as the men thought, perhaps not working) in the union office. It was alleged that management never checked up on them to see whether they were there or not. A steward in a good position, I was told, could claim 'twenty hours' bloody overtime a week', and yet hardly ever put in an appearance working a shift on his own plant.

The animosity felt for stewards generally because of their perks was directed with particular intensity at the leading stewards who were said to form a tight little ring of twelve men enjoying spectacular advantages. These stewards were alleged not merely to have enjoyed an above-average share of perks but also to have exercised unjustified power (it was a circle that might properly be referred to as the 'quasi-elite'[1]). It was said that whenever any issue arose they formed a sub-committee which met officially to consider the matter; and if they had to meet management representatives at such a meeting they would get together privately first for an official 'pre-meeting' before the main one. For every such meeting they were allowed time off, and for any meeting on a day on which their shift was subsequently due to work a night-shift they were allowed to take the complete shift off. It was alleged that they spread their meetings out so carefully that some of them never had to work night-shifts.

It was indicative of the dissatisfaction that all this caused, that any management action seen as being taken against the stewards personally was treated by the operators as a cause for celebration. For example, although the men regretted that a recent management economy measure had led to a significant cut-back in the works' own transport system that, until a short time previously, had supplemented the inadequate public transport available, they were nevertheless delighted that this economy had at least had one good result – it had led to the elimination of the stewards' 'site-transport sub-committee' and, therefore, to the elimination of one excuse the leading stewards had had for not working their shifts.

In these circumstances it is scarcely surprising that it had been impossible to create an acceptable 'democratic' structure in the works within which, by operating in conjunction with the stewards, management could persuade men to its way of thinking. Far from accepting the 'representative' nature of the stewards' role, the men expressed considerable resentment when stewards did take action without consulting them. The company did little to improve its image with the men by being 'nice' to the stewards, for this was seen simply as the result of a weak management trying to curry favour with the newly powerful unions. If the ultimate objective was that the stewards should be able to persuade the men of the wisdom of management policy, the strategy failed because it destroyed the basis of any authority the steward might have had.

A chance incident convinced me that men were very quick to regard independent decisions taken by the stewards as high-handed, and resented them deeply. I had wanted to attend an important meeting between a plant manager and senior operators. The manager said he had no objections to my going if the others would agree. I asked several senior operators personally and they were all quite happy that I should attend; nevertheless, to be on the safe side, I felt it necessary to make sure that the steward would also agree. As I could not find him, I asked a supervisor who got on well with him, to ring him at home to ask his permission. The answer was a flat 'No', for reasons I was never able to discover (the steward had not previously objected to my attending other meetings). I thought it wise not to make an issue of the matter, since it had been made clear to me that all my research depended on the agreement of the stewards; I, therefore, did nothing further about it. After the meeting however, I was asked by the others why I had been absent and when I said the steward had forbidden it there was an angry reaction. Why, it was demanded, should the steward have the power to impose his will without reference to what the others wanted? The plant manager, to whom the question was addressed, replied with the stock management defence of stewards in such circumstances, saying 'He is your representative, and therefore he doesn't have to ask anyone before he makes a decision.' I joined in, trying to pour oil on what I saw were troubled waters by saying, as was true, that the steward had been asked rather bluntly, out of the blue, and had not been told what anyone else might have thought. I was taken aback when I instantly became the target of the men's anger: I was just one of those who defended the steward whatever he did – it was inexcusable of me. Only when the manager left did the men relax, grin because they had been half teasing me, and begin to tell me why they felt so annoyed, recounting a string of objections they had to the behaviour of stewards.

Moreover, and this is relevant to Burawoy's (1979) arguments, criticism directed at stewards caused resentment against management. Significantly it was the plant manager at whom the question about the steward was directed, for to a considerable extent the men blamed the management for the shortcomings they saw in the stewards. Despite any changes in legislation regarding industrial relations, the problems regarding the unions in general and the stewards in particular were blamed by the men on the fact that, in their view, the management had voluntarily given up managing. The men did not see management as having set out to corrupt the stewards but, rather, as having, like Frankenstein, created a monster they could not control, but could only placate.

The men blamed management for changes in the rules regarding the selection of their 'safety representatives'. Formerly the men had been free to choose any of their number (and we have met one such operator who had never been a steward). Recently, however, they had been told that their shop-stewards would henceforth take on this role. The men believed that this was because the stewards had pressed for the change because they wanted the associated advantages. Protests had been made to management but, as usual, they had been told that the stewards were their proper representatives. The operators I spoke to on both Plant X and Plant Y were particularly indignant because, they said, it was inevitable that as stewards spent less time on their plants than other operators, they would have less genuine interest in safety and would know less about it than other men.

The men also resented what they saw as management's willingness to promote an influential shop-steward from operator to senior operator for no better reason than the desire to pander to someone powerful in the union. I was told that normally men would be promoted to the position of senior operator only on the recommendation of a plant's supervisors, and that a plant manager would disregard their advice only in the most exceptional circumstances. However, I was told, one shop-steward had been promoted even though none of the supervisors had supported the idea. What further proof was needed that management unfairly favoured the stewards? I was asked to reflect on the enormity of such a promotion when considered from the safety angle. Such a man was no better, basically, than an ordinary operator; indeed, in practice, he was probably less skilled because his time might normally be more taken up with union business than with looking after the plant. Yet because of such political promotion, he might be found in charge of the whole plant at night, and in an emergency. At such a time disaster might be a hairsbreadth away.

It is relevant to the argument that will be developed about the relative influence of steward and supervisor, that it seemed that where a steward lacked power he totally lacked the ability to get men to do as he wanted. For example, sometime previously there had been a short strike in one of the bagging plants in the works (a plant where a strike was not something inherently dangerous). The union chairman and the senior stewards had been against the strike, but the men on the plant concerned had been adamant and had asked other plants for support. No other plant had come out in sympathy, but as a token gesture the union had asked for an overtime ban. I was told that on Plant X, despite the steward's opposition, the manager there had easily persuaded the men to work overtime. He had 'talked to the lads', telling them that it would be such a disaster if anyone did 'throw the switch' on it that to avoid that possibility he had decided that they should start shutting the plant down in an orderly way. Moreover, as this would mean a great deal of work if it were to be done swiftly, he offered overtime to the outgoing shift if they would stay to help the incoming shift with their work. To a man they accepted the offer and stayed on. The most remarkable thing about this story was that there was no condemnation of the shift for agreeing to work overtime when their steward was calling for a ban on it. Indeed, it was taken so much for granted that no comment at all was made on the men's action. On the contrary, what was stressed to me was that it was mean behaviour on the part of the plant manager. The steward had promised him that, whatever happened, the men would not just walk out. He should have accepted the steward's word that there would be no lightning strike and not have asked for the plant to be shut down. It was therefore assumed that he offered the men overtime deliberately, in order to shame the steward in the eyes of his fellow stewards by exposing the lack of support he could command on his own plant. I was told that the steward himself was bitter, not against his members because he had known what to expect from them, but against his manager whom he held to be entirely responsible.

For our present discussion, what is significant is that given evidence like this there seems to have been no basis for management's expectations relating to the stewards. If this was the extent of the steward's influence, how could management rely on a steward's authority to get the men to accept company policy, even supposing the stewards wished to do this? I heard a steward try, with real conviction, to persuade some of his men that the five-shift system the company was proposing was desirable. He said there was a lot to argue about but that in some form it would come and it would be a good thing. It would, he said, be to everyone's advantage, for the company would, even if there were no pay rise, be giving the same money for a week of thirty-seven-and-a-half hours as they were currently giving for a forty-hour week. The only response he got, however, were complaints that the new system would entail a considerable loss of overtime and, therefore, a fall in living standards. Angrily he retorted that the works was one of the very few sites in the company still working overtime at all, and that not all the plants even in this works could get overtime. They must, he said, get out of the habit of expecting a standard of living that came from working a sixty-hour week! The argument went on for some minutes without the steward's points making any impression on his listeners. As they said afterwards, as he was getting twenty hours' easy overtime himself, what right had he to tell them they should not want it?

Against the argument that the steward was their 'democratically elected representative', and that they therefore ought to support him, the men had a simple answer if anyone wanted to hear it, the assertion if they disliked the steward, that his election had somehow been rigged. The men did not assert that all stewards were elected on crooked ballots, but it sometimes happened. The operators admitted that it was often difficult to find anyone willing to stand for election. What they argued was that perks grew with the influence that came to a steward through seniority, and that once a steward had achieved a position in which he began to get real benefits from his position, he would strive by all means, fair or foul, to get himself returned. He might seek to get in 'unopposed' by hiding from his members the true date of an election; if they asked he might say only: 'You'll know soon enough,' until the date had passed and it was too late for anyone else to stand. If things looked really dangerous for him, however, then a steward might arrange a rigged vote. In one case, I was told, when a steward thought he was likely to be defeated he arranged for the ballot box to be opened in the union office when there was no witness except for his pal, the chairman. In this case, it was said, the official story was that there had been nine votes for the sitting steward, nine for his opponent, and two spoiled votes, so the chairman had properly given his casting vote for the sitting man. There were other views, of course, on what had really happened in this case. A supervisor said that he thought the really official, and in his opinion correct, story was that the vote against the sitting steward had been split so that although there had indeed been a strong vote against him, it had been useless; the sitting steward had indeed scraped back by two votes. The first story, about the chairman's casting vote, was given more credence, with the difference that it was widely assumed that the count had been incorrect and unfair and that the chairman had improperly supported the re-election of his friend. If such stories as these are believed then clearly the men, as a group, feel no obligation towards their steward consistent with that which management presume they ought to feel.

It can also be argued that it is inherent in the structural situation of the plants that any steward was likely to find it almost impossible to do anything, no matter how disinterested his motives, that would not lead him to incur the resentment of some of his men. Process operators were divided into shifts and subdivided by grades. As the result of chance circumstances, these subgroups might develop mutually conflicting interests. Their shop-steward, if he took action on behalf of one subgroup inevitably found that he incurred the wrath of another. Indeed, I talked to one operator who had resigned from being a steward over precisely such an issue. His first act had been to succeed in raising the grade of his own group, and this had made him popular; but then, with crusading fervour, he had gone on to give similar help to another group, and this had resulted in the cutting of the differentials his own set had previously enjoyed. The consequence was that he encountered the bitter opposition of his closest mates.

At this stage it is important to our general argument to consider whether, and if so to what extent, management may be held to have willed the difficulties and the anomalies of the situation in which the stewards found themselves. Is management naive or machiavellian in apparently assuming that stewards represent their members, yet, by its actions, nevertheless helping to make this representation impossible? Nichols and Beynon (1977) certainly, and Burawoy (1979) possibly, would argue the machiavellian case. I argue a different case. Obviously it was intended to influence stewards, that is unquestionable, but how far can it be said that all the consequences of managerial actions were desired by senior managers? It would be particularly unconvincing to argue, as Nichols and Beynon do, that the unions were without real power *and* to go on from there to suggest that management deliberately worked behind the scenes to destroy the influence of the shop-steward that, overtly, they seemed so intent on building up. If it is acknowledged that the unions have actual power, it would be possible, in principle, to argue that it might be in management's interest to win over the union representative and at the same time make an effort to undermine his influence with his members. But success in such an enterprise would presuppose a very extensive insight into all those complexities of the steward's situation that have just been discussed; and of that I found no evidence.

I find it both simpler and more convincing to believe that management actions were not devilishly cunning but the result of men acting from mixed motives in complex situations and producing results that, often enough, were not what they had expected. As an example of this kind of situation, let me turn to the case of a plant manager who supported the promotion of a shop-steward to senior operator against the wishes of his plant supervisors, and the other operators. In this case I feel I know enough to be sure that the manager did not believe that he was promoting a steward who could easily be made to do management's bidding or that he was seeking to make the steward unpopular. On the contrary, I think the manager believed himself to be promoting a tough man, but a man of real potential who was the object of unfair prejudice on the part of the supervisors. It was not, after all, unreasonable for the plant manager to assume that supervisors might be unfairly prejudiced against a man who was a shop-steward, because in practice they often were. Consider the occasions for tensions to arise between steward and supervisor. Obviously supervisors must tend to be jealous of the privileges of a steward, especially an influential one. But such a steward would have to be outstandingly perceptive and well balanced if he were to cope with the change of roles he must experience between his union office and his shop floor position. In the one role even senior managers listen deferentially to his views; in the other role his supervisor, the lowest of the low on the managerial scale, might in a crisis, bark an order at him, expecting immediate obedience and scolding him should he be inept for lack of practice at his official job. It is a situation that might have been designed by someone with a malicious sense of humour, but was inevitable once stewards were given representative status. However, in such a situation it was scarcely likely that a steward should be the object of his supervisors' unbiased opinions. In these circumstances, and given that the manager thought the steward worthy of promotion, the case seemed to him to be clearly one of those rare exceptions when it was justifiable to flout the supervisors' opinions. But the consequence was that a manager, from motives that so far as I could judge were quite proper, did something that to others on the plant seemed to be a clear case of management toadying to union power, and caused a great deal of resentment against the steward.

NOTE

1. See Batstone, Boraston, and Frenkel (1978: 7): '[The] steward network focused upon the conveners and a key group of leader stewards – the quasi-elite (QE) – who acted as an informal cabinet to the conveners.'

7
The sophisticated eye

In this chapter I want to look again at an earlier suggestion I made as to why Plant X seemed more ready to co-operate with management than did Plant Y; but this time I want to consider that idea in the light both of the data that have since been discussed, and of the arguments of Nichols and Beynon (1977) on the one hand, and Burawoy (1979) on the other. I want, that is, to take up and examine further the suggestion that a major factor in Plant X was that of the formal influence of the supervisors and that this influence was something that had arisen out of a variety of contingent factors and not as the result of some management plan.

To my suggestion there are a number of objections. First, my own data on Plant X make it clear that the supervisors could have had no easy task in influencing opinion informally since it is obvious that the workers there did not constitute one big, happy family in which the views of authority would find automatic, or even ready, acceptance. There were many tensions between the different groups of operators, with the consequence that what pleased one set was not necessarily pleasing to another. Moreover, we have seen that between the supervisors and the senior operators there were considerable tensions, resulting from their obviously conflicting interests over pay and working conditions – and since senior operators were identified with the men in a way that the supervisors were not, this cannot have helped the supervisors' general position. Second, there is the objection, implicit in the argument in *Living with Capitalism* (Nichols and Beynon 1977), and fitting in well with the problems just outlined relating to my own material: Nichols and Beynon are thought to have made a major improvement to the 'Bravermanian' Marxist position because they give evidence for the existence of class warfare by 'proletarians' acting outside any union structure (Elger 1982). At Riverside this warfare apparently shows itself particularly in hostility between supervisors and men, and for its existence specific evidence is given. Third, there is the objection that may be called the Burawoyan Marxist position. Given Burawoy's (1979) arguments, it follows that even if there should be a reasonable case for arguing that despite what Nichols and Beynon say, supervisors did exercise considerable influence on Plant X, it still remains to show that this was the result of contingent circumstances and had not been brought about as the result of senior management strategy; and this will have to be argued even if it could be shown that the supervisors themselves were not conscious of being manipulated. Since the evidence for class warfare between supervisors and men that Nichols and Beynon present is central to any discussion about the supervisors' influence (for if their men feel little but hostility for them it is scarcely worth considering how far supervisors may be tools of some senior management strategy) we shall look at this data first, and then go on to consider the material in the light of Burawoy's arguments on the ways by which management gains 'consent'.

One point, however, must first be clarified: what are we are to understand by 'acceptance' or 'rejection' of 'managerial authority'? Gallie (1978) was referring to the explicit acceptance or rejection by men of 'management's right to manage' in the abstract. Nichols and Beynon (1977), in their account of Riverside, concentrating on the search for evidence of the existence of 'class warfare', found it in cases in which men were explicitly, or constructively, disobedient to managerial wishes, so their criterion must be obedience. Burawoy (1979) sees 'consent' in any action of the men that results in the raising of productivity, even when this is not their intention. I agree with Burawoy but for his last clause; for me the best evidence of 'consent' is effective dedication to the job.

In much of the preceding account, however, I have presented the case for saying not only that many men were apparently concerned to do a good job but that the operators effectively accepted the authority of management in a very obvious way, in that they appeared to obey very readily instructions given them about their work; moreover this was so even when strict enforcement of an instruction would not have been easy. This is where my findings seem to conflict markedly with those of *Living with Capitalism*, for Nichols and Beynon specifically make the case for saying that the men they studied at Riverside rejected the authority of management in general, and of the supervisors in particular. If I am to question their interpretation of their evidence it is obvious that I must set out their evidence in some detail.

Nichols and Beynon's case is that the unions obediently co-operated with management, and sought to encourage the men to do so, because the union officials had been in one way or another rendered unwilling to fight the bosses, but that the individual men set out to subvert management's plans. Nichols and Beynon are not here discussing, as I have done, resistance to, say, accepting a drop in overtime for they do not mention this subject. Rather they talk in general terms of the 'anti-work' and 'anti-management' behaviour of employees acting 'spontaneously' and outside the union structure, and their behaviour is set in sharp contrast to the spineless behaviour of the majority of union officials and stewards. The evidence given for such attitudes of hostility to capitalist authority relates to instances, described as acts of 'sabotage', personal acts of hostility against superiors and collective acts against the right of management to take decisions, and these collective acts are seen as most significant for a revolutionary future.

Nichols and Beynon (1977) seem to imply that management authority was rejected *in toto* by the men they studied. In their most general summary of workers attitudes to management they say:

'At Riverside the men we talked to on the plants were working for ChemCo in name only. They didn't believe in the company in any real sense . . . At work they resisted. They did what they had to do but no more. They were industrial spoilers. And in this respect we found there to be no substantial differences between the men on the band end (in the packing sheds) and those in the control rooms (i.e. the process operators). The actual content of the work obviously made *some* difference. It affects what you have to do and how you can get by.'

(Nichols and Beynon 1977: 166)

It is said that the operators felt they had better jobs, and some felt more important jobs than those of the packers, but Nichols and Beynon said they found no evidence that the operators saw themselves as being in a different category from the ordinary labourers when it came to considering their relationships with their employer. They were equally hostile. This hostility was not primarily expressed through the trade unions for obvious reasons, because the union organization had become so linked with the structure of capitalism. Nevertheless there was still a struggle against management but it was being carried on at an informal level, in confrontations between individual workers and the management (Nichols and Beynon 1977: 139).

Discussing this informal conflict in a chapter actually called 'The Workers' Struggle', the main focus of the authors' attention is on the men in the packing sheds, but it is said explicitly that their behaviour differs in degree only from the operators. The operators too had their games with the foreman.

'Anonymous notes are written in the log books, the foreman's boots are filled with water – "just to cool him down" and any additional work is resisted . . . The monitoring, the "responsibility" – all the pressures toward "integration" and "self-discipline" – cannot prevent control room operators coming into conflict with management; and their conflicts contain all the elements of antagonism that the packers experience.'

(Nichols and Beynon 1977: 138–9)

Citing particular instances in which antagonism was generated, the case is mentioned of the manager who could not resist coming into the control room and 'altering the bloody running of the plants, the flow of the compression – if it dropped he was altering the bloody flow' when he should not have 'fiddled about down here'. Even worse was the new manager, inexperienced with the running of machinery, who kept issuing potentially disastrous orders telling the men to run them flat out to increase production. In the end one man, fed up with having to disobey orders to prevent breakdowns, did exactly as he was told, with the result that 'a couple of hundred tons' of fertilizer were spilled and wasted. In an extreme case a cocky young manager made it so clear that he thought his men were idiots that the resulting 'accidental' loss of production became obvious and he was removed from the plant; in effect the men 'got rid of him'. This is seen as a rare situation in that he so upset the normally calm surface of industrial relations (resulting from the managerial strategy of tact that in effect limited extreme behaviour) that the underlying resistance and hostility of workers clearly emerged (Nichols and Beynon 1977: 138–40).

Nichols and Beynon (1977) do not seek to exaggerate the significance of this behaviour, which they call 'covert anti-work activity'. They say regretfully that such individual acts represent 'only a *muffled* challenge to capital . . . it doesn't penetrate too deeply into the structure of corporate power' (p. 141); indeed, if it were to have more than a limited effectiveness it would have to be co-ordinated and organized. It did not threaten, they thought, the overall control of management, 'but it represented, nevertheless, an important ideological "distancing" from the hegemonic embrace of capital' (p. 166). As such it indicates a potential class-based antagonism to management as the representatives of capital.

Any such behaviour that came to the notice of the works manager, although he might describe it in somewhat different terms from those used by Nichols and Beynon, might strengthen in his mind also the assumption that there existed a fundamental dichotomy within the works, with the managers on the one side, and the workers on the other, with the latter being generally hostile to management. Against this kind of evidence, it might seem that it must be foolish to talk about the widespread existence of 'goodwill'. Here, any works manager might argue, was the relatively objective evidence of sociologists that the workers were inherently hostile to management, and that it was not just managerial prejudice that might lead him to think so.

Here I would go back to what I said earlier, and argue that a very significant factor in all this is the model of authority in industrial relations that is implicitly being used. If it is the simple power-structure model described earlier, then anything less than prompt compliance with the wishes of those senior in the hierarchy must be evidence of some deeply hostile resistance to the whole concept of managerial authority. Any deviations such as those just discussed must constitute behaviour that is 'anti-management'. There is, however, another possible interpretation of such behaviour. This model is essentially transactional, and argues that the *normal* conditions for exacting obedience to instructions are different; they depend on negotiations between the people concerned. As a normal part of the relations of production, and not just to prevent antagonistic behaviour, those possessing formal authority enter into complex exchanges with those below them, and since the latter are not really powerless, these transactions are not one-sided affairs, even if they are not evenly balanced. Once the idea is accepted that authority has to be transacted then it becomes imperative, in the case of any apparent disobedience to authority, to ask about the context in which it occurred. It can be accepted that the particular wishes of a particular superior may be flouted because he is held somehow to have been at fault and deserving of punishment; there is no necessity to assume that the whole basis of his authority is being rejected. That this latter model is the better one in terms of which to understand the situation at Riverside can be seen if we cease to focus exclusively on instances of obstructon of managerial authority but, instead, take a rather wider view of management/worker relationships, and consider all the evidence I have given about the extent to which there is willing co-operation with management in the functional requirements of production. Opportunities for serious sabotage abound and are very seldom taken; those supposed to impose discipline often have very little ability to compel prompt compliance and yet men carry out their wishes; men, on their own initiative, and without being thanked for it, try to improve productivity. This does not look like the wholesale rejection of management authority, and it is against this background that it would seem reasonable that anyone considering cases of a lack of co-operation at the works should at least ask whether men are trying to achieve something other than the downfall of management.

It makes sense to Nichols and Beynon (1977) to write of the existence of 'class warfare' at Riverside because they focus only on negative acts, but even on this basis their evidence is weak; there are many reasons for opposition to authority, and total hostility is not necessarily implied. They say that some foremen were harassed and deceived by their operators but this tells us little because we know nothing about the context of such action. The importance of context was shown by the case I gave of the supervisor who was tricked into signing a form that allowed three men to 'work their ESOs' against the practice agreed for Plant X.

These men clearly set out to punish this supervisor for being, as they thought, unfair to his own senior operator; it was, however, significant that their behaviour shocked James just because he knew he could trust them never to behave like that with him. This is scarcely evidence of any general antagonism to authority. For Nichols and Beynon to tell us that a new manager, by his arrogant and ignorant directions about the running of the plant, so angered one of his workers that he obeyed his instructions literally and caused a minor disaster is no evidence of hostility to all management; the mysterious events that led, they say, to the transfer of a young manager might well have been a much-needed lesson to a 'whiz kid', not the forerunner of revolt in any general sense. Arguably, the operators did the company a favour.

Here, however, surely we have a phrase on which Burawoy (1979) would pounce and argue that while my evidence may contradict Nichols and Beynon, the effect, if it is accepted, is only to provide a nice case that tends to support his position. Burawoy, I think, would argue that indeed the workers were doing the management a favour, and that somehow, if only I had been theoretically sufficiently sophisticated, I would have seen that they were being manipulated by management. If it is to be argued that there was negotiation between supervisors and operators in the sense I have described, and this negotiation had the effect of creating the climate of consent in which men worked relatively happily at the tasks management had set them then, from Burawoy's standpoint, it may be assumed that senior management knew what was going on and had created this situation. I will seek to counter such a suggestion by saying that Burawoy's argument must fail because the kinds of relationships between supervisors and operators were highly complex, so that it would be inherently unlikely that senior management really appreciated fully the subtleties of the situation. Moreover I can show that supervisors often felt hostile to senior management and most certainly did not set out to use any informal influence they might have possessed to manipulate their men for the sake of pleasing senior management. But again, Burawoy would almost certainly return confidently to the attack, asserting that his theory does not demand that low level management, such as foremen and even plant managers, should consciously wish to co-operate with senior management; all that is necessary is that they shall be committed, for whatever conscious reason, to the productivity of their plant. If they are so committed, Burawoy seems to say, then the assumption must be that this situation has been produced by senior management because, in the last resort, it is in capital's interests that such commitments shall exist. We will concern ourselves later with the logic of this argument. For the moment I wish to set out the evidence on the subject in order that we may see, in the particular case of Riverside, just what has to be assumed if we are to accept Burawoy's position here.

To recap, my argument is that an important factor making Plant X a notably co-operative plant from management's viewpoint was the extent to which supervisors had informal contacts with operators. Such contacts enabled supervisors to motivate their shifts so that their time-keeping was better than on Plant Y, and their sickness rates, and therefore certain overtime rates, were lower. Moreover, if the plant manager could persuade his supervisors that changes in working practice had to be made, even if they were disagreeable, then it seemed that the supervisors had a fair chance of bringing the men round to agreeing to alter their practice. I am not, of course, suggesting that there was no actual or potential hostility between operators and supervisors on Plant X; indeed, I have shown how easily a supervisor who might try to exercise his authority by flaunting his formal 'right' could land in trouble. I am suggesting that there was scope for a supervisor to act through informal channels and that through such means a supervisor could get a reasonable response, as James found when he sought to make it 'illegal' on Plant X for any operator to work a 'doubler' on the morning shift.

To recap further, I have argued that the Plant X supervisors were not motivated by any particular desire to stand well in the eyes of senior management, but that they were deeply committed to their plants, in complex ways. I have made it quite clear that supervisors saw their own careers as being essentially bound up with the continuation of their plants, and therefore with their profitability, but that the evidence was clear that there was more to their concern than sheer economic self-interest – their very perception of themselves and their self-respect seemed to be linked to their ability to prove their technical competence in the eyes of their peers, the other supervisors. To achieve success, however, the supervisor also has to be socially successful, because he must get his men to follow his instructions in a situation in which he has very little power; he must, in effect, negotiate his position.

It is essential to the argument here presented that it should be recognized that the supervisor/operator relationship is complex and very vulnerable to bad 'performances' and to outside influences. If the supervisor plays his role badly, for whatever reason, he is very open to sanctions that can be used against him; indeed, the remarkable thing is not that supervisors were sometimes punished, but that for the most part they were willingly obeyed despite the inherent weakness of their position. The supervisors were, however, keenly aware that they were also dependent on the existence amongst the operators of a general atmosphere of goodwill towards management, and that if the men were to be made to feel really resentful then there would be very little that even the best supervisor could do to keep up morale. That was why the Plant X supervisor quoted earlier was so concerned that a new plant manager might 'upset them out there'. Only if the operators wanted to do a good job were they open to suggestions from anyone with managerial status; only if a supervisor had some degree of standing in an operator's eyes could he exert real influence with them. We have seen this to be so in the case of particular supervisors, but if supervisors in general had lost their standing then their ability to influence operators would have been very much reduced. In other words the social situation was very delicate. What I question is the extent to which senior management, who had many other things to worry about, appreciated either the vulnerability of the supervisors' position or the extent to which the productivity of the plants really depended on what the supervisors did.

If it is to be argued that senior management really did fully understand the social situation of the supervisors and had created it in capital's interests, then it has to be said that they had exceptional sociological gifts in that they must, apparently, have created this enormously complex social situation through what amounted to a double bluff, for they have to be credited both with giving the false impression that they no longer much valued the supervisors, and with trying to create the presumably equally false idea that they did seek to support the shop-stewards. They had certainly fooled the supervisors, who were convinced that they were not appreciated by senior management; and, indeed, they had fooled the operators also. Everyone thought, for the reasons outlined in the last chapter, that senior management was more concerned with building up the shop-stewards than with standing by the supervisors. Moreover, by 'everyone' I include here both Nichols and Beynon, and myself.

If senior management is to be credited with playing such a complex game then it has to be said that it was a rather dangerous one in so far as considerable risks were being run of losing the committed enthusiasm of the supervisors. It seemed doubtful to the supervisors, even to those on Plant X, that any loyalty they might show to ChemCo would be repaid with loyalty. Rather they thought they had reason to believe that their efforts were unappreciated: they thought that senior management had let them down by giving preference to other men; that they had been singled out for unfair treatment; and worse, perhaps, than anything else, that their efforts to keep the plants running well were disregarded because management were no longer concerned about this. Everything that has been said about the management's apparent preference for shop-stewards rankled with the supervisors, and they were rather bitter that to save a little on labour costs their position relative to the senior operators had been undermined. That they had been treated particularly badly they thought was shown by many things. One example was the commonly cited fact that while operators could choose the time of their holidays the supervisors could not; they also thought it galling that while other groups had been successful in efforts to gain by having their jobs regraded they, the supervisors, had not merely not gained but had actually lost out in their efforts. As we saw, when Plant X supervisors had negotiated over regrading with the company's Review Committee they had had their case rejected, which perhaps was fair enough; what was worse was that having said, in the hope of improving their case, that they would be able to supervise Plant X with six men rather than with the seven they had employed, the committee had seemed to behave like sharp lawyers, taking advantage of this admission, so that not only were the supervisors not up-graded but they were forced, henceforth, to manage with six men only.

Since that experience there had been the second case in which the supervisors had tried to be up-graded, and when they had eventually decided not to fall in with the management scheme of combining the supervision on Plants X and Y, top management had stepped in, supervisors thought, to punish them, filling the posts of shift manager from outside the works. They had had the clear message that as ammonia plant supervisors they now had little hope of further promotion. (It is perhaps not without significance that Jack, the indolent supervisor who took no action to check the waste of hydrogen, was one of the supervisors who had expected promotion and whose hopes had been dashed.)

Only their concern for the future of their plants, and the pride that they still took in the good opinions they could earn from one another seemed to me to keep them ready to go beyond what could have been demanded of them. It is at least possible, therefore, that if the numbers of supervisors were in the future to be so reduced that they no longer provided a 'reference group' that expressed such opinions, then a major influence on the morale of supervisors would have disappeared. If they were to cease to believe in the importance attached to the plants, this would probably have a devastating effect on this morale. They prided themselves on their technical competence. This might, as we saw in the case of the shift-fitter dispute, lead to supervisors showing hostility to management policy, if it was believed to be incompetent or ill-advised. But the supervisors' pride in this technical ability might also, we saw (pp. 153–54), lead them to devote all their skill over a long week-end to solving the problem of the arsenic leak on Plant X. Once, perhaps, foremen might have expected to have basked in the commendations of management; but supervisors were no longer convinced that senior managers were really concerned about productivity. It was even believed that the works manager had actually said, in the context of an industrial dispute, that he would be unconcerned if production were stopped. This was probably simply a tactical ploy and did not represent what he really thought, but it had shaken the supervisors' belief in the importance of their efforts. From management's viewpoint there was clearly a risk that if supervisors' self-esteem were to be entirely eradicated they would no longer be much concerned with productivity. This would most certainly not have been in the interests of the company, because of the considerable influence that the supervisors wielded with the men. Let me stress again that there was a context in which operators trusted supervisors as they could trust no 'real' managers. Operators knew themselves to be concerned for the welfare of Riverside but doubted whether 'they' were. 'They' in this case meant all managers above the level of supervisors, just because 'they' had careers that were not limited to Riverside. Supervisors, just because their very limited promotion possibilities focused their interests on the works, were the one element within the management structure whose attachment to Riverside was credible to the men. Of course there were contexts in which operators believed that a sharp division existed between themselves and the supervisors, but on the crucial issue of the future on the works they knew that they and the supervisors were on the same side.

It is at this point that I have to say, unambiguously, that I simply do not think that senior managers or, indeed, even plant managers, did fully appreciate many of these social complexities. For the reasons that I have given earlier (pp. 178–79) it was axiomatic amongst managers that it was *they* who were interested in the future of the plants whilst the men, and some thought the supervisors also, were too short-sighted to pursue anything but their own immediate financial advantage. I am not arguing that none of what I have been discussing was known to management, nor that plant managers were not very perceptive in some of their relationships with their supervisors and operators. Even Nichols and Beynon (1977) note that the conflict they thought they saw existing between management and workers was in some ways strictly limited, and that 'both managers and workers find themselves covertly negotiating the reality of corporate production. Conflicts and antagonisms are contained beneath the surface by way of tacit understandings and unmentioned limits.' (Nichols and Beynon 1977: 140). They imply that it was only the plant manager who was young and foolish who ran into serious trouble. In their experience only the very inexperienced and truculent manager apparently thought he could rely on compulsion to get his men to do as he wanted and totally ignored the importance of their goodwill. Certainly it was my experience that some managers were very sensitive to the issues involved. What I am doubting is that all the issues were fully understood, and still more that they were the result of deliberate manipulation by management at any level. I think it much more reasonable to assume that senior managers, their minds often taken up with other and more pressing matters, did not fully understand the social situation in which they found themselves.

It was, after all, not perhaps very surprising that senior managers and even plant managers might doubt the dedication of the supervisors. I have noted that they were often highly critical, and openly critical, of management policy. Those who made no secret of their dissatisfaction might well be assumed to be disloyal. They showed obvious reluctance to fall in with many managerial plans: in the case of the shift-fitter dispute the supervisors were loud in their condemnation of management policy. They openly objected to it on the grounds that it was a mere accountancy gesture which involved raising real costs and lowering output, and simply showed that the accountants did not know their job. To senior management, the supervisors seemed unreasonable in their opinion that in a time of some recession, the ammonia plants should operate at full production, whatever the labour costs involved. I will give one final example to show the kind of evidence that might make even a perceptive manager doubt that supervisors could be wholly relied on to act in the interest of the works.

It could well have been argued that doubts about supervisors' reliability had been proved by what had been done to frustrate senior management's plans to prevent men earning very high overtime pay by working their own ESOs. (It will be remembered that these are 'extra shifts off', formally a holiday but for a considerable period almost invariably worked by the men at the special 'holiday overtime' rates.) To understand what happened I have to explain the situation in some detail; but I make no apology for doing so since the issue in the end has to come down to the question of the extent to which senior management are aware of the complexities of the social 'relations of production'.

The story starts with a plant meeting on X. In response, I was told, to the plant manager's manipulation, the operators voted to accept the management suggestion that they should avoid excessive overtime and agree to take their ESOs as actual days off, with the proviso that an operator might work his ESO, and get the premium overtime rate, if the alternative was that another operator would have to be asked to work overtime to provide cover for the absent man. This seemed a sensible compromise between what management wanted and what the men wanted, but in fact it led to resentment between different shifts. The overall manning rate for the plant had been agreed with the union, but as it did not divide neatly into four, it meant that two shifts each had one more man than did the other two. The more fully manned shifts always had a so-called spare man, so that when any of their members had an ESO he had to take it off because it was unnecessary to ask for help from another shift, and no overtime was generated. The situation was different on the two other shifts: they would always have had to call for help from another shift, so their members were allowed to work their ESOs as they always had done. Now, by agreement with the union, a shift with an extra man was always followed by a shift without such a man. This meant that when, not long before I started my research, the plant manager ask the men to vote for the total abolition of the practice of working the ESO, he got the men's agreement. This, a surprising result to the outsider, is simply explained as due to 'ani', that animosity that we met earlier in the analysis. Given the pattern of shifts, if the vote for the abolition of all ESO working was accepted then the tightly manned shift would always have to call for help from another shift whenever one of its men had his ESO off, and such help would always come from the preceding shift that would be a fully manned one. Thus, the positions of the two pairs of shifts would be reversed at a stroke, and those previously disadvantaged became the advantaged ones. Moreover, by definition they had more men than the other two and, therefore, when a vote was taken, their wishes carried the day: the two larger shifts voted solidly for the change.

Now, the opinion of the supervisors on Plant X was that the vote, whilst not dishonestly manipulated by the plant manager, was organized by him with the full understanding on his part of the issues involved and the way in which the men would vote. He might well be said to have been engaged in 'manufacturing consent'. Nevertheless, the result was scarcely what he had foreseen. I was present when James bluntly told the plant manager that it was morally wrong of management to have instigated this change because while the man who worked his own ESO incurred no abnormal strain, the new system significantly raised the number of 'doublers' that were worked and, therefore, the strain on the men. The manager smiled, a little helplessly, at me and said, 'I know, but that is what the lads wanted.' James only snorted. However, when the manager went out, James told me the background I have just related, and gave it as his opinion that the manager 'must' have known what would happen if he put the matter to the vote. He thought management had wanted the change perhaps because of the small saving in overtime payments that resulted, but more probably because it fitted in with the attempt that was being made to abolish totally all overtime that was worked under the premium rate for so-called 'holiday working', the category under which ESOs had been worked; he assumed it would 'look good on paper'. (My hunch, it is no more than that, is that this may have been true; I suspect senior Riverside management, fighting for the existence of an inherently somewhat uneconomic works, felt it necessary to show the company decision-makers that the situation at the works was now very different from what it was in the perhaps profligate earlier days of the 1970s.)

Now apparently the sequel of the drive against ESO working, and the reason for discussing it here, is that James had been so concerned that he had tried to reverse management's manoeuvre by using the only weapons he thought would be effective. Some supervisor (I was told it was James but I made no attempt to verify the story and it may have been another man) had realized that there was a way of making the new rule very expensive in overtime payments. He had spread the word to the operators that there was a rule, agreed with the unions, that if any man worked an unexpected doubler on a night-shift immediately before a day on which he was to be on holiday, then, in addition to his ordinary overtime pay, he could claim payment, at holiday overtime rates, for necessary sleeping time (eight hours) on his first day off. This the operators (supervisors could not participate) now knew, lovingly, as 'the golden nugget'. They now planned the timing of their ESOs with the finesse of hunters spreading nets for game. The best ploy was for an operator to book an ESO for a Monday on which he should have worked a night-shift. He missed a night-shift; by the pattern of shift sequence he would have been at work on the previous Sunday afternoon, beautifully placed to volunteer (and he would be the only one) to do a doubler on Sunday night when there was a high chance, often a betting certainty, that some operator would 'phone in sick'. With only a little luck the canny planner would get overtime for his doubler night-shift, and then overtime at premium rates for 'sleeping' on the day he had claimed his ESO. It was far more lucrative than it had ever been to work the ESO.

What I have to stress is that if indeed James were behind this I am absolutely certain that his motive was not to enable the operators to milk the company. He said repeatedly, to anyone who would listen, that the new system was bad for the men and bad for the plants, and that for the sake of health and of safety they should revert to the old pattern of the men working their ESOs. I know, because he said so, that he was baffled as to why, given the obvious expense involved in the golden nugget, that management policy had not been reversed. Knowing all that we do know about his concern for an alert shift, a concern that had made him ready to take an unusually firm line with his operators over the killer shift, there seems to me to be only one conclusion to come to, that he was not out to make a nonsense of management strategy, but had a genuine doubt about the wisdom of one particular strand of management policy, and wanted to change it.

This may have been a somewhat unusual case in that a wily plant manager was confronted by a supervisor who, in some ways, was just as wily. Nevertheless it would seem to me to be nonsense to do other than accept the fact that managerial plans, however manipulative in intent, are just as likely to go astray when dealing with the work-force as when dealing with fellow capitalists.

The remarkable thing, perhaps, is that it has been necessary to present the evidence with such care to support the contention that all that happens with regard to the relations of (or in) production, is not somehow willed by management. Yet that seems to be the inevitable consequence of the high academic standing of structural Marxist theory in this field. Let me repeat that I am not suggesting that management does not try to avoid confrontation and to get the willing agreement of its work-force to the measures that it wants to bring in. (Only structural Marxists would regard this as necessarily deplorable.) What I am arguing is that it is wildly improbable that every aspect of shop floor relationships that can be construed as ultimately increasing productivity exists as the result of the machinations of management. To prove this point it is necessary to take a last look at the theorists who have been discussed.

8

Conclusion: theory and evidence

I want to look again at some of the theories that have been discussed in the course of this book in order to see what comments may now be made on them in the light of the evidence gathered from the Riverside ammonia plants. I began this account with a description of the two plants that, so far as possible, was based on observation devoid of theory, but structured round an interest in the relationship between technology and social patterns in industry. Since that opening chapter, however, we have discussed a number of theories on this theme, and it is now time to try to examine them again.

First, we may look at Braverman's (1974) ideas, especially as seen through the prism provided by Nichols and Beynon's earlier book on Riverside, *Living with Capitalism* (1977). In a sentence, Braverman's thesis is that relationships in industry are not structured by technology, but on the contrary, capitalist management designs and adopts particular forms of technology in order to control the work-force; its principal tactic is to use machines to deskill work in order to render the work-force powerless, and indeed, Braverman assumes that the work-force does lack power. As we saw, Nichols and Beynon implicitly accept most of the

Bravermanian thesis, but deviate from it in that, while they believe the formal union organizations to have been rendered so ineffective by management as to be of no use to the workers, the latter, can nevertheless fight back in informal ways. Every example of operators failing to work as management would wish, and every case of hostility they showed to foremen was taken as evidence of this informal fight, which is seen as class warfare manifesting itself on the shop floor.

I believe that in the pages of this book I have provided ample evidence for saying that this particular structural Marxist view of industrial relations is too simple, and is forced to be very selective of the data considered if it is to be crammed into what is something of a theoretical strait-jacket. Indeed, that it leads to something that amounts to distortion was demonstrated by the passage quoted from *Living with Capitalism* that sought to suggest that the Riverside site was chosen for the works in the hope that the labour force recruited might be 'green'; quite apart from thus impugning the good sense of the workers, it was simply disingenuous totally to omit any reference to the many advantages of the site in relation to communications and markets. Note that I am not suggesting that Nichols and Beynon's general 'ethnography' is inaccurate, but that having been gathered with the intention of illustrating Braverman's thesis, a lot of data must simply have been passed over as irrelevant, excluded because the authors were not interested in 'mere empiricism'. The result is that instead of a analysis that might have shown the complexities of the relationships between different categories of Riverside employees, we are given a vision that essentially focuses on a dichotomy that the authors see manifested in the class warfare fought between exploited workers (below the level of foremen), and the agents of capital (the foremen and management above them).

Burawoy's *Manufacturing Consent* (1979) provides a structural Marxist view that is very much more subtle than Braverman's thesis, and one that is much more convincing in its readiness to look honestly at data that do not, at first sight anyway, appear to support a Marxist analysis. Burawoy is ready to acknowledge that in the workers' experience, all is not gloom and doom on the shop floor, that men even apparently enjoy their work and the 'games' they play; in fact he provides evidence for the view that workers can even enjoy working hard and that their enjoyment is not directly related to the thought of the pay-packet that they will eventually get. Further, Burawoy is ready to depict foremen not as mere 'agents of capital', but as those who readily help their men in the fiddles they are running, or at least connive at them. Burawoy (1979) does not reduce those he studies to mere stereotypes. He is even ready to acknowledge the evidence he saw that the managers of the machine shops he studied sympathized with their men and sought to protect them from attempts made by the 'work engineers' (the modern form of time-study men) to tighten up regulations in order to prevent the fiddles that were being carried on.

Most striking of all, when Burawoy is compared with Braverman (1974), is the fact that Burawoy is prepared to acknowledge that trade unions, even American trade unions, have exerted a considerable influence on relationships between management and workers. Writing of what he saw in 1975 and comparing the situation with 1945, he comments on the decline of unfettered management power and the growth of real, if limited, power in the hands of the unions. He comments that large corporations are like 'internal states' in their power, a simile that was earlier suggested from a very different political viewpoint by Jay (1967: ch. 2). However, like modern capitalist states, modern corporations, Burawoy notes, are restricted by the growth of bureaucratic structures and rules to which management is bound to adhere in its dealings with its workers; if management breaks these rules then the unions can force a climbdown in the workers' interests.

Burawoy's (1979) structural Marxism, however, informs all his analysis, and in its light he interprets all the complex data he presents. In effect, he is like Braverman in that he seems to have implicit faith in capitalist managements as omniscient and omnipotent. A non-Marxist commentator like Jay (1967) can comment caustically on management ineptitude: for example, he describes a case in which a splendid chance to profit by its main rival's temporary discomfiture was lost by a corporation simply because its managers, when they should have been taking action, were too happily involved in internal jockeying for power; and he notes in another instance how a new corporation chairman lost $425 billion in six years just because he allowed groups of which he was supposed to be in charge to go their own divergent ways (Jay 1967: 45). For Burawoy, at least when he is considering management action in relation to workers, one might almost imagine that the managements of corporations have the attributes of deity. Burawoy assumes that they know all that is going on and that they intend all the consequences of their actions. What workers do may, apparently, have unintended consequences, since things that they think are against management's interests turn out to be to its advantage. All that managements do would seem to be ultimately for capital's benefit, and this is known to senior management even at the very moment that they appear to be losing out.

For all this Burawoy (1979) has not so much an explanation as a phrase that recurs throughout his book almost like some hypnotic chant, which when repeated assures him, and is supposed to assure his readers, that he has received enlightenment. What he writes, whenever he seeks to explain why something that seems to act against management's interest is really in its interests, is, 'This is due to the simultaneous obscuring and securing of surplus value' (Burawoy 1979: 25–30). We may begin to unpack this statement by taking 'surplus value' to mean, very roughly, 'profit derived by the company ultimately through the workers' work'. If we bear in mind that Burawoy argues for various reasons that happy workers are more productive than unhappy ones, then 'obscuring surplus value' is that action that management are assumed to have taken in order to make workers enjoy what they are doing; 'securing surplus value' is any action of management that involves them in the broadest sense in improving productivity. Under certain circumstances, according to Burawoy's arguments, the securing and obscuring are done simultaneously with ease, simply because happy workers, even if they are piece-workers who think they are running a fiddle, tend to work harder than dejected ones. Sometimes, however, things are not quite so simple, and Burawoy explains apparent conflict between different sets of managers by suggesting that one set is busy obscuring while the other set is securing surplus value; it may not be apparent to them, but they are really both pulling in the same direction in the interests of the greater accumulation of capital. It is worth exploring these ideas in somewhat greater detail.

One excellent illustration of Burawoy's position is to be seen in his account of the relationship between foremen and men in the engineering machine shop he studied in the 1970s. He says it was very different from that described for the same firm in 1945 (Burawoy 1979: 61–2, referring to Roy 1952: 102, 290). Burawoy (p. 170) says that in his experience foremen were not seen as hostile because the whole situation relating to 'the labour process' had changed. Because of the limited extent to which management, now bound by agreements with the union and armed with computers instead of stop-watches, intervened directly to alter piece-work rates, friction with management generally had been very much reduced. In 1945 foremen had to some extent suffered as the result of the antagonism generated by brash time-study men. In 1975 management kept to the rules and changed the 'rate for the job' only if some worker blatantly and persistently exceeded the accepted maximum bonus rate. The result was that on the rare occasions when rates were cut by management, foremen could convincingly put the blame on particular transgressors; the men accepted such reasoning and would react simply by trying to impose sanctions on individual rule-breakers. This was a case of 'simultaneously obscuring and securing surplus value' because management restraint 'strengthens consent to its domination', for when the norm about the rate was broken the reaction was such as to serve to 'restore or reinvigorate commitment to the rules', that is, the informal rules that said that management action against blatant rate-busters was fair, which meant, in effect, that the normal rate for the job was regarded as just. Moreover, instead of leading to worker solidarity against management, the action of management in altering the rates for a job, under these conditions, merely turned the workers against one another (Burawoy 1979: 167–70).

Burawoy is scathing about those who would seek to explain as due to some misapprehension any apparently self-defeating efforts by management to extract efficiency from workers by imposing tighter rules. To say that 'management does not understand the requirement of efficiency' is, he says, to make the same kind of error that was made in reverse by Elton Mayo when he argued that workers acted as they did because they did not understand where their best interests lay. In engineering firms of the kind he had studied, he argues, managers had often come up from the shop floor and must be presumed to know that it was counterproductive to tighten rules. It might, perhaps, be that rule tightening is a kind of ritual reaffirmation of the fact of managerial domination: that is, the workers may think they have control, and need to be reminded of their subordination through a period of increased discipline (Burawoy 1979: 174). More probable, he thinks, is the suggestion that such periodic tightening of the rules is due to a struggle between shop management and higher management. Shop managers are not directly involved with the ultimate problem of securing surplus value by selling the product to customers; therefore costs are allowed to go up and quality to slide, as foremen, subject to social pressures from their men, turn a blind eye to much that is going on. To restore the situation higher management exerts pressure in the only way it can, by imposing new rules; but these are incompatible with the shop's 'labour process', so after a while, shop management relaxes the new rules until in time another profit crisis arrives. All this Burawoy sees as an example of the shop managers' concern to secure the co-operation of their men – as he puts it, their concern with 'obscuring surplus value'; higher management being concerned with profitability for the corporation has to be concerned with 'securing surplus value', thus they seem to be at loggerheads, but in reality, of course, overall profitability depends equally on the 'obscuring' activities of the shop management.

Somewhat similarly, according to Burawoy (1979), a corporation's overall profitability depends also on the action of the union leadership, even when it would appear that what they do is against the firm's interests. He argues that a corporation as an 'internal state' can exist only if it allows in its government a 'limited participation by representatives of labour', that is union representatives. These must be strong enough to impress their membership by their power in relation to management, and responsive enough to their members' wishes to command their allegiance; but the union representatives must not really be strong enough to challenge management prerogatives in relation to 'the labour process'. Management knows, however, that if it is going to negotiate successful bargaining agreements with the union, it must allow these leaders enough apparent power to appear legitimate. Indeed, in order to enhance the members' confidence in their union, it is to management's advantage from time to time to appear to break the rules of some collective agreement so that the union may appear to force it to retreat and so be seen to act independently of management interests (Burawoy 1979: 112). It does not really matter if individual union leaders incur members' antagonism, for so long as complaints are directed at errant individuals, the institution is spared from their criticism (p. 113). In Burawoy's opinion, even violent condemnation of shop-stewards and other union activists only reinforced the normative assumptions about industrial government; since such criticism, by implication, is directed against the special privileges such men receive, this criticism only reinforces 'the normative assumptions of industrial government, namely that everyone is equal before the law'. This law, of course, serves management's interests (p. 114). This again is an idea that needs further elucidation.

Burawoy (1979: 112) argues that the role of the union is to preserve the *status quo*. It does this by acting as an umpire, protecting the rights of industrial citizens and overseeing the punishment of offenders against contractual obligations. With obvious irony, Burawoy quotes a statement to the effect that 'the union is an attempt to extend the democratic processes in the industrial community' – the idea that people who make up a society should work out rules and regulations to govern the relationship of one to the other.

The flaw for Burawoy is that this involves the *de facto* acceptance of the contract of employment because, if there is a grievance, it is considered as an individual case and its merits are assessed in the light of the 'rules of industrial government laid down in the contract' (Burawoy 1979: 114). Moreover, collective bargaining not only removes conflict from the shop floor to a level at which it is unlikely to cause disruption but it *generates a common interest* (my emphasis) between union and company in the survival and growth of the enterprise. There is, says Burawoy, an element of class struggle in collective bargaining, since workers are on one side whilst capital is on the other, but what are in contention are merely 'marginal changes'; hence, he says, it is merely a game and revolves around accepted rules (p. 115).

Even if the machinery of collective bargaining breaks down and there is a damaging strike, this will serve merely to 'reinforce' the commitment of others to collective bargaining. Indeed, ultimately, collective bargaining supports the capitalist system since even if it sometimes leads to the bankruptcy of a particular firm (because the company commits itself to a certain wage that proves in the end to be more than can be covered by its profit margins) this merely means that the representatives of labour become aware of a common interest with capital in the growth of profits (Burawoy 1979: 115). Similarly, bureaucratic procedures that prevent management from taking arbitrary action, rightly understood, support management power by preventing it from forfeiting the consent and goodwill of its work-force. This ensures the continuation, relatively unchanged, of the pattern of relationships that exist between those engaged in the labour process. Such bureaucratic procedures require a relatively autonomous union structure that can be seen as a legitimate bargainer on behalf of the workers. To preserve this illusion, collusion must not be obvious; union officials must not get too obviously preferential treatment; however, if they do, and this is sometimes difficult to avoid, their members will, with luck, ascribe the frailty of the leadership to the weakness of human nature rather than to the structural conditions in which leaders have to operate (p. 119).

I said at the beginning of this section that for Burawoy management, or at least senior management, has the attributes of deity, that is omnipotence and omniscience; I think this case has now been made out, for it is clear that in his view, the management of a large corporation organizes everything relating to the work-force in such a way that all things work together for its greater good. Specifically anything and everything that reduces conflict between workers and management is brought about ultimately by senior management in the interests of capital accumulation through a process that smooths the path of production by conning workers into imagining that they share a common interest with management. All collective bargaining by unions, and the institutionalization of machinery for dealing with grievances are properly interpreted as being organized by the corporation in its own interests, and by implication against that of the workers. In summary we can say that, from Burawoy's viewpoint it is impossible for the workers to win, for:

1. If there is no trouble between workers and management then conflict has been removed from the shop floor, to management's advantage.

2. If there is trouble and the company wins, then this, naturally, serves to remind workers that they are subordinate.

3. However, if there is trouble and the union wins, then the legitimacy of the union is strengthened, which is of course in the company's interests.

4. All successful collective bargaining, being merely about trivia, commits the unions to the rules of the capitalist game.

5. If collective bargaining collapses, the bad results of this breakdown merely reinforce the commitment of others to the system.

6. If collective bargaining results in a company's bankruptcy,

this makes unions in general aware of a common commitment to capitalism.

7. If workers detect bias in the conduct of the negotiations involved in collective bargaining, this directs their attention to the imperfections of the system rather than to the underlying relations upon which the system rests.

8. If workers become antagonistic to union representatives this is either immaterial to, or beneficial to, the company, because it directs hostility to individuals and not to the system.

At this point in considering Burawoy's position, any anthropologist familiar with work done in this field in the southern African area would find the arguments just outlined very reminiscent, although in an exaggerated form, of Max Gluckman's (1954) studies on royal ritual and especially the rituals of rebellion. There too would be found the idea that bitterly hostile outbursts against individuals (Gluckman was writing about local kings) did nothing but good for the system as a whole because, by implication, the condemnation of a bad king inevitably suggested that the institution itself was fine, if only the right person could be found to fill the role. Gluckman, too, argues that if norms are broken and condemnation follows, then this strengthens the system because the result is that everyone unites in agreeing that the norms are good. Gluckman was arguing not about capitalism but about 'society' as a cohesive institution – one that could gain the consent of its members and so endure, even in the absence of a really strong central government that could force compliance with its wishes. Anthropologists had a genuine problem in explaining why societies lacking powerful governments did not break apart into some Hobbesian chaos in which every man's hand was against his neighbour. It is ironic to find that an anthropological argument that was persuasively argued, but is now regarded as resting ultimately on an untenable and old-fashioned theory of society, and one based on assumptions about the significance of *unintended* consequences of actions, should be brought out again as a bright new theory of capitalism, this time with the explicit assumption that senior managers always know what they are doing in the sense that they fully foresee the consequences. It seems very likely that Burawoy, since he worked in Zambia, which theoretically was very much Gluckman's country, must, consciously or unconsciously, have been influenced by Gluckman's ideas. For an anthropologist it is fascinating to meet them so transmuted.

Nevertheless, I have to argue that even in their new guise of functional Marxism the ideas are still functionalist, still teleological and rest on assumptions that remain to be proved. In the case of their application to the analysis of the relations of production and the work process, I think they cannot stand up to the test of empirical evidence. I am aware, of course, that mere empiricism is no substitute for theoretical sophistication; but theories must stand up to rigorous empirical testing. It was, after all, a naive but empirically observant child who pointed out that the emperor's attire left something to be desired.

Let us, therefore, think about the empirical situation in which the Riverside works manager was placed at the time of which I am writing. I must make it clear at the outset that my analysis is not based on detailed discussions of these issues with the then works manager. I did have a number of conversations with him in which he did, amongst other things, talk about the general position of the works. Nevertheless, much of what I shall say is the result of building up a picture from what different people said in many different contexts. What I am seeking to do here is to present, as clearly as possible, what was the actual position of an actual senior manager and point to the contrast between what it was possible for him to do in the Riverside situation, and what Burawoy's 'senior management' is supposed to accomplish in the field of 'obscuring' surplus value.

In looking at the position of the works manager, it must be remembered that he had overall responsibility for the entire works. He was not, of course, an entirely free agent since he was an employee of ChemCo and had to follow certain directives that came to him from higher up the chain of command and ultimately he was responsible to those senior to him for what he did at Riverside. Nevertheless he had been appointed to get on with the job of managing the works without detailed interference. Therefore, to a large extent, the buck stopped with him, and it was up to him to organize the day-to-day running of Riverside so that it made a profit for the company, and so that its work was not disrupted by strife. In other words, in Burawoy's jargon, the works manager was charged with both 'securing and obscuring surplus value', and it is for this reason that the examination of his position is theoretically of value. As an actor in this situation he had to undertake both roles.

One obvious point that has to be stressed is that the works manager was not necessarily free to pursue policies most calculated to win the consent of the work-force because of the constraints he faced in other directions. Let us assume, for the sake of argument, that he had total knowledge of all the social complexities of the 'relations of production': even this would not mean that he was free to implement policies that were designed solely to make friends and influence these people. (I am aware that the structural Marxist argument usually involves making assumptions based on the absence of scarcity, and this may have its uses in the same way that under certain circumstances it may be desirable for a physicist to ignore friction – but that assumption is not usually of help to the engineer, and like the engineer, I am here explicitly making an empirical analysis.) Let us start, therefore, by exploring briefly those constraints that were placed on the works manager by his responsibility for 'securing surplus value'.

First of all there was the task of keeping viable a works which, as we have seen, could not produce as cheaply as newer plants even within ChemCo and this task was made more difficult by the general market conditions. The demand for Riverside's main product, artificial fertilizers, was not directly hit by the recession but nevertheless demand was likely to fall for farmers were indirectly influenced by it, particularly because, as they tend to borrow heavily from banks, they are very vulnerable to high interest rates and must cut costs if these rates rise. One obvious way for a farmer to cut his expenses in the short term is to cut his fertilizer input. Moreover, it was already obvious by 1981 that the EEC intended to do something pretty drastic about cutting milk production, and since one of the main uses of artificial fertilizers is to increase the yield of grass to be grazed by dairy cows, farmers had every reason to cut back; selling Riverside fertilizer was not going to be easy.

Any Riverside works manager was also constrained by the requirement that he should satisfy the senior managers in ChemCo. Managers external to Riverside had the ultimate power over the future of the works, and they also had the ability occasionally to do things that interfered with aspects of its day-to-day running. They made major policy decisions that affected Riverside, especially, of course, decisions about investment. Also, specific cases of more direct intervention were cited: there was the example quoted (p. 22) of the plant that was shut down without warning, allegedly even to the then works manager, when all the men working on it were confident that its future was assured because it was profitable; a more recent example was the decision to appoint, to the posts of shift managers, men from other ChemCo works – a decision which was said to have been taken without reference to the wishes of the Riverside management. Apart from such unusual interference, it was clear that the works manager had to make a case for the continuation of Riverside to a potentially critical audience. I am not suggesting it was a basically hostile audience. Much had been invested in Riverside and there is no evidence that more was required than a 'reasonable' return on capital. Moreover the technical improvements that had been made to the works, in order to make it more economical to run, had been effected with the help of the resources and engineering expertise of the parent company. On the other hand there was no evidence that the top managers were in business to support lame ducks out of sheer beneficence. To keep Riverside going the works manager had to make a good case in two main ways. First, he had to show that production was as cheap as technical efficiency could possibly make it. Second, it is likely that he also felt he had to show that the people working at Riverside deserved top management's sympathetic understanding. In other words I think he had to make a 'moral' case: he had to show that everyone was 'pulling his weight', doing 'a decent job' and in particular, perhaps, the works manager had to avoid losing sympathy by avoiding any suggestion that the employees were selfishly concerned to 'milk' the company by any 'improper' means of raising their labour costs. In the interests of all, therefore, it was the works manager's task to concern himself with, and prevent, unwarranted extravagance from whichever quarter it might come. For this reason he had to spend considerable time thinking about the elimination of such expense. If necessary, in the course of pursuing this thankless task, the works manager had to be ready to make unwelcome decisions at whatever cost to his own popularity.

In seeking to cut costs the works manager had to face constraints imposed by the unions. We have already dealt at some length with the question of whether or not unions have real power. I am not here concerned with questions of ultimate power but with the works manager's experience. It seems unquestionable that to the Riverside works manager, union power was a very significant restraint on his ability to achieve a really flexible work-force that would have cut operating costs. However much management may have tried to build up stewards for its own purposes, it was clear that the works manager and his closest associates spent much time worrying about shop-steward reactions and felt them as an inhibiting influence. The opposition of union officials was even more serious. There was evidence that management would very much have liked to have brought in a system of apprenticeships that would have trained youngsters in the combined skills of electrician, fitter, and instrument artificer. All the relevant craft unions were, however, opposed to the idea and it was, in consequence, dropped. To those who would say that 'really', in capital's interest, it was probably a good thing to keep the old union structure and so divide up the workers, it is surely relevant to say that in Germany, where the union structures are different, many firms in fact have just such combined apprenticeship schemes, and apparently find it in their interests to do so. In other words there is no reason to doubt that had the unions not prevented this action, Riverside too would have had combined apprenticeships. Moreover, if the ultimate in power is to prevent opponents from even contemplating altering the *status quo* then, arguably, the unions at Riverside were very powerful for despite all the desire for flexibility no manager, so far as I know, had ever contemplated, as a practical proposition, the idea of introducing flexibility between process workers and maintenance men; yet, as we have seen in New Jersey, a recent study by Halle shows that where the unions make no objection to such flexibility, flexibility was brought in that allowed any man to switch from being a process operator to being a skilled maintenance man. Thus there seemed good evidence for the argument that the works manager certainly was constrained by powers the unions possessed and sought always to effect his economies in ways that did not involve a head on clash with the unions.

All these constraints imposed by the economic situation, the need to present a good case to senior company officials, and the need not to provoke the unions into retaliation, seemed to have influenced the works manager in his dealing with his work-force. Clearly, given the economic situation, the technical drawbacks of the works, and its 'political' position in ChemCo, he had to make economies. He would have liked co-operation from the men; but if they would not give him active support then perhaps he felt he had to *make* them comply for the long-term good of all. Forced compliance, however, could easily erode that goodwill on which high productivity depended and it is at this point that Burawoy's arguments fall. Even supposing, for the sake of argument, that the works manager was both insightful and machiavellian, this would not enable him to avoid the problem that what he had to do to succeed in some of his tasks inevitably prevented him from succeeding in others; he could not act in such a way as always to preserve the men's 'consent' for to preserve the works it seemed necessary to do things that they resented.

Let us look at the consequences of the need to cut costs and show good intentions to senior managers, which meant that the works manager felt bound to cut at least the more expensive forms of overtime, and all other costly ways of using labour. It was in this cause that he had decreed the drastic cutting of the shift-fitters, encouraged his plant managers to eliminate that most expensive form of labour, the so-called 'holiday overtime' (so that they sought to prevent men from working their own ESOs) and encouraged them to try to cut down overtime working by achieving at least that 'flexibility' that allowed substitution of a 'cheaper' man for one who was more expensive, and in so doing hit the interests of senior men. In taking these courses of action, the works manager had taken care to avoid arousing significant hostility from union officials. It was not that they had been in any way bought off but that national union policy in the first place regarded overtime in a period of recession as something that was not to be encouraged (for the aim should be to increase the numbers of jobs available rather than to increase the earnings of those in work), and the general union aim of raising the position of the lowest grades had meshed with the management desire to achieve flexibility between grades. It was obviously inevitable that these actions would, however, encounter the opposition of the men, and the works manager knew it. Why did he decide to take this risk?

I would argue that on the basis of what seemed to be the general reaction of the men to any economizing efforts, their reactions to such economies may have been regarded as just one of those unfortunate factors about which little could be done. In other words the works manager knew some of the likely reactions to what he was doing but thought that he had to risk them. In the dilemma he faced some risk had to be taken, and that of incurring the men's hostility may have seemed the least bad choice for two reasons. In the first place their antagonism may have seemed something that was inevitable anyway. Second, the full extent of the risk may well not have been realized; it seems very doubtful to me that management recognized just how much the productivity of the plants was dependent on the goodwill of the workers, and therefore there was almost certainly an underestimate of the likely costs of forefeiting their consent.

Opposition from the men may have seemed inevitable in any case to the management since many workers, operators, and maintenance men clearly put considerable efforts into circum-venting management's wish to economize on labour costs. Quite apart from the more subtle cases of resistance that have been discussed there were many very open cases that came to the works manager's attention. We have seen that operators were much attached to their 'doublers' and that some, like Richard (p. 114), seemed to be able to fiddle overtime opportunities if they wished to earn extra money; it was obvious to me that senior management knew that this was going on but, despite Burawoy's assumptions, did not know how to stop it, given the men's legal right to three days' sick-leave without having to produce a doctor's certificate. We have also seen, for example, that there was open hostility being expressed towards the proposed five-shift system that management was trying to introduce; despite the genuine advantages from such a system, the proposal, because it would lead to cuts in overtime, led to the 'strike' on Plant Y. There could not have been more obvious evidence of resistance to management policy. Even where the works manager had been successful, as he had been in eliminating much of the labour costs that had previously been involved in the 'shift-fitter' system, he had encountered a lot of obvious resentment in consequence, including, in this case, a union-backed overtime ban. It was, perhaps, not surprising in such circumstances that managers seemed, like Nichols and Beynon, to assume that they had, indeed, to operate with a dichotomized works in which only managers were concerned about such crucial considerations as economic viability and the necessity of cutting costs, and men showed not goodwill but a kind of generalized hostility to management.

I believe that management's perception of this hostility had very significant results. I have argued that men accepted managerial authority, but they certainly did not do so by manifesting docile and unargumentative obedience. So far as the works manager was concerned, if the main reactions to what he thought were urgently necessary commands or requests for economy seemed to be only cries of loud discontent, and more or less astute moves to sidestep any new ruling that he might make, then it was not unreasonable, perhaps, for him to assume that generalized hostility to management authority existed and conclude, however reluctantly, that the workers were concerned only with maximizing their own wages; uninterested in the welfare of the works, they might seem simply set on opposition. In these circumstances I argue that the works manager, and other senior managers, those who according to Burawoy should have been concerned with 'obscuring' as well as 'securing' 'surplus value', that is with seeking the voluntary co-operation of workers as well with making a profit, were in fact underrating the significance of the resentment caused by their economies, and assumed it to be solely concerned with the loss of wages and to be unconcerned with losses in efficiency. The consequence was that complaints about losses of this type were regarded as mere camouflage for more self-interested gripes.

It would, after all, not be so surprising if management overlooked the extent to which goodwill or consent affects productivity; with the exception of the recent work by Burawoy and those associated with him, it has been often underplayed in studies on industrial relations, due, it seems probable, to the habit of mind that focuses attention on what men fail to do rather on what they achieve. A rare exception is to be found in Halle's (1984) study, which centres on an automated chemical works complex in New Jersey. What is relevant to our present argument is that in treating Braverman's arguments with some scepticism, and underlining the extent to which the men he studied had achieved a great deal of freedom in the way they ran their machines, Halle shows their concern for productivity. They were 'not Taylorized automotons, operating in a work setting dominated by management. On the contrary they have seized a fair degree of control over their work . . . management has attempted to specify precisely what each worker should do. But . . . there are clear limits on how far this can be implemented' (Halle 1984: 126). This was possible in part simply because no manual about the machines they operated could tell the men precisely how they should work. Each machine had its own quirks and peculiarities, knowledge of which was crucial to operating it efficiently, and only the men on the job had this knowledge (p. 119). Moreover, and even more important, something else that could only be learned on the job was the knowledge of the danger zone for particular machines.

'The instruction manual may state that certain levels of pressure and temperature are dangerous, but given the variability of equipment even on installation, and the modifications it undergoes over time, this information is unlikely to be precise. It may be possible to operate quite safely within a formally designated danger zone, and there may be danger areas that are not formally designated . . . All this can be discovered only by experience, and it is workers who have this experience. . . . Management has little choice but to rely on workers' expertise.'
(Halle 1984: 119, 124)

Halle argues that their grasp of this knowledge was one way in which workers escaped managerial control, but he also says of their production patterns, 'But batches do meet specifications, which would not always be the case if production workers rigidly followed the formulas.' Thus, even though they were opposed to certain management rulings, men not only did not act against the essential management objective of being able to sell a product of a good standard that would satisfy the customer, but used their own secret inside knowledge to help in this aim. Halle's account is, however, unusual, and often the subject of goodwill scarcely enters theoretical discussion.

In my earlier discussion of the role of the supervisors I have already argued that even plant managers seemed unaware of the extent to which productivity was dependent on the work-centred-ness of supervisors, and how much less likely it was that the works manager, who depended for his information on the plant managers, should have realized the situation. Yet on the ammonia plants, too, there was much about the way in which the machinery was run that was the private knowledge of men and supervisors and was used to maintain productivity. Indeed, it was the failure to know these 'secrets' that marked one of the Plant X supervisors as a social outsider, and the mark of this status was that he could not, in the estimation of the other supervisors, keep the plant from 'tripping' (see pp. 151–52). Indeed it is obvious, if we reflect on the large influence on a supervisor's self-esteem played by his ability to run the plant efficiently, not allowing it to trip despite any technical problems encountered, that there was a very direct influence here on productivity. Because a supervisor's pride was bound up with his ability to keep his plant running it was in itself an asset to management. It exerted its influence not simply in the technical field, but, as we saw, in the supervisor's interest in taking the trouble to run his shift well, which in the cases of the best supervisors meant that they were concerned not simply with getting obedience, but with getting it tactfully, and with actually deserving the trust of the operators. I have suggested that much of the difference in goodwill between Plant X and Plant Y may have been due to the greater scope on Plant X for supervisors to influence their shifts; and this seems further evidence of the contribution made to productivity by the fact that a supervisor's self-esteem was linked to his ability to run his shift well.

Yet, contrary to what Burawoy would have us assume, I found no evidence whatever that senior management had any real understanding of the supervisors' outlook, and, for all the reasons I have previously given, it would seem simply absurd to suggest that this attitude had been deliberately 'manufactured'. Of course senior management wanted the supervisors' goodwill and tried to maintain good relationships with them but only within limits set by factors such as the apparent need to keep in with shop-stewards. Therefore, if necessary, the supervisors' pride was affronted and risks were taken with their goodwill. Far from such decisions being taken with a full knowledge of the social situation that I have described, it was apparent to me that the works manager was not even fully aware of the differences in detail between the working practices of the two ammonia plants. He had confidence in his plant managers and having delegated responsibility for the plants to them, he did not examine microscopically everything that went on, for after all he had many other things which demanded his attention. Since the reasons for the differences between Plant X and Plant Y had not been carefully examined, the assumption seemed to be that the explanation must lie in some difference in ability between the two plant managers concerned – a perfectly reasonable assumption given incomplete knowledge of the 'relations of production', but not a springboard for successful machiavellian intervention by the works manager.

I would argue that if senior management was ignorant of the extent to which productivity was dependent on the goodwill of supervisors, there was even greater ignorance about the extent of dependence on the day-by-day goodwill of the ordinary workers. Let me stress again how common this goodwill was. In the course of this essay I have noted particular instances: the young operator on Plant Y who rushed off from his meal because he had heard a change in the sound 'his' compressor was making; the very notable case of the control room man terribly frustrated because he could not get his supervisor's permission to cut down on the intake of his feed and so reduce the waste of raw material; the other control room operator who said how much interest he got from trying to make the plant run more efficiently while he was in charge; the Plant Y operators who were personally irritated by the careless operator, and put in extra efforts during their turns of duty to try to restore the balances he upset. Once the significance of this kind of data is understood and noted it becomes evident that it is very widespread. Wherever there was occasion, earlier in this account, to note that managerial authority was accepted despite the absence of power to compel obedience then that acceptance may be said to have been due to goodwill. Even those who rejected certain aspects of managerial authority nevertheless displayed this goodwill in other contexts.

Let us look again at the case of Basil, who was at the bottom of the hierarchy of process operators because he would not do control room work. Basil, as we saw, exploited the possibilities of his position with considerable imagination. He scorned the implicit claims to superiority of the control room operators, demonstrating his independence. Nevertheless, in his own way, he took good care of the plant. He resented, and was ready ultimately to defy, a supervisor he thought was treating him badly; but he entertained no animosity for James, even though James had had to report his conduct to the plant manager. Wise supervisors made little effort to make Basil do his work in the ways that the rules laid down because they knew that even if his performance were unorthodox, he would keep his part of the plant running efficiently and they could be sure of his competent co-operation in a tight corner. He combined an almost insolent rejection of inessential instructions with an alert awareness of the real functional requirements of his job. It would be very easy to select examples of his behaviour and say, 'Here is a man who rejects managerial authority.' Of course, this would ignore all those characteristics that made him the best of the operators in the opinion of some of the supervisors. Basil, indeed, was a kind of walking example of the complexities involved in men's attitudes towards authority, and the unlikely people who manifested goodwill. Can we assume, however, that this was at all obvious to the works manager? Or can we assume that he really knew about the other consequences of goodwill that have just been outlined? If he did not, if he focused more on the obvious antagonism that he often encountered, would it have been surprising? If this were the situation, then I can only repeat that it seems to me most unlikely that he could have taken into consideration all the costs that might be incurred by action likely to arouse resentment.

It seems to me, having now examined the empirical position of an actual works manager, a man responsible ultimately both for the profitability of the works and for the policy pursued towards the workers, that it impossible to accept as reasonable Burawoy's hypothesis that in so far as workers consent to managerial authority, this consent has been 'manufactured' by management. It is an interesting and perhaps useful idea if taken as a kind of Weberian ideal-type position, in terms of which really existing situations may be examined – but as with all ideal-types it is a fundamental error to think that the situation described in the theory actually exists. Burawoy's hypothesis allows no room for actual flesh and blood managers – not only have they the attributes of deity, but like certain African high gods described in the anthropological literature, they lack all real qualities. Burawoy's managers are even devoid of any ambitions except of those securing or obscuring surplus value. It would, perhaps, have been better if he had noted Jay's comments on junior managers:

> 'You might think that if you take a man on, give him a guarantee of employment, a fair salary and a well defined job, you can assume from then onwards that he will work for the good of the corporation which is employing him. Perhaps there are some who do, but on the whole it is safer to assume that, while the good of the corporation will always been an important consideration, it will not be his first loyalty: that is reserved for himself, for his present status and rewards and his future career. And it is only too possible for them to come into conflict with it.'

(Jay 1967: 205)

Burawoy's hypothesis demands, in addition to all the other factors that have so far been discussed, that managers in charge of plants should be above all concerned with 'obscuring surplus value'. Those we have met at Riverside were, I thought, competent men trying to make their plants highly productive places but, as we have seen, there were occasions when their own career interests seemed to be placed before that of the organization they were paid to lead – a phenomenon not unknown amongst academics, even left-wing ones – so even here the theory meets difficulties.

The works manager is actually a real man who has to come to decisions in situations of conflict. For his information he must rely on that supplied to him by other managers, who are also actual men with conflicting aims and ambitions, whose perceptions of any situation are likely to be less that one hundred per cent perfect. Theories of industrial relations in general, and even those about the 'relationships of production', really must take such empirical factors into consideration.

In this book I have attempted to show something of the complexities hidden within the term 'managerial authority', and something also of the complexity of the situation within which, at Riverside, it had to be exercised. If I have suggested that management had a less than perfect understanding of what was really involved in this 'authority' that is scarcely surprising. White and Trevor comment:

> 'Western management thought, exemplified particularly by the "behavioural science" school, appears to have persistently trivialised the subject of authority. It is often portrayed as a one-dimensional problem, in which the choice is simply between being relatively authoritarian or relatively participative (or democratic). It is more realistic to regard authority as a highly complex and many sided affair. It is not merely its strength, but its form, its purpose, and its method of legitimation which are at issue.'
>
> (White and Trevor 1983: 11)

This book began simply as an exercise in the application of the techniques of social anthropology to the study of industry. I hope that it will turn out to have shed perhaps a new light on this very under-researched topic of managerial authority.

References

Abrams, P. (1981)*Historical Sociology*. Wells, Somerset: Open Book.

Batstone, E., Boraston, I., and Frenkel, S. (1977) *Shop Stewards in Action: The Organization of Workplace Conflict and Accommodation*. Oxford: Blackwell.

Batstone, E., Boraston, I., and Frenkel, S. (1978) *The Social Organization of Strikes*. Oxford: Blackwell.

Blackburn, R.M. and Mann, M. (1979) *The Working Class in the Labour Market*. London: Macmillan.

Blauner, R. (1964) *Alienation and Freedom: The Factory Worker and His History*. Chicago: Chicago University Press.

Braverman, H. (1974) *Labour and Monopoly Capitalism: The Degradation of Work in the Twentieth Century*. New York: Monthly Review Press.

Burawoy, M. (1979) *Manufacturing Consent: Change in the Labour Process under Capitalism*. Chicago: Chicago University Press.

Crozier, M. (1976) Comparing Structures and Comparing Games. In G. Hofstede and M. Kassen (eds) *European Contributions to Organization Theory*. Amsterdam: van Goram.

Doeringer, P. and Piore, M. (1971) *Internal Labour Markets and Manpower Analysis*. Lexington, Mass.: Heath Lexington Books.

Elger, T. (1982) Braverman, Capital Accumulation and Deskilling. In S. Wood (ed.) (1982) *The Degradation of Work? Skill, Deskilling and the Labour Process*. London: Hutchinson.

Gallie, D. (1978) *In Search of the New Working Class: Automation and*

Social Integration within the Capitalist Enterprise. Cambridge: Cambridge University Press.

Gluckman, M. (1954) *Rituals of Rebellion iŋ South-East Africa* (the Frazer Lecture 1954). Manchester: Manchester University Press.

Goldthorpe, J. H., Lockwood, D., Beckhofer, F., and Platt, J. (1969) *The Affluent Worker in the Class Structure* (Cambridge Studies in Sociology). Cambridge: Cambridge University Press.

Gospel, H.F. and Littler, C.R. (1983) *Managerial Strategies and Industrial Relations*. London: Heinemann.

Halle, D. (1984) *America's Working Man*. Chicago: Chicago University Press.

Jay, A. (1967) *Management and Machiavelli*. Harmondsworth: Penguin.

Lazonick, H. (1983) Technological Change and the Control of Work: The Development of Capital–Labour Relations in the U.S. Manufacturing Industry. In H. F. Gospel and C. R. Littler (1983) *Managerial Strategies and Industrial Relations*. London: Heinemann.

Mallet, S. (1969) *La nouvelle classe ouvrière*. Paris: Editions de Seuil.

Naville, P. (1961) *L'automation et le travail humain*. Paris: CNRS.

—— (1963) *Vers l'automatisme social? Problèmes du travail et de l'automation*. Paris: Gallimard.

Nichols, T. and Beynon, H. (1977) *Living with Capitalism: Class Relations and the Modern Factory*. London: Routledge & Kegan Paul.

Radcliffe-Brown, A.R. (1952) *Structure and Function in Primitive Society*. London: Cohen & West.

Roy, D. (1952) Restrictions of Output in a Piecework Machine Shop. Ph.D. dissertation. Chicago: University of Chicago Press.

Taylor, F. (1947) *Scientific Management*. London and New York: Harper.

Turner, V. (1957) *Schism and Continuity in an African Society*. Manchester: Manchester University Press.

White, M. and Trevor, M. (1983) *Under Japanese Management*. London: Heinemann.

Wood, S. (ed.) (1982) *The Degradation of Work? Skill, Deskilling and the Labour Process*. London: Hutchinson.

Name index

Subject index